D0849541

DEVELOPMENT ECONOMICS
ON TRIAL

DEVELOPMENT ECONOMICS ON TRIAL

THE ANTHROPOLOGICAL CASE FOR A PROSECUTION

POLLY HILL

FELLOW OF CLARE HALL, CAMBRIDGE

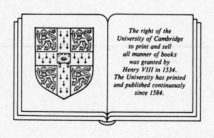

The right of the
University of Cambridge
to print and sell
all manner of books
was granted by
Henry VIII in 1534.
The University has printed
and published continuously
since 1584.

CAMBRIDGE UNIVERSITY PRESS

CAMBRIDGE

LONDON   NEW YORK   NEW ROCHELLE

MELBOURNE   SYDNEY

Published by the Press Syndicate of the University of Cambridge
The Pitt Building, Trumpington Street, Cambridge CB2 1RP
32 East 57th Street, New York, NY 10022, USA
10 Stamford Road, Oakleigh, Melbourne 3166, Australia

Cambridge University Press 1986

First published 1986

Printed in Great Britain at the University Press, Cambridge

British Library cataloguing in publication data
Hill, Polly
Development economics on trial:
the anthropological case for
a prosecution
1. Rural development –
Developing countries
I. Title
330.9172′4   HC59.7

Library of Congress cataloguing in publication data
Hill, Polly, 1914–
Development economics on trial.
Bibliography.
Includes index.
1. Rural development – Africa, West.
2. Rural development – India, South.
3. Economic anthropology – Africa, West.
4. Economic anthropology – India, South.
5. Technical assistance – Africa, West – Anthropological aspects.
6. Technical assistance – India, South –
Anthropological aspects. I. Title.
HN820.Z9C64   1986   307.1′4′0966   86-2613

ISBN 0 521 32104 2 hard covers
ISBN 0 521 31096 2 paperback

'To the extent that economics is a source of legitimacy for government actions, the modern discipline constitutes in itself a major obstacle to development in backward regions.'

J.K. Hart   *The Political Economy of West African Agriculture*

CONTENTS

༺✦༻

ACKNOWLEDGMENTS

I received much support in writing this book from those who kindly agreed to criticize one or other of my numerous drafts, making many constructive suggestions; in this connection I particularly need to thank Drs Keith Hart, Peter Loizos and Piers Vitebsky, Mr David Williams (great scholar and journalist of West Africa), and my editor at the Cambridge University Press, Dr Peter Richards. I am also grateful to Drs Christopher Bayly, Patrick Chabal, Carol MacCormack, Peter Skalnik and Teresa Spens; and I am especially appreciative of the encouragement I have received over the years from Professor Michael Lipton who, like some of the other economists at the official Institute of Development Studies at the University of Sussex, is well aware of the relevance of economic anthropology. The usual disclaimer that none of these people is responsible for anything that I have written is insufficient: it is rather that I am aware that some of them disagree with various aspects of my approach or presentation. Indeed, my most severe critic is myself, for contrary to appearances I am a reluctant polemicist who has been loath to embark on the vigorous assault I believe the subject demands.

Finally, I want to thank members of Clare Hall, Cambridge, for the congenial academic environment they have continued to provide; and to say that all my published work within the past twenty-five years has depended on living within a reasonable distance of the great Cambridge University Library, which is enlightened enough still to permit the borrowing of books.

PREFACE

For many years I have been waiting in vain for someone else to write this book. While it is common knowledge that so many of the assumptions on which rural development economists base their work are thoroughly unrealistic, owing to their general lack of experience of the tropical world, no one seems to be prepared to assume the role of outside professional critic. Given the failure to appreciate the significance of professional division of labour, it is generally believed that there is no role for a mediator who seeks merely to build bridges between economic anthropology and development economics. But just as an art critic seldom gives artists practical advice on how to improve their work, so it would seem the height of arrogance for an anthropologist like myself to make practical suggestions on working methods or subject matter to economists. Nothing like that is to be found here.

My approach is at once polemical and constructive: my polemical purpose is to expose what I see as the old-fashioned, stereotyped, Western-biased, over-generalized crudity and conceptual falsity of so many conventional economic premises, as well as economists' complacent attitude to bad official statistics; my constructive purpose, which takes up much more space, is a practical demonstration that many of the findings of the less esoteric branches of economic anthropology ought to be regarded as highly relevant to development economics although, as any glance at economists' bibliographies shows, they are habitually ignored. The fact that anthropologists usually pursue their work by means of detailed enquiries in the field has led to a refusal on the part of economists to believe that such detail is not usually an end in itself but rather the empirical basis for generalization.

I am well aware that many complex issues have been discussed in very simple terms (or neglected altogether) in this book, which I have sought to keep brief in order to appeal to as wide a public as possible.

As I thought it would be confusing if I drew my anthropological findings from many different regions of the rural tropical world, I have chosen to concentrate mainly on Anglophone West Africa (all of which lies south of the relatively sparsely populated Sahel) and on south India, the two regions in which I have undertaken prolonged fieldwork myself – place names are listed in the Glossary. This is not to say that the themes and arguments that are presented here could not have been equally well developed using information from other parts of the world, or that I was obliged to make so much reference to my own publications. But like every other author I find it advantageous to work with the material I know best. I am concerned with arable farming so that pastoral societies fall outside my scope. Some four-fifths of the entire population of south India and possibly also of West Africa (for which the figure is not known at all precisely) consists of rural dwellers, who live either dispersedly on their farmland or in settlements with populations of under some 5,000, where the very great majority of households are dependent on farming or farm-labouring for their livelihood. Accordingly, it is certainly the countryside, not the towns and cities, which should be regarded as providing the definitive ways of life in those regions. Nor has the definition of *rural* presented any difficulty for, except in the immediate vicinity of very large cities, which are surprisingly rare in both regions, there is no urban-rural continuum, which takes such subtle and complex forms in some other world regions, notably China.

The justification for examining a few elementary textbooks on economic development in my polemical chapters is that they reflect 'prevailing orthodoxy', such as is adhered to by many economists, often unwittingly; given the enormous influence of these texts on the minds of students, in particular, it is unfortunate that they seldom receive the reviews they deserve.

Owing to their acceptance of bad official statistics, relating particularly to the value of crop production over wide areas, development economists must be regarded as mainly responsible for the contemporary mood of demoralization over third-world prospects, which has overwhelmed the public in the Western world – a public which so often feels that 'it is too late for anything to be done'. Since the famines in Ethiopia and Sudan became public knowledge, *Africa* has become a doom-laden word. Two of my main polemical purposes are to argue that much third-world 'doom-mongering' has no sound intellectual basis and to affirm the viability of tropical economies. The situation is not helped by the widespread use in India of such jargon as *semi-arid tropics* (a synonym for non-irrigated, rain-fed farming regions); or by shifting the boundary of the West African Sahel (properly the zone where pastoralism, not arable farming, has long defined the mode of existence) some 400 miles south into the heart of Nigeria.

Since my purpose is not didactic, my constructive (non-polemical) chapters 6 to 14 are not intended to form a linked, coherent whole; they are rather a set of essays on particular practical subjects, such as rural credit-granting, inheritance systems and farm-labouring, on which it would seem that economic anthropologists have much of interest to say to development economists. This would not be so were anthropologists devoid of a concern for economic development. Many of us (and I speak emphatically for myself) have long had the presumed needs of development economists in mind when conducting our work. Yet the number of economic anthropologists (as distinct from urban sociologists) concerned with the third world is now so tiny relative to the colossal number of development economists that it would seem that we ought to continue to concentrate on our fundamental research in the field, where most matters are unexplored, rather than converting ourselves into 'development anthropologists'. But such a conclusion is perhaps conditional on our persuading the economists to start reading our books. Will the university students, whom I have had particularly in mind when writing this book, please use their influence to help?

PREAMBLE
HOW THE FARMERS OUTWITTED
THE BUREAUCRATS: A TRUE TALE

∽∾

One of the underlying themes of this book is that farmers in the rural tropical world are commonly not the docile, subservient or angry 'peasants' portrayed in many textbooks and official publications, but rather men and women with a proper and controlled contempt for external authority – a contempt which they often delight in concealing under a veneer of acquiescence. So I start this book with a Preamble relating to a particular case in which the clever farmers completely outwitted the gullible bureaucrats in the latter's political game.

The bureaucrats were officials of the notorious Gold Coast Cocoa Purchasing Company (CPC), an essentially political body which had been established by Nkrumah in 1952 for the purposes of gradually ousting all existing expatriate licensed buying agents[1] for cocoa, as well as the highly successful Co-operative Marketing Association (based on local cocoa-buying co-operative societies) which was later to handle even more cocoa for export than the United Africa Company – only to be subsequently rewarded by liquidation. Being effectively a political arm of government, though disguised as the Cocoa Marketing Board's own licensed buying agent, the CPC was able to offer lavish blandishments to farmers who would support them.

What form should these blandishments take? By the time of which I write (1953), it was fairly well known that if cocoa farmers received official grants for the replanting of their cocoa farms, many of which had been devastated by swollen shoot disease,[2] they usually devoted the cash to some 'more profitable purpose', such as building a house in Accra for letting. Wanting to be more

1. Only licensed buying agents appointed by the Cocoa Marketing Board were entitled to buy cocoa for export on the Board's behalf. See Beckman (1976: Chapter 4).
2. A virus which destroyed many of the cocoa farms, particularly in southern Ghana; it had first been identified in 1939. See Hill, 1963. Most of the cocoa farmers in this zone were migrants – see Chapter 11, Appendix A.

'constructive', the CPC therefore hit on the idea of using their funds to relieve the indebtedness of cocoa farmers, which was rightly known to be endemic. Everyone, including the officials of the CPC, all of whom were Africans although Ghana did not attain her independence until 1957 – everyone knew that indebtedness was 'bad' and ought to be 'relieved'. Everyone, or nearly everyone, also knew that most of the creditors, the misnamed 'money-lenders',[3] were cocoa farmers like their debtors – from which it was supposed to follow that creditor farmers were apt to be the mortal enemies of their debtor farmers.

In accordance with these beliefs, this 'wicked debt' was 'relieved' by transferring it from the creditor to the CPC itself, whose local Seven-Man Committees, composed of farmers believed to be loyal to Nkrumah's Convention Peoples Party (CPP), notionally assumed charge of the cocoa farm which had originally been pledged as security for the loan. This relief could only be achieved by paying the creditor a lump sum down: never mind that the creditor would probably immediately lend this windfall to someone else, for at least the CPC would have done its best to purify the economic atmosphere.

Everything was above board so far as the CPC was concerned. Grants to relieve indebtedness were made by a CPC official, associated with members of the local Seven-Man Committee, at a public meeting; an account of a loan-granting session which I myself attended in 1953 is given in the Appendix to this Preamble. The two parties were required to appear together before an official and his attendant farmers (who preserved silence) and to present supporting documents, of a type which, for some decades, had conventionally been drawn up by local letter-writers when farms were pledged. If, then, the debt was adjudged genuine, a cash sum, usually less than that recorded on the document, was immediately paid to the creditor. The maximum sum that could be granted to an individual was as high as £1,500.

Actually the farmers themselves did not share the belief that debt was 'improper': it was not necessarily even 'unfortunate', since most farmers did not pledge all their cocoa farms, of which

---

3. Moneylenders proper, who lent cash on interest and not on the security of cocoa farms – see pp.84–5 below.

they usually had several, and since relatively few farms went unredeemed by debtors.[4] Debtor and creditor were commonly friends and never enemies, the general attitude being that creditors were 'helpful people'. And as the two parties were necessarily thrust into each other's arms by the CPC's loan-granting procedure, what more natural than that they should have been inclined to act collusively from the outset, sharing out the 'swag' between them as they walked back to their village? Nor was there any reason why the unexpected windfall should affect their financial relationship – why should they regard the debt as liquidated? Since, in addition, there was no reason to believe that the local Farmers' Committees would take the faintest interest in the pledged farm which had been notionally transferred to their charge, or would demand repayment of the loan, for which they and the debtor-farmer were jointly responsible, it made good sense for the original debtor/creditor relationship between the farmers to remain intact.

The farmers being clever people, it soon dawned on them that the respective roles of creditor and debtor could easily be played by anyone, provided a local letter-writer, the equivalent of a petty lawyer, could be persuaded, as of course he could be, to compile a conventional Promissory Note. Such bogus Notes named the two parties; claimed, falsely, that one was indebted to the other to the tune of a certain sum; identified the boundaries of the pledged farm, which was presumably usually owned by the party identified as the debtor; and specified the terms for redemption of the debt – which was fairly commonly self-liquidating in terms of the share of the cocoa from the debtor's farm to which the creditor had become entitled. The (genuinely) innocent loan-granting officials, who had neither the time nor the inclination to inspect the farms which were supposed to have been pledged, had no means of distinguishing false from genuine applicatons, and many thousands of bogus debtors were 'relieved' of invented 'debt'.

For this well-organized deception, which readers may find hard to believe, there is much hard documentary evidence.[5] It is not

---

4. See Chapter 8.
5. See also Beckman, 1976:66 *et seq.* 'The scheme was wide open to manipulation by prospective beneficiaries, as well as by administrative officers' (p.62).

merely that the Jibowu Commission of Enquiry[6] into the affairs of the CPC reported (p. 32) that the Promissory Notes were apt to be 'false, antedated and prepared purposely for obtaining CPC loans', but that as late as 1957 the CPC itself had so little idea of the extent to which it had been hoodwinked that it actually granted me permission to examine its whole collection of original loan dockets, for the genuine purpose of studying the various systems under which farms had been apt to have been pledged in different regions. After examining several thousand Promissory Notes, I was indeed convinced that most of them had been concocted to deceive the CPC if only because a very high proportion of them bore dates just preceding the visit of the 'debt relieving committee' to the particular area. Moreover when, as so often, the CPC arbitrarily scaled down the original 'debt', fresh Notes were at once provided for the smaller sum, showing that the letter-writers were obedient, tame creatures, who were presumably always privy to the deception. Presumably, there were many cases such that the two parties already happened to be 'united by debt'; when they were, there was no reason for them to abandon their original relationship of 'mutual assistance', which each found advantageous.

Of course the farmers also outwitted the bureaucrats by neglecting to repay[7] the great bulk of the sum of nearly £3 million that had been granted (i.e. loaned) in this way before the scheme ended in 1956, as a result of the critical attitude of the Jibowu report. This they had always intended, rightly supposing that the dangers of prosecution, or of farm seizure in the event of default, were virtually non-existent. Ultimately, of course, as the Jibowu Commission reported, a procedure based on the idealistic colonial ideology (see Chapter 8 below) regarding the impurity (the impropriety) of debt – an ideology which had been uncritically inherited by that spearhead of anti-colonialism, the CPP – was sullied by the granting of loans for political services rendered. But that is another story.

6. An official enquiry chaired by Mr Justice Jibowu which reported in 1956.
7. This situation was not unique. 'The Nigerian Agricultural and Cooperative Bank will give no more loans to farmers through the River Basin Development Authorities until outstanding ones are settled. The chairman Group Capt. Usman Jibrin (rtd), said that the Authorities owed the bank Naira 55m disbursed to farmers through them, and had done little to settle the debts.' *Nigeria Newsletter* (1985: 9 March, 77).

Although the great bulk of the Promissory Notes which I examined were 'forgeries', the consistency of the geographical pattern that they revealed regarding the terms on which cocoa farms were apt to be pledged in different districts, showed that, in this general way, they were authentic documents, which were useful for research purposes, since they incorporated the sorts of terms familiar to the three parties, particularly to the letter-writer, whose experience told him what was customary. I shall make use of this material in Chapter 8.

APPENDIX
The Creditors Come Too[8]

The small octagonal house, somewhere in the southern Gold Coast, was full of gaily-clad farmers talking excitedly but not clamorously. A central table was covered with American cloth of loud design, around which reclined in very low easy chairs, of the type issued by the Public Works Department, the members of the local farmers' Group Executive. At the table was a big man from the Cocoa Purchasing Company (CPC) with his assistant and interpreter.[9] On the table were many brown files each containing, among other papers, an application on a stock form for a loan from the CPC – money which would relieve a cocoa farmer of his indebtedness.

Much work had been done locally in the past two months preparing applications for the busy man from the CPC and now all was set. Today he was here and tomorrow he would be off elsewhere. So today was a big day and all the local farmers who wanted relief from their burdens were congregated. All their creditors were congregated, too, some being distinguishable by their dress, which, for some unexplained reason, was more often shorts than the common long cloth.

The first farmer-applicant was accompanied, as required, by his creditor. The big man from the CPC perused the case file with rapid efficiency. 'Why', he asked, addressing the creditor through his interpreter, 'did you lend £195 without interest?' 'Because we are members of the same family.' 'Tell me the *actual* sum, the *actual* sum lent.' 'One hundred and ninety-five pounds.' 'The *actual* sum . . .?' 'One hundred and

---

8. An edited and shortened version of an article by the present writer published in *West Africa*, 21 November 1953, soon after the meeting described.
9. Many different languages are spoken by the migrant cocoa farmers of southern Ghana.

ninety-five . . .' 'I put it to you, you black Shylock you,[10] that the sum *actually* paid was £150 and that you charged £45 interest.' The man from the CPC thumped the file. Neither creditor nor debtor flinched; neither of them denied the charge. 'And how many loads [of 60 lbs] of cocoa have been taken from the farm so far this season?' 'Twenty loads have been sold to the CPC.'[11] The man from the CPC did some quick arithmetic on a small sheet of paper. 'I will give you £160,' he said, addressing debtor and creditor jointly as though they were one, 'one-sixty pounds, that is all. You creditors are a menace to the community. How can one of us Africans treat another like this? The reason I pay you only £160 is that £150 was the *actual* sum lent. I will pay you £10 interest.[12] The cocoa farm will remain in the possession of the CPC until the loan is paid off.'

The second applicant was a dignified, handsome, massive woman of prosperous demeanour. She was weeping because her creditor had refused to accompany her and because a certain document had been mislaid. The man from the CPC spoke gently to her, saying he was willing to consider her application on the next day in a town some thirty miles away. She departed somewhat comforted.

The third and fourth cases were quickly dismissed. One because the applicant had not provided himself with authority to represent the absentee creditor – and was not the sum of £1,000 perhaps too much?; the other because the creditor was not there at all. As the fourth 'applicant' withdrew he disdainfully unfurled his old black umbrella.

The fifth case was interesting due to the admission that the application had been prepared by the creditor, a young and innocent-looking man in khaki shorts. Five months ago he had lent the farmer £450, interest free. 'Why interest free?' 'Because we are friends.' 'And you have the use of your friend's farm – the farm is pledged to you for eight years?' 'Yes.' 'I put it to you that the *actual* sum, the *actual* sum paid out, was £300 and that you were to receive £150 in interest?' And so, conveniently, it proved to be. So far this season the creditor's profit from cocoa-selling from the pledged farm had been about £47. The man from the CPC did the arithmetic; the crowds outside shuffled in the sunlight; a very old, nearly toothless, member of the Group Executive stared, as it were, into the future . . . 'I give you £259 2s 5d,' the man from the CPC said suddenly. (There were no protests, though no one understood the arithmetic.) 'And I order you to take possession of this man's farm,' he said, addressing the Group Executive.

10. These were, of course, the actual words used although the official, like the farmers, was a Ghanaian.
11. The creditor hoped to ingratiate himself with the CPC official by saying this.
12. As we shall see (Chapter 8), the pledging of cocoa farms often involved no cash interest, but the official did not know this.

After the delivery of a suitable lecture on the unseemly behaviour of the creditor, the pair withdrew.

The sixth applicant was accompanied by his brother-in-law, to whom he had pledged a farm for ten years; both considered that it was in the public interest that the debtor should be released from bondage. In this case it was actually agreed that £350 had been honourably lent without interest. 'I pay you £250 15s,' said the man from the CPC, after his usual scribbling. How this sum was computed was perhaps not clear to the applicants (let the word stand in the plural), but it did allow for the fact that the rapacious creditor had taken from his innocent brother-in-law the profits from 75 loads of cocoa. Ten per cent interest was awarded to the creditor, who was commended for his transparent honesty.

The next applicant and his creditor were both smiling broadly – collusively. 'Is he your very good friend?' 'He is my very good friend.' 'And you lend money to your very good friend?' 'I lend money to my very good friend.' 'Why have you so much money?' 'I am big cocoa farmer. *If I have money I lend money.*' It emerged that both the applicant's farms had been pledged for eight years to his very good friend and that the sum borrowed was £400 *actual* with £200 interest. No cocoa from the farm had yet been sold by the creditor, so the arithmetic was simple. 'I pay you £440, including interest of £40. Your farm will be taken over by the CPC, but as it is a good, big farm it should be possible to pay off in one season.'

The farmers outside were now waiting somewhat more passively. Reports were good as far as they went: there was no need for the debtors to keep an eye on their creditors, or *vice versa*. The evening shadows were lengthening, the queue shortening.

CHAPTER 1

WHY COUNTRY PEOPLE
ARE NOT
PEASANTS

༄

The vogue word *peasant* suddenly entered general usage in relation to the rural tropical world in the late 1960s. Before that we had all been content to be more specific, employing *farmers*, *agricultural labourers* and the like; and we had been under no obligation to identify whole rural populations as *peasantries*. Certainly, there had been some academic discussion regarding African and Asian peasants and peasantries before that date, notably by Firth,[1] who held that *peasant* was 'a broad descriptive term of an empirical kind, suitable only for demarcating rough boundaries in categorization' (p.17)[2] and by Fallers, who concluded that the word denotes 'among other things, a degree of rusticity in comparison with his betters which we do not feel justified in attributing to the African villager';[3] but such discussion was not associated with any general attempt to differentiate rural populations by employing *peasant*. Even the French, who are more familiar than the British with peasants in their home country, remained quite content, for example, with *cultivateur*.

In this brief chapter,[4] I try to show why the sudden and universal adoption of *peasant*, as a kind of synonym for *countryfolk*, has done so much damage to our proper comprehension of the operation of rural tropical economies. The power of single words in human affairs is, of course, astounding; as they can trigger wars and revolutions and lead to the exoduses of whole populations, we should not perhaps be surprised that the sudden switch to *peasant* should have had such far-reaching consequences. In any case, many students of underdevelopment suddenly felt a need for this word for ideological reasons: they were obliged to replace pre-

---

1. Firth and Yamey (eds.), 1964.
2. He pointed out (p.18) that the term might usefully include non-cultivating countrymen 'so that we can speak not only of peasant agriculturists but also of peasant fishermen, peasant craftsmen and peasant marketers, if they are part of the same social system'.   3. Fallers, 1961:110.   4. See also Hill, 1982.

vious terminology with *peasant*, just as *African* had necessarily replaced the colonial *native* in the post-war years preceding Ghanaian Independence.[5] Authors employ, or are manipulated by, the words they deserve. And *peasant* in its contemporary usage is the semantic successor to *native*, incorporating all its condescending, derogatory and even racist overtones, especially in its usage by educated town-dwellers in the third world itself.

Despite the absurd waste of effort that has gone into attempts in the past fifteen years or more to qualify *peasant* appropriately,[6] its power to confirm our primitive ideas[7] of an amorphous, undifferentiated mass of tillers of the soil, labouring against overwhelming odds to provide sufficient food for their families, remains undiminished. But, curiously, although the word is necessarily very derogatory in many contexts, it also has cosy, even sentimental, connotations which tend to conceal the extremities of individual poverty. In European literature and tradition, though mainly outside Britain, a peasant is a hardworking, suffering, independent man, who tills his own plot and maintains his livestock with a little success; in India the word is desecrated by stretching its meaning to incorporate landless Harijans, whose squalid circumstances are mainly dependent on the whims of others.

For several cogent reasons the only possible definition of *peasant* in ordinary tropical conditions is a countryman or woman.[8] 'When

5. Thus, the (then) Imperial Institute in London was obliged to change, at a moment's notice, all the captions on its exhibits which used the word *native*.
6. I think that a majority of all the articles on the third world in certain scholarly journals, such as *The Journal of Peasant Studies*, have been concerned during that period, though perhaps not so much quite recently, with the futile task of defining and qualifying *peasant*. At the same time certain authors who might be expected to attempt to define *peasant* fail to do so, Klein (1980) being an example. In the introduction to his *Peasants in Africa* he implies, though does not state, that peasantization has something to do with colonialism and is content to criticize named 'liberals', including myself, on the grounds (which would apply as well to himself) that 'they focus more on the effect than on the cause', 'fail to account for the form and function of peasantries' and 'do not adequately describe the relation of the peasantry to the larger economy' (p.11).
7. I feel entitled to use this expression since, as an experienced anthropologist, I was so inappropriately surprised by the great degree of economic inequality which I found in Batagarawa, where there was uncultivated land which could be taken up by anyone (Hill, 1972).
8. I have even seen an absurd attempt to argue that in Hausaland *peasant* cannot be defined in terms of households since Hausa women, who own little land, 'are not part of the peasantry as it has usually been defined'.

is a peasant not a peasant?' we may enquire, to which the sensible
reply is, 'When he/she lives in a town or city.'[9] Assuming that we
adopt the *Shorter Oxford Dictionary*'s definition of *peasant* as 'one who
lives in the country and works on the land; a countryman a rustic
(*sic*)', then in rural West Africa and south India there are very few
non-peasants, for nearly everyone has some connection with
agriculture or the care of livestock. Even in south India[10] most
artisans and village traders are also farmers or farm labourers and
there are very few occupations, such as fishing, which are at all
likely to be all-absorbing or sufficiently rewarding on their own.
Whereas in medieval Europe and imperial China there were in the
villages specialist artisans, such as cobblers and builders, who did
no farming, this is not so in West Africa, where most rural blacksmiths[11] aspire to be farmers. In Hausaland in northern Nigeria,
which is surely not anomalous in this way, there is a very strong
tendency for the most successful farmers to have the most
remunerative non-farming occupations and *vice versa*. Non-
farming occupations, which may be pursued at any time, provide
farmers with some insurance against the unreliability of the
climate; yet few of those who discuss the riskiness of peasant
agriculture mention their existence.

9. But now that the multinationals (denoted, for some reason, as transnationals) have
   moved into West African agriculture, an alternative reply is 'When he is a
   multinational corporation'. On moral grounds the British colonialists, unlike the
   French, staunchly resisted the establishment of expatriate-owned export-crop plantations in West Africa. Fortunately the magnificent victory won in the early 1920s by
   Governor Clifford over Lever Brothers (later Unilever), on the matter of Nigerian oil-
   palm plantations, was grandly recorded by Hancock (1940); thereafter 'peasant
   agriculture' remained basically undisturbed. But no longer. According to Oculi
   (1984), American-based 'transnational corporations', in conjunction with Nigerian
   interests, have recently moved directly into Nigerian rice production, poultry farming
   and cattle rearing. The American poultry companies, who bring their own stocks of
   fowls, are reported to be 'very happy' (p.89) to import US grain for feeding the birds.
   Oculi comments that the 'new social category' of Nigerian businessmen, civil
   servants, military personnel and 'rural elites', which is associated with these ventures,
   has no 'creative orientation to agriculture' (p.91) and that it has effectively passed 'a
   vote of no confidence in the small farmer' (p.90). In its issue of 25 March 1985, *West
   Africa* reported (p.580) that the Ghanaian government and the multinational Lonrho
   were to form a joint company to establish plantations for the cultivation of foodcrops.
   'Having co-operated in mining for so long, Ghana and Lonrho should operate in
   . . . agriculture.'
10. Although the old idea of a close association between specialized occupation and caste,
   especially such as would exclude farming, is now generally outmoded, it is true that in
   south Indian villages there are apt to be very small numbers of people, such as washer-
   men (but not 'sweepers', who are solely urban), who have no concern with
   agriculture.
11. I mention blacksmiths because they are, perhaps, the most prosperous of all
   'traditional' artisans; they are apt to be notably successful farmers.

Just as the various social classes in any Western community have little meaning unless defined in relation to each other, so if tropical peasants are to be regarded as a 'class' they must be related to non-peasants. But if, as I have argued, there are no (rural) non-peasants, we are thrown back on the *Oxford Dictionary*'s definition of *peasant* in its early use as being 'antithetical to noble', for surely no one would argue that *all* townspeople stand in opposition to *all* countryfolk?

Yet, even if we admit that peasants are to be equated with countryfolk, may the word not be useful in facilitating categorization? I would argue that this is emphatically not so since, owing to the likelihood of overlap between categories, verbal classifications employing *peasant* are usually much inferior to statistical classifications (in terms, say, of the sizes of farm-holdings) and are much less informative than straightforward words such as *landlord* or *tenant*. It is astonishing that so little heed has been paid to Lenin's warnings[12] of the dangers of obscuring differentiation by dealing in terms of average peasants of various categories.

What then becomes of the common belief that cultivators who never employ farm labourers should be rigidly contrasted with those who do,[13] either by denoting the latter as non-peasants or by differentiating peasants into these two 'classes'? Certainly, I would argue that, a peasant being a countryman, the latter course is impossible, especially as labour employment is much more common than is often supposed (see Chapter 10). As for the former possibility, this may easily lead to absurdity, for instance where impoverished widows are obliged to employ labourers to clear or plough their land,[14] or where many cultivators employ labourers very occasionally. Again, one may ask, if labour employment is so crucial, ought not landless farm labourers to be regarded as non-peasants?

A further objection to *peasant* resides in its common evolutionary connotations. Even if there is no contemporary rural 'class' standing in opposition to the peasant, and thus defining

12. In *The Development of Capitalism in Russia*, Vol. 3 of the Collected Works of V.I. Lenin, originally published in 1899.
13. Thus, Shanin in the introduction to his influential *Peasants and Peasant Societies* (1971:14–15) insists that 'The family and nearly only the family, provides the labour on the [peasant] farm.'
14. Mencher (1978:201) notes that even relatively poor farmers with holdings of under an acre may employ others to help with ploughing.

him, many writers seem to imply that there must have been a time, not so long ago, when those who are peasants today were *pre-peasants*, because they were unconnected with any wider cash economy;[15] these are the writers who would virtually define the peasant in terms of his exploitability by the wider capitalist world. Three points need making here. First, that it is more straightforward to emphasize 'urban bias', in the numerous senses of that expression; second that many urban non-peasants are likewise exploited; and third that the dates at which cash started to percolate into village economies vary by many centuries, as any comparison of south India with Tanzania shows.[16] So I am convinced that *peasant* is misleading unless it be equated with country-dweller. It should therefore be abandoned as otiose and old-fashioned.

To illustrate some of the difficulties of categorizing *peasant*, let us consider those enterprising and wily migrant cocoa farmers of southern Ghana who were the subject of my Preamble and will be discussed further.[17] Does such a farmer, who had bought half a square mile of uncultivated forest for clearing and planting, conform to any conventional notion of a peasant? And if we insist on denoting some migrant farmers as such, where are we to draw the statistical line? Certainly, many of them farm such small acreages (see pp.161–2 below) that they are able to dispense with farm labourers; but in a polygynous society much depends on particular family circumstances and there is no possibility of indicating the maximum area of planted cocoa which might be cultivated by family labour, especially as farms are often so widely dispersed that different members of the family are in charge at each place. For such reasons as these and also because labour employment may be so small-scale and casual, it is certain that *peasant* ought not to be used as a differentiating criterion in this context.

As we shall see, not all cocoa farmers, even in southern Ghana, are migrants who had bought their land. Some of them are 'sedentary farmers' who cultivate land belonging to their local matri-

15. Writers vary greatly in the significance they attribute to the degree of involvement in the cash economy implied by *peasantry*. *Peasants* by Wolf (1966) led the way in this discussion.
16. Iliffe (1979:132) states that in Tanzania the use of money was surprisingly rare before 1890.   17. See Chapter 11, Appendix A.

lineage, nearly a half of whom are commonly women cultivators in their own right. Enough is known about such farmers and about similar people in Ashanti,[18] to be sure that the graph relating acreages cultivated to numbers of farmers is reasonably smooth and well extended. Some of these farmers are creditors, some debtors – some even both; some employ labourers, others do not; some have a large number of dependants to help them on their farms, others have few; some are efficient cultivators, others are not; some are lorry owners, others have no transport. These categories overlap. How can some of these men and women be denoted peasants and others not?

The notion of *peasant* is peculiarly inapposite in many south Indian villages where rich high-caste farmers, living in large cement houses, and owning large acreages of farmland, irrigation equipment, sufficient plough animals and so on, and with educated sons in the city, cannot be compared, by any stretch of terminology, with the impoverished Harijans in their squalid huts just round the corner, even if the latter happen to own a little land. The primary classification of members of these strictly endogamous castes, each of which is proud to maintain its identity, must be in terms of caste, *peasant* being as inappropriate to the rich high-caste farmer as to the Harijan.[19]

The fact is that, wherever one looks, the various expressions of economic inequality within a rural community are almost certain to render *peasant* an incongruous word if applied to all house-holders, however elaborately it may be qualified. How can it simultaneously embrace both a famous Hausa Koranic teacher[20] who has twice made the pilgrimage by air to Mecca, and has twenty students who assist him on his large area of farmland, and a man who owns no more than a ramshackle habitation, half an acre of land and one donkey?

18. See Fortes (1950) and (1970).
19. This is not only an outsider's view. Thus, Cassen (1978:287) notes that the Indian anthropologist Béteille 'has argued persuasively that if we were being careful, we would not even use the word 'peasant' to describe agriculturalists in India'.
20. The fact that many of the most famous Hausa Koranic teachers (Malams) reside in the countryside, often in remote places, makes us realize that, in a sense, Hausaland *is* the populous countryside, the few cities being anomalous conglomerations, including large stranger-elements. (And who has ever heard of a whole country composed of peasants?)

Finally, one must, of course, recognize that many of those who make such heavy weather over defining *peasant* are primarily concerned with the peasantry as a political entity. But the uses of such a category in most, though not in all, regions of the tropical world are very limited, partly because individual country-dwellers do not regard themselves as defined in relation to their opposition to urban 'non-peasants'. (President Nkrumah of Ghana was not alone in finding his inability to 'mobilize the peasants' both surprising and unfortunate, especially as they were not averse to paying lip-service.) Primarily owing to the significance of intra-village economic inequality, individual households in any community usually lack a common political purpose. Certainly, in a general way, they may deplore the patronizing attitude of townsmen, many of whom are poorer than themselves, to countryfolk *per se*;[21] and they resent low prices for farm produce and high taxes on some of their own purchases.[22] But this does not usually mean that they are an organized political force to be reckoned with, despite their numerical predominance, or that they are able to challenge the 'small, interlocking elites of . . . business men, professionals, bureaucrats who "substantially control" the distribution of resources'.[23]

The weakness of 'the peasantry' in relation to external forces is demonstrated by the recent World Bank irrigation schemes in Hausaland. These have imposed 'a new risky, expensive farming system . . . on a silent population', states Wallace,[24] and are the consequence of an *international 'peasant denigrating' conspiracy*. No one asks the farmers' opinion; 'no one taps their knowledge'. Much natural marshland (*fadama*) has been unnecessarily inundated; many of the smaller farmers have already been totally dispossessed. If the schemes do not fail altogether, as so many have before them, this will be because of the success of a policy which scorns and ousts the knowledgeable and efficient indigenes in favour of powerful external interests.

---

21. Thus, Hausa countrymen will often wryly refer to themselves as *talakawa*, an interesting word meaning *commoner* which derives from *talaka* (poor), and which is often employed derogatorily by townspeople. Mote (1977:103) suggests that Chinese civilization may be unique in that its word for peasant has never been a term of contempt.
22. See Lipton, 1977:Chapter 13, 1980:15 and 1984 on rural-urban terms of trade.
23. Lipton, 1982:143.   24. Wallace, 1980:70.

Perhaps the most deleterious effect of the contemporary compulsion to define *peasant* is that the matter of economic inequality within rural communities, which is of over-riding significance, is considered intellectually dissatisfying unless categories of peasant can be properly identified – as they usually can not be, leaving the notion of the amorphous peasantry intact. This results, for example, in a failure to realize the need for reliable and informative statistics of land-holdings by household, such as do not carelessly bundle all those owning (say) less than five hectares in one class;[25] to a lack of serious interest in the landless, who are omitted from many statistical tables and often falsely identified with farm labourers; and to the neglect of important non-farming occupations, such as trading, which are often wrongly presumed to involve 'non-peasant specialists' only.

The search for universal generalizations relating to the rural tropical world, in all its diversity, is a vain one. One of the main reasons for this is intra-village economic inequality, to which I turn in the next chapter.

25. As is quite usual in India: indeed, the majority of households are fairly commonly in the smallest size-group.

CHAPTER 2

THE VAIN SEARCH FOR UNIVERSAL GENERALIZATIONS: 1. THE RELEVANCE OF ECONOMIC INEQUALITY

〰️

One of the few important socio-economic generalizations which may safely be made about rural tropical economies is that a significant degree of economic inequality always exists within any rural community in which cash circulates.[1] This inequality may be so pronounced that the economic behaviour and motivations of the poorest farmers are entirely different from, even the mirror images of, those of the richest. Yet the economists' need for generalizations relating to all farmers in the village necessarily ignores this essential fact. This means that contrary to appearances the village community as a whole, not the household, is effectively the unit of investigation. I shall justify my 'inequality generalization' in Chapter 6. In this chapter I try to expose the confusion resulting from ignoring village inequality by reference first to a recent textbook; then to an attempt by two economists to verify various hypotheses by means of fieldwork; and finally to the work of some world-renowned development economists.

The textbook is *Agriculture and Economic Development* by S. Ghatak and K. Ingersent (1984),[2] in general a respectable work which may come close to achieving the authors' ambitious aim of being 'essential as a main text for courses on development economics and agricultural economics'. I start with Chapter 2, 'Structure and Characteristics of Agriculture in LDCs',[3] in which (pp.5 *et seq.*) the authors examine the main attributes of 'traditional agriculture',

1. I put the matter this way (see, also, pp.71 below) merely because I am not concerned with those rare contemporary economies in which cash does not circulate. Incidentally, why does Rimmer assert (Peil *et al.*, 1982:56) that 'there are *a priori* reasons for expecting inequality in income distribution not to be pronounced in most African countries'?
2. I chose this textbook because it is both well organized (its conventional diagrams and algebra being exceptionally clearly presented) and up-to-date. However, such is the gulf between economists and economic anthropologists that, so far as I can tell, no anthropological work is included in its lists of references at the end of each chapter, which may run to some 200 titles altogether – allowing for overlap.
3. Less Developed Countries. The fact that not all LDCs are within the tropics is hardly relevant, for most of them are and the authors' main interest is clearly in that zone.

defined as 'the characteristic farming type in countries[4] where agriculture is the dominant employer (including those who are self-employed)'. Their first point of emphasis is that 'peasant agriculture', which they use as a synonym for 'traditional agriculture', is 'typified by the *small, family* farm' (their italics) – a view which implies instant dismissal of the significance of inequality. ' "Small" in relation to what?' is the inevitable query: small in relation to existent simple farming technology, or small by comparison with the developed world?

Then, what can be the meaning of 'typified' in this context? Is a farmer who cultivates 40 acres 'small' if, as is commonly the case, there are many in the same community who cultivate less than 2 acres? If the graph relating acreage (on the X axis) to the number of farmers (Y axis) declines reasonably smoothly between (say) 2 acres and 25 acres, as it often does, what is 'typical'? The fact is that one of the most salient economic characteristics of a rural community is likely to be the actual shape of this graph, which has to be drawn to have meaning.

The authors' first 'attribute' of traditional agriculture is that the '[agricultural] production unit' is characterized not only by its small size but by its high degree of self-sufficiency. If this implies that most *households* produce most of the food that they require, then it is a dangerously misleading statement, for research has revealed that the riskiness of agricultural life in the rural tropics is apt to be such that a fair proportion of farmers in any community fail to provide at all adequately for their households, even where there is no scarcity of farmland. Indeed, as I have pointed out elsewhere,[5] in well-populated localities the only self-sufficient farmers in a community may be the richest. This lack of appreciation of the significance of inequality is all the odder considering that the authors allow themselves (p.7) the highly debatable, though common, generalization that in third-world countries land is generally 'scarcer' than labour – this being one of those blanket statements which is, paradoxically, either meaningless or untrue, as we shall later come to realize.[6].

---

4. Can this mean that they are considering countries as a whole?
5. Hill, 1982:123.
6. Presumably, it is often meant to imply that the community *as a whole* would cultivate more land were it available?

The authors' second point is that 'few purchased inputs are employed', which implies *inter alia* that 'the farm workforce consists principally of family labour'. Again, such a generalization ignores inequality. In localities where most farmland is cultivated every year and there is no fallow, as in much of south India and in parts of savannah West Africa, high proportions of richer farmers are apt to buy 'inputs' of organic manure and/or chemical fertilizers. As for the extent of labour employment, while it is usually, though not necessarily, true that there is more family than hired labour *in the community as a whole*, the crucial question relates to the propensity of richer farmers to employ poorer men or women on their farms (see Chapter 10). In adding, rather apologetically, that there may be 'some hiring-in and hiring-out of labour ... amongst neighbouring farms (*sic*)', Ghatak and Ingersent overlook such massive long-distance migrations of labourers as virtually created the cocoa-growing industries of Ghana and the Ivory Coast – which certainly fall within their definition of 'traditional agriculture', not only because agriculture was the 'dominant employer', but also because 'traditional techniques' were employed.

The authors' third substantial point is that 'the emphasis on self-sufficiency implies that a proportion of farm output is not sold', but consumed by the farmer's household, which means that the significance of inequality is overlooked. While it is true that such richer farmers as have some reasonable hope of producing all the food that they require may be generally hesitant about selling foodstuffs, especially in the period before they are able to assess the size of the next harvest, poorer farmers, on the other hand, are sometimes obliged to sell their entire output in order to meet their pressing debts and consumption needs. The latter are the farmers who sell produce immediately after harvest when seasonal prices are lowest. Indeed, when my Batagarawa farmer-assistants (see p.74–5 below) were asked to expatiate on the distinguishing characteristics of impoverished farmers, such enforced grain-selling was often mentioned.

Such are the difficulties in handling that vague term *subsistence farmer* that I have long abandoned its use. The basic ambiguity (see also p.53) is that it may be defined by reference to whether the farmer sells any produce or to whether he buys any; these and other difficulties attaching to *subsistence* are well illustrated by Ghatak and Ingersent, whose attempt to identify the main attributes of traditional agriculture becomes confused when they try to differentiate farmers or communities using this embarrassing word.

They begin by referring to *purely subsistence agriculture*, which is such that no household sells any produce; they do not mention that such communities are statistically so rare in the world that they could be ignored in a textbook of this type with scarcely any loss. They then turn to *semi-subsistence agriculture*, which is such that some produce is self-consumed and some sold, but they fail to add that virtually all *communities*, as distinct from individual households, are of this type. They imply[7] that such cultivators produce sufficient food for their own requirements, thus presuming, as is usual among economists, that food sales are to be equated with 'surpluses'.[8] After discussing whether households may eat more than they minimally require, either because there is no market, or because 'the farmer does not require a cash income' (both unrealistic possibilities), they then distinguish pure from semi-subsistence farmers on the basis that the latter are farmers-cum-'businessmen'. But because, presumably, the quaintly inappropriate 'businessmen' might be thought to imply some element of wealth, they at once throw all caution to the winds, affirming that 'cash income is typically very low'. Readers will realize that I have no further need to criticize *typically very low*; but I must protest that *typically* is immediately forgotten in the text, it being concluded that *in general* 'risk-aversion' takes 'precedence' over 'profit maximization' in deciding which crops to grow.

One reason for the general neglect of inequality in underdevelopment theory is the common misconception, shared as we have seen by these authors, that *peasants*, such as grain cultivators, concentrate so exclusively on arable farming that the relationship between agriculture and such occupations as trading and craftwork (which are apt to be engaged in by various members of the

7. This seems to be fair comment within the general context of the statement that *pure* subsistence farmers are not necessarily self-sufficient (p.7).
8. On p.189 the authors use the conventional, and misleading, term 'marketed surplus', meaning output less 'own consumption'. See p.75 below.

farming household) require no analytical investigation. It is seldom realized, for example, that in many tropical regions most traders are male and/or female farmers, who may engage in long-distance as well as local trading. As we shall see, the evidence suggests that it is usual for the richest farmers to enjoy the most lucrative non-farming occupations, so that the matter of inequality assumes even more importance than if farming were the sole, or invariably the main, pursuit.

To such an extent do these authors presume that *peasants* are interested only in farming that they would even deny them the possibility of making cash profits from crop storage. In regions such as northern Nigeria, where normal conditions of pronounced seasonal price fluctuations are nowadays compounded by severe inflation, the logistics of grain storage deeply concerns the farmers, to the extent that large-scale storage of bought grain for sale at a price rise is one of the chief 'remunerative non-farming occupations' of richer farmers.[9] The farmers not only provision the cities with grain, but are responsible for storing much of that grain on the stalk for many months. Most of the grain threshing is carried out slowly by hand in the villages throughout the year; and most grain traders handle threshed grain only. Compared with the immense stocks of unthreshed grain held in village granaries, city stocks and storage facilities are relatively tiny. Yet we learn (p.23) that 'there is little scope [for farmers] for accumulating stocks to bridge periods of low prices'. Why must the functions of cultivators be thus over-simplified and denigrated?

Finally, I would object to the statement (p.24) that 'most rural households are restricted to only a very small plot of land'. I would do so on three grounds: first, because of the implication, on p.6 and elsewhere, that household self-sufficiency in foodstuffs is usual; second, because it ignores variations in the shape of the 'inequality graph' referred to on p.17 above; and third, because it overlooks the fact that high proportions of all farmers in many regions own several scattered plots.[10]

Some readers may feel that, in using a textbook to illustrate my contentions, I am not doing justice to the work of development

9. See Hill, 1972.   10. See p.103 below.

economists whose work is directed rather at their own colleagues. For in their efforts at simplification are not such writers justified in using *typically* when they ought to draw a graph? I would argue, on the contrary, that elementary tasks, such as that of pointing out the dangers involved in the misuse of averages, are one of the first duties of those who take on the education of students. I would argue, also, that this textbook reflects 'prevailing orthodoxy'[11] reasonably reliably.

I now turn to a research study, by two established economists, in support of my contention that the grand development theories are far too generalized to be testable in the field. *Palanpur: The Economy of an Indian Village*[12] reports on an attempt to show, by means of village fieldwork,[13] that 'theories of development economics should have the power to explain what one finds in a village such as Palanpur' (p.4). The authors sought to choose between: first, Schultz's contention that 'given its constraints of knowledge the village economy makes efficient use of its assets'; second, Hirschman's argument that 'entrepreneurial decision-making is in short supply and substantial and clear incentives are necessary before investment commitments will be made'; third, Lewis's emphasis on 'the importance of incentives and the price mechanism in the allocation of resources and the generation of growth'; and fourth, Myrdal's belief that 'markets and prices play a minimal role in the agriculture of South Asia', so that an institutional emphasis is required.[14]

The authors frankly admit that they found themselves frustrated in their general purpose: 'We did not find that the village accorded with any single simple theory and we had to draw upon several models[15] to explain its various features.' Plaintively, they report that there was 'wide variability' (p.119) in the practices and attitudes of Palanpur farmers; while they sometimes imply that economic inequality in part accounted for this bewildering diversity,

---

11. See pp.68–9 below.   12. C.J. Bliss and N.H. Stern, 1982.
13. Rapidly undertaken as long ago as 1974.
14. Schultz, 1964; Hirschman, 1958; Lewis 1955; Myrdal, 1968.
15. The notion of drawing on 'models', rather than offering explanations, has many implications with regard to those economists' approach to fieldwork. Quotation from Bliss and Stern, p.299.

this matter received little systematic, analytical discussion, though they did examine the theory regarding the inverse relationship between yield and scale of farming (see p.73 below), finding yield roughly invariable.

An astonishing innocence informs their fairly detailed discussion of factor and commodity markets, in the general sense, for they seem somehow to have assumed that certain grand generalizations ought to have emerged and they were, therefore, disappointed. ('As we have surveyed a number of different markets ... and found in them disparate features it would be pointless to attempt a summary of our findings ...' (p.122).) They do admit that 'the perfectly competitive market of the textbook is an unlikely object to look for in a small village' (or anywhere?); but, alas, each market had its own 'peculiar features', and there was no market at all for bullock hire – they failed to note the reason which is that, as a precaution, bullocks were always hired out with their own ploughmen! Had they read any economic anthropology[16] they could hardly have concluded (p.123) that the lack of perfect competition was a matter of real interest.

On the question of the labour market they stumblingly discuss the tendency for daily wage rates, for any particular task, to remain roughly standard throughout the season, but seem to regard this as virgin country for they make no reference to the similar findings of numerous other investigators (see Chapter 10). Although much sophisticated mathematics is included in their chapter on tenancy and share-cropping,[17] their conclusions are, to their own admission, impressionistic; thus, for example, assuming that farmers in general[18] had 'a high degree of risk aversion', share-

16. So far as I can tell, there are no publications by anthropologists in this book's bibliography – as with Ghatak and Ingersent. Did the great 'Polanyi debate', of which one hears little nowadays, become generally known to economists in its heyday in the late 1960s? For this would at least have familiarized them with the idea that the existence of 'the market principle' cannot necessarily be taken for granted in Africa. There were two camps: the 'substantivists' who, influenced by Karl Polanyi (see Dalton (ed.), 1968) contended that traditional exchange depended on reciprocity and redistribution; and the 'formalists' who were in favour of the *selective* application of Western economic theory. See Hopkins, 1973:6 and Dalton, 1971.

17. While they claim to have been helped by the 'substantial literature' on share-cropping (*métayage*), they refer only to 'Marshall and Cheung' who appear to be the two economists Alfred Marshall (1890) and Cheung (1969). See Appendix to Chapter 14.

18. I think, but am not certain, that this is the correct understanding – see p.165.

cropping would commend itself as spreading risk between land-lord and tenant.

Much attention is devoted to wheat,[19] which occupied 42% of the cultivated land in the *rabi* season of 1974–5, but their con-clusions are disappointingly lame. 'We are unable to confirm that neo-classical economics is alive and well and residing in Palanpur, at least in its simplest form' (p.291). 'Farmers were not doing the best that they could do given their resources. But one should not, and we did not, expect the world to be that simple' (p.293).

'Credit', we are told, 'is not an input like labour and bullock power but it enables the farmer to buy inputs and it therefore plays a central role in agriculture' (p.105). In briefly analysing the type of credit-granting which involved private farmers, the authors generally disregarded inequality, though they did reveal (presumably correctly, see Chapter 8) that the richest farmers were the most indebted. On a return visit to Palanpur in 1977 they interviewed twelve farmers about private borrowing, as a result of which they concluded that 'it does seem inaccurate to think of the farmers of Palanpur as typically facing unyielding credit constraints. That they do not attempt to commit more resources to agriculture must then reflect an unwillingness to change established practices, undertake risk, or whatever' (p.319).

It is largely because they ignore social factors that Bliss and Stern are so often baffled by diversity: thus, 'Why it is that some factors are traded rather than others we cannot explain' (p.305). They are confused and self-contradictory on the matter of land-selling; this is important since no single theory, incorporating any degree of detail, can possibly apply to land-selling and non-land-selling economies alike – each of which is common in the rural tropical world. Land-buying having been (at least until recently, see Chapter 13) one of the main ways by which richer farmers aggrandized themselves at the expense of poorer farmers in some economies, here again the significance of economic inequality is overlooked.[20]

---

19. Two highly mathematical chapters (pp.222–93) relate to this crop; one presumes that they will be of much interest to agronomists.
20. Ghatak and Ingersent are equally casual on land-selling.

More surprising than their lack of knowledge of anthropological factors is Bliss and Stern's almost total neglect of their fellow economist Myrdal's monumental work on South Asia, *Asian Drama*,[21] particularly of his findings on farm labouring (see p.108 below). Why has *Asian Drama* had such a marked lack of influence on other economists, even though Myrdal very modestly considers (p.1843) that many of his arguments may apply outside South Asia?[22] I suggest this is mainly because of his great degree of emphasis, at hundreds of points in his three volumes, on problems of inequality and his consequent refusal to present 'final truth' (p.xiii). He wrote with much insight on 'the village hierarchy' (pp.1052 *et seq*.), remarking that 'no accurate statistical picture' of the various social groups within a village existed for any South Asian country. And, most unusually for an economist, he had some interest (p.1100) in the relationship between craftwork and agriculture. But his frequently expressed distrust of official statistics would hardly have endeared him to his fellow economists. He was convinced that 'in twenty or even ten years' time we shall have different approaches and use quite different concepts and theories from those we have been accustomed to using' (p.xiii). He must be disappointed at the lack of progress that has been made since 1968 in speeding up 'the reorientation of economic and social research in South Asia'.

Finally I turn to look very briefly at the theories of three grand generalizers with special reference to economic inequality; I shall argue that their theories are not only basically untestable in the field but are essentially ambiguous. Tempting though it might be to examine some more up-to-date theories, the example of Bliss and Stern shows that 'the old masters', Schultz and Hirschman, still exert much influence on development economists – and Boserup, my third generalizer, continues to be very widely cited.[23]

Schultz claimed, as we have seen, that village economies make efficient use of their assets, given their constraints of knowledge.

---

21. Myrdal, 1968 runs to 2284 pages.
22. Defined at that time as including 'Pakistan, India, Ceylon, Burma, Malaya, Thailand, Indonesia and the Philippines, and sometimes South Vietnam, Cambodia and Laos as well' (p.41).   23. See also reference to W.A. Lewis on pp. 51–2 below.

'*There are comparatively few significant inefficiencies in the allocation of the factors of production in traditional agriculture.*'[24] This assertion is based on the belief that the organization of traditional agriculture tends towards a 'particular type of equilibrium' (p.29) – an equilibrium such that no outside expert could discover any major inefficiency in the allocation of factors and that no productive factor remains unemployed. Such static economies are 'incapable of growth except at high cost', to the point that it does not pay to invest in agriculture unless the farmer is given the opportunity 'to transform the traditional agriculture of his forebears' (p.23).

Schultz tested his hypotheses by reference to Tax, whose work relates to a Guatemalan village, and to an unpublished thesis on an Indian village by Hopper, two authors who were unconcerned with economic inequality.[25] He was gratified to learn from Tax that 'competition is present everywhere in the way products and factors are priced';[26] that there was 'no disguised unemployment or under-employment';[27] and, even for child labour, 'no such thing as a zero marginal product'.[28] His primary confirmation from Hopper was that the farmers' 'implicit prices' for various crops, i.e. the relative prices implied by their respective allocations of various resources including land and bullock time, closely matched such actual market prices for products and factors as were available, so that there was no evidence that improvement in output could be achieved by altering farmers' factor allocations.

These two publications can hardly be regarded as confirming Schultz's grand generalizations.[29] In the case of Tax this was mainly because his village pursued trade rather than traditional agriculture; since it produced no foodstuffs for household consumption it was not 'typical of a large class of poor agricultural

24. Schultz, 1960:37 – his italics.   25. Tax, 1953; Hopper, 1957.
26. No anthropologist would ever agree with such a general attitude. Nor is it necessary to be in the least esoteric in refuting it. One may just affirm that where reliable units of measurement, such as acres or bushels, are lacking, there are technical reasons for imperfect competition. (Indigenous units are never as standard as local people and others suggest.)
27. The inevitability of such under-utilization of labour in south Asia is one of Myrdal's major themes, which he deals with most interestingly and at great length.
28. Schultz, 1964:42–4.
29. Schultz himself referred (p.40) to the 'paucity of usable data' to test his hypothesis.

communities' as Schultz claimed; and it was, indeed, most exceptional in its total lack of under-employment. As for Hopper's
material, there is no mention of the relevance of economic
inequality to agricultural performance: it is implied, though not
stated, that rich and poor are similarly motivated and well
informed.

This is, of course, the general charge one has to levy against
Schultz's work, to the degree that at best his conclusions could
relate only to better-off cultivators, though one would still be left
with the misbelief regarding the ubiquity of competition. *Severely
impoverished individuals, who exist in all communities*, as we shall see, *are
necessarily inefficient if only because they lack the resources to set themselves
to work effectively in either farming or non-farming occupations*. As the
poorest farmers often obtain very poor yields from their farmland
owing, for example, to their inability to buy manure or fertilizers,
so from the point of view of the village community as a whole the
fact that they cultivate any land at all means that Schultz's notion
of the optimal allocation of resources is unsustainable. Accordingly,
any concept of the inevitability of inequality is entirely at variance
with Schultz's idea of equilibrium, which is a deliberate abstrac-
tion, reminding one of the pre-Keynesian belief that stable
equilibrium implied full employment.

Turning to Hirschman, it is perhaps odd that Bliss and Stern
should have sought to test his view that 'enterprise' is in short
supply in rural communities, since he was primarily concerned
with industry. (Hard put to it to find an example, they state (p.51)
that farmers would be 'enterprising' in Hirschman's sense if they
continued to use fertilizers after the subsidy, which had first
encouraged their use, had been withdrawn.) Here I merely want to
insist that the notion of 'the unenterprising peasant', which
prevailed for so many decades, is now right out of fashion, there
being a great deal of evidence that certain 'peasants' respond to
incentives. So what should one nowadays make of Hirschman's
view that it is not the resources themselves but the ability to bring
them into play which is lacking? We can retort by citing Lipton
who, goaded by Hirschman's unsupported generalities, asserts
that 'the impoverished rural sector does not have, because it can-

not afford to have, anti-economising, non-innovating attitudes'; and that 'local rural traditions are surprisingly modern'.[30] Or one can repeat Chambers's view, which is based on much sound practical experience, that 'innovations which farmers can manage, and find are good, spread very rapidly indeed, through innumerable personal trials'; perhaps, as he says, 'the least recognized aspect of rural people's knowledge is its experimental nature'.[31] But whomever we cite, we always find ourselves reflecting that poorer villagers, who have small farm-holdings and cannot borrow, may be precluded from exerting any latent propensities to be 'enterprising', however that tricky word is defined, so that one can seldom speak of enterprising communities.[32] It seems that, so far as the countryside is concerned, Hirschman's views have lost any relevance that they ever had, so that Bliss and Stern would have saved themselves the trouble of testing them had they looked more widely at recent literature.

I have chosen Boserup as my third 'grand generalizer' owing to the extraordinary appeal her contra-Malthusian views have exerted – an appeal which is altogether out of proportion to the rigour of her theoretical arguments.[33] Boserup believes that third-world farmers do not actually adopt more efficient technologies, which are potentially available to them, until declining yields resulting from population pressure persuade them to do so. But the farmers themselves, together with their friends the rural blacksmiths, have always been the great innovators so far as their own tools are concerned[34] and her notion (p.38) of *unutilized knowledge* of superior tools and intensive agrarian techniques is not convincing.

It seems that her astonishing persuasive powers were partly due to her well-timed optimism, there being remarkably little firm evidence that increasing population density *in itself* induces favourable technical change – though the Anloga shallot farmers

30. Lipton, 1977:214.   31. Chambers, 1983:92.
32. An example is, however, provided by the shallot farmers of Anloga in south-eastern Ghana – see p.159 below.   33. Boserup, 1965.
34. This is taking a long view because, of course, colonial Departments of Agriculture were responsible for introducing metal ploughs during this century in both south India and parts of savannah West Africa; these are now sometimes made by local blacksmiths. See Hill, 1982, Appendix II (3).

(n.32 above) are a rare and anomalous example favouring her thesis. Her basic idea that the state of agricultural technology, systems of land use and methods of cultivation are all primarily determined by population density would seem to be confounded by the vast areas of the West African savannah where all three variables are remarkably standard although population densities are very variable. But to Boserup such questioning would be irrelevant since she expresses herself in general evolutionary terms. A statement such as that *as population pressure increases more intensive cultivation methods offset any tendency towards decreasing returns*, output per head being maintained, can be neither confirmed nor refuted, the time-scale being unknown. And, of course, her beliefs fall within the context of this chapter since she overlooks the plight of the most impoverished cultivators who would be bound to lack the finance to improve their technology.[35]

Boserup also considers that there are certain circumstances in which farmers are only forced to abandon their high 'leisure preferences' when population density is high. But in the third world the economists' concept of 'leisure' ought always to be used with great caution, if at all, partly because conditions of economic inequality are vitally relevant and invariably overlooked, but also because the work/leisure dichotomy was developed in Western societies where *men* were apt to work for set times away from their homes. As for *women*, the leisure concept is apt to have poor application to them throughout the world, but especially in the rural tropics where they, and their children, are so commonly the household beasts of burden. At the very least, the age and gender of the person enjoying leisure should be specified (see Chapter 12).

Perhaps the main reason why economic generalizations should never cover both rich and poor cultivators is that the latter are not free to choose between various options, being always under duress; the small minority of rich people are those who make all the important decisions, while the others trail behind for ever adjusting themselves to hopeless situations. The point is that the

---

35. Tenancy and share-cropping being generally lacking in West Africa (see p.155 below), the poorest cultivators would not benefit from improvements introduced by rich landlords. Interestingly, however, the Anloga shallot farmers are again an exception.

struggling poor are a universal phenomenon, not an anomaly. It is the failure to appreciate this, and the refusal to study 'ordinary village poverty' for what it is, on the ground, which accounts for the general panic aroused by the thought that externally encouraged 'rural development' invariably enhances incipient inequality to an unacceptable degree.[36] But *existent* inequality is not incipient but grossly actual. The brake imposed on development for fear of the inequality it would be bound to *create*, has enhanced our ignorance of third-world realities and ensured that the great bulk of the population should continue to feel that there is little hope.

36. Naturally, I am not here referring to massive irrigation projects, such as those sponsored by the World Bank in northern Nigeria – p.14 above.

CHAPTER 3

THE VAIN SEARCH FOR UNIVERSAL GENERALIZATIONS: 2. THE POOR QUALITY OF OFFICIAL STATISTICS

Those economists who search for grand generalizations on the socio-economic organization of the rural tropical world may adopt one or more of four basic approaches. They may rely on their own 'basic commonsense', in the manner of Schultz or W.A. Lewis;[1] they may adopt an evolutionary approach, in the manner of Boserup – and, incidentally, of many neo-marxists; they may themselves undertake fieldwork designed to test the generalizations of others, as did Bliss and Stern, or use other peoples' field material; or they may primarily rely on official statistics.

If this book has one main theme it is that of the weakness of the first of these approaches (that of basic commonsense), so that many of its chapters deal in a practical, empirical way with specific subjects, such as indebtedness or migration, which are particularly apt to lead the 'commonsense adherents' astray. The second approach is gravely hampered by the lack of appropriate historical material, especially in tropical Africa. This is not, I need hardly add, because third-world countries 'have no history',[2] but that the history is the wrong sort – political, dynastic, urban, rather than rural and economic.[3] As for the third approach, rather few economists or even agronomists attempt much wide-ranging socio-economic fieldwork themselves;[4] and it is, alas, most

1. For instance, in his famous article, 'Economic Development with Unlimited Supplies of Labour' (1954), which necessitates the assumption that marginal productivity in the rural sector is lower than subsistence requirements. See, also, Lewis, 1955 and pp.51–2 below.
2. Certainly not such a region as northern Nigeria, even though it had always rigorously turned its back on the colonial Atlantic, continuing to stare northwards until it was colonized as recently as 1903.
3. While one hesitates to make such a generalization about India, with its vast and learned historical literature on the countryside, at the same time one must remember Myrdal's dismay when he discovered the 'extremely frail basis' (1968: xi) for contemporary factual knowledge on the economy of South Asia – India not excepted: 'wherever I turned, I found that any statistics available had to be scrutinized most severely before being used; at best they were highly uncertain. . .'
4. Unlike Myrdal, who spent the larger part of three academic years living and working in South Asia.

unusual for economists, with the notable exception of several at the official Institute of Development Studies at Sussex University, to use the findings of field anthropologists[5] – presuming them to be myopic, trivial, irrelevant and disinclined to generalize. This chapter is concerned with the fourth approach: with the reliance on official statistics relating to the rural tropical world. I shall argue that such statistics are usually of far worse quality than their users purport to realize, and that it is commonly with their aid that economists, and others, do so much to mislead the world.

The reasons for the poor quality of such statistics are so numerous[6] that I shall start by stressing some basic causes, allowing others to emerge in the course of the subsequent discussion, taking most of my detailed examples from south India,[7] for there is nowadays such a dearth of official statistics relating to Anglophone rural West Africa[8] that I have little alternative.

What, then, are some of the main general reasons for the present calamitous state of affairs? In offering the following limited selection, I refer readers to Chambers's witty, perspicacious, saddening and detailed account of 'the pathology of rural surveys',[9] which is based on bitter personal experience. And we must constantly remember that the problem of 'informant inaccuracy' is most certainly not peculiar to the third world:[10] thus, Bernard *et al.* report in relation to certain Western sociological studies that 'about half of what informants report is probably incorrect in some way'.[11]

5. Why, for example, do Ghatak and Ingersent (1984) ignore the excellent *Green Revolution*? (ed. Farmer, 1977), which records the results of one of the few successful attempts to relate the findings of members of an inter-disciplinary research team – in this case in both Sri Lanka and south India? It is hard to disagree with Geertz (1984:57) that 'social theorists' believe that 'the function of research is the aggrandisement of theory rather than the function the enablement of research. . .'
6. While the distinct and professional field of demography is necessarily outside my scope, I shall criticize some features of the Indian population census. See also Chapter 15.   7. As in Hill, 1984.
8. This was not always so. Ghana, for example, had reasonably good statistics on a fairly wide range of subjects around 1960 – the year, as it happens, when a most superior population census was conducted.   9. Chambers, 1983:52–5.
10. We learn from *The Times* (23 August 1985) that the official statisticians concerned with UK national accounts have their own grading system for the accuracy of official figures, grade D figures being 'more than 20 per cent away from the truth'; also, it is *arbitrarily assumed*, for example, that 8 per cent of all wines and spirits consumed is charged to company accounts, 'and so does not count as part of consumer spending'. See *United Kingdom National Accounts, Sources and Methods*, 3rd edition, HMSO, 1985.
11. Bernard *et al.*, 1984:503.

First is the general failure to realize the degree to which statistical procedures are based on conditions peculiar to first-world countries – where, after all, only a small minority of the world's population lives. Having reported elsewhere on my inability to find any professional general literature which makes creative suggestions for the improvements of statistics relating to the rural third world, where there are many peculiar problems outside the experience of Western-trained statisticians, I shall not repeat that discussion here.[12] However, I must mention that the *Programme* of instructions issued in 1976 by the Food and Agriculture Organization (FAO) for the 1980 world census of agriculture made no reference to the special problems of tropical countries, apart from stating that 'farmers might be ignorant of their areas under cultivation' – as, indeed, they commonly are. In many tropical regions crop mixtures, involving inter-cropping (usually on unirrigated land), are far more common and productive than pure stands,[13] yet the FAO's instructions were to ignore the possibility of the greater productiveness of mixtures![14]

Second is the extremely poor quality of the basic statistical series issued monthly and annually by the FAO on crop production etc.; this agency gives the impression of refusing any responsibility for the reliability of the figures it presents, merely accepting the offerings of its member countries at face value and providing hardly any notes. There is no evidence that the FAO

12. See Hill, 1984:493–5. But since that article was drafted, *Estimation of Crop Areas and Yields in Agricultural Statistics* (FAO, Rome, 1982) has reached the world's libraries. This mentions (p.43) earlier unsuccessful attempts to measure crop areas in developing countries using indigenous units, and pays attention (pp. 92–8) to the problems presented by tropical mixed cropping. See also n.16 below.
13. For part of northern Nigeria, Norman (1973:130) estimated that the yield per acre of crop mixtures, which were very common, was no less than 62% higher than that of sole crops. See also Rourke in Kotey *et al.* (1974:20 *et seq.*) on inter-cropping of food crops with cocoa. Inter-cropping on unirrigated farmland is very common in south India; in the course of discussing the numerous varieties of crop mixtures, B. Harriss (1984:86) suggests that the crops have 'different maturing lengths, different sensitivities to the quality and timing of rainfall, differing resistance to disease', etc.
    After completing this book, I was fortunate enough to be invited to an FAO conference held in Harare, in November 1985, on 'production statistics of subsistence food crops in Africa', at which official representatives of many African countries were present. The enlightened conclusions of this conference are likely to prove highly influential both in official statistical organizations in African countries and within the FAO itself; perhaps I may be permitted to add that the conference showed that many African statisticians have a sophisticated awareness of their special problems, which has been insufficiently utilized up to now by the FAO and other UN organizations.   14. See Hill, 1984:292.

gives much practical statistical advice to its member countries over the collection of the figures on which its series are based.

Third is the false belief that sophisticated statistical processing necessarily improves the quality of the basic material collected in the field. Allied to this attitude is the common adoption of over-meticulous sampling procedures, as in the All-India National Sample Survey.

Fourth is the failure to realize that this field material (I would not call it data) is not a kind of pure substance with an inherent validity, which drops readily into the hands of those who are well organized, but rather matter which has commonly been extracted from unwilling informants by resorting to many convolutions, blandishments and deceits, including sheer guesswork which is not necessarily particularly inspired. Then, at later stages, the field material is commonly fudged, cooked and manipulated by officials at higher levels, the main purpose being to ensure that the trends will be found satisfactory and convincing by those with still greater authority, as well as to compensate for presumed biases, which are usually unrelated to the realities of tropical conditions.

Fifth is the fact that the ground-level workers, who question respondents, are often expected to perform impossible tasks, which may take no account of respondents' genuine ignorance. Those in remote control are often unaware that ground-level workers are not necessarily the honest, professional, knowledgeable people, with a real understanding of local conditions, which their over-romantic notions of rural realities would suggest: but are commonly under-trained, lonely, under-supervised, over-worked, ignorant, bored, underpaid strangers, who may be forced into corruption, including collusion with respondents who have rightly persuaded them of the futility of their task.

Sixth is the over-valuation of questionnaire techniques, the 'results' of which tend, by their very nature, 'to err in the direction of ideal stereotypes'.[15]

Seventh is the failure to realize that in rural tropical conditions there are many types of statistics which are conventionally presumed to be indispensable, which cannot possibly be collected

15. Leach, 1967:85.

with a sufficient degree of reliability to justify the trouble involved. An example is the very important root crop (or tuber) known as cassava or manioc, which is necessarily stored in the ground for varying periods since it will keep no more than a couple of days (or so) after harvesting, and which is often cultivated on tiny plots and in mixtures so that no West African country can have the faintest idea of how much is produced; yet the FAO issues regular figures of annual *African* production, largely built on its own estimates, the basis of which goes unrevealed.[16] There is often a compulsion to quantify material which had much better be described; for 'there is a wide range of sociological phenomena which are intrinsically inaccessible to statistical investigation of any kind'.[17]

Eighth is the unwillingness of economists to engage in public discussion on their doubts about the quality of the material they use, an example being Indian livestock figures – see pp.44–5 below.

Ninth is the political demand for 'impossible figures',[18] such as 'league tables' for countries, showing *per capita* income or the proportions below an indefinable 'poverty line'. So strong is the pride of each independent country as well as the world demand for aggregates, that each country must have its national income estimate: in the third world such *estimates*, which are never, of course, denoted such, are necessarily largely based on bad agricultural statistics.

Tenth is the false belief that it is always better to have some statistics than none. Of course we all suppose ourselves to be so compassionate that we must demand, for example, statistics concerned with the incidence of under-nourishment, despite the risk that they may paint too rosy a picture: Cassen reports that a certain All-India National Sample Survey estimate of calorie intake *per capita* for Kerala state may have been 40% too low.[19]

16. The FAO publication (n.12 above) expresses considerable realistic despair about cassava statistics (pp.6 and 102–3), especially in relation to 'incomplete harvesting'.   17. Leach, 1967:77.
18. As pointed out by a *Times* leader (4 June 1983): 'Sadly, figures have come to replace words as the medium of ideas in politics.' The following reference to British politicians from the same source might well relate to the international community of development experts: 'They have failed because they are impaled on this obsession with statistics, whereas the real issue is the changing nature of work and the whole pattern of working life. . .'   19. Cassen, 1978:95.

Eleventh would be the impossibly high cost, in terms of skilled manpower and other scarce resources, of estimating reliable countrywide statistics of crop output on the basis of crop-cutting samples and area estimates. This is especially true in Africa where root crops (cassava, yams and cocoyam), bananas and plantains, are far more important than in India and present such appalling statistical problems.

Twelfth is the failure to realize that 'it is not necessary to know everything to know anything'.[20] So there is an urge to collect far too many statistics: a condition which Geertz appropriately characterizes as *quantophrenia*.[21] This is nothing new in India where (see n.32) the British Raj was far more concerned with statistical quantity than quality. There is a failure to appreciate that *qualitative trends* may be both informative and reliable.

Such is my selection of general explanations for the poor quality of many official statistics. Before examining particular instances I must develop further the idea of 'respondents' genuine ignorance. Why are third-world respondents liable to be very much more ignorant about the affairs of their households, for example, than is realized by Western office-statisticians or their counterparts in the third world?

I start with the fact that 'the householder', from whom investigators are usually instructed to obtain all the information required, may have little or no knowledge of the various day-to-day economic activities of other household members, notably those of his wives in polygynous West Africa. The difficulty is not so much that 'households' may be hard to define statistically, though this is a fact, as that certain of their members may be close to being 'individual economic entities', people who may attach so much importance to privacy that intrusive questions, even by their husbands, will inevitably result in lying, so that the husband is obliged to guess. The unfortunate fact is that enquiries of the 'household budget type', which are conventional in the West, are

---

20. Geertz, 1984:523.
21. *Ibid.*, 528, n.17. According to Stansfield (1981:278), the term *quantophrenia*, which is popular in operational research circles, dates back to 1956; the diagnostic system of this disease, he tells us, is 'the appearance of numbers purporting to be precise, whereas really they are of little meaning because the definition of what they measure is imprecise'.

based on notions of integrated economic activity and asset-sharing
within the household where the apparently subservient wife may
be quite capable of rifling the household granary, incurring
embarrassing debts, secretly selling her jewellery and so forth.

As for West Africa, there are many regions where most of the
trading, and much of the food processing for sale, is undertaken by
women, strictly on their own account (see Chapter 12). Women
are invariably obliged to cook and carry water for their husbands
(maybe with the help of their children), and they may have other
compulsory household tasks, but their 'economic autonomy' is
shown by the frequency with which they farm separately and
demand 'payment' for marketing their husbands' farm produce;[22]
and there are many societies in which mothers are responsible for
providing much of their children's food.[23] Then, large extended
households,[24] which include (say) two or more married sons and
their dependants, may present particular difficulty if, for instance,
the economic relationship between members varies seasonally:
thus the household may form a more integrated socio-economic
group in the farming season than in the dry season, when married
sons may be expected to fend for themselves.

But ignorance of other people's affairs is only one of the
unhappy respondent's difficulties, when faced with an investigator
wielding a long questionnaire, for he may also be incapable of
answering questions relating to himself in an approved manner.
Perhaps most serious of all for students of rural inequality is the
fact that, in both West Africa and south India, most cultivators
cannot report their total acreages with any accuracy, unless
perhaps they are very small, partly because this acreage, or *farm-
holding*, usually consists of what one may call a 'portfolio' of
separate, scattered, *farm-plots* (see p.103 below). As, in both continents, it seems that the vernacular words relate to farm-plots
only, holdings and plots often become hopelessly confused in
conversation. No doubt many desk-bound statisticians have a
European notion of a compact 'peasant farm', with its associated

22. While this often involves a cash element, it may also include food-stuffs and/or
    concessions, such as the right to cultivate certain land cleared by their husbands. See
    Hill, 1975 and 1978.
23. Thus, mothers may provide the ingredients for certain meals, fathers for others.
24. Such households are common in some West African regions, but not in others.

yard, cowshed, etc., so that this is reflected in the wording of questionnaires.

It is true that in south India a few householders in any village do take an interest in farm acreages, especially if they own paddy fields; but even though the village land records, which are maintained for revenue purposes and are open to inspection, have always expressed areas in acres, in my experience most farmers continue (as one would expect) to *think* in terms of indigenous units of area,[25] such as those based on seed requirements or the time taken to plough a field. In any case, farmers have a 'disinclination to aggregate' the areas of their several plots, an aspect of a general matter which I discuss below.

In West Africa generally, though cocoa areas are exceptional, the situation is far more intractable, especially in the southern forest zone. In that zone, where food farming is usually based on systems of bush fallow[26] with no manuring (such that cultivators seldom own the land they cultivate in any year but enjoy temporary usufructural rights only), the abstract 'maps' of land use for any community undergo continual change and individuals never know the arithmetical area of their holdings, though they may well have a good practical idea of relative plot, or even holding, sizes. Needless to say, official cadastral surveys are very rare there and anthropologists have seldom found it practicable to assess acreages.[27]

So far as I know, only one serious attempt at a cadastral survey was ever undertaken officially in Anglophone savannah West Africa – and this proved so unsuccessful that it had to be abandoned.[28] Even if enumerators are sometimes trained to measure plots, their accuracy is another matter and cultivators have certainly never had any opportunity of learning to think in terms

25. I make this assertion, which is apt to cause provocation, on the basis of much detailed comparison of respondents' estimates of their own (and their sons') holdings with recorded land revenue statistics in the Karnataka villages (see Hill, 1982).
26. Such sedentary systems ought to be rigorously distinguished from systems of shifting cultivation, which (in West Africa at least) involve population movement; but unfortunately modern statisticians insist on employing 'shifting cultivation' in all circumstances.
27. But see Forde (1964), Chapter 1, for an assessment based on counting yam mounds.
28. This was in northern Nigeria (see Hill, 1972:312–13). But did the recent massive, and often suspect, irrigation schemes in northern Nigeria usually involve mapping the farmers' plots before they were inundated? This is not entirely clear from the excellent article by Wallace (1980).

of acreages, not even the migrant cocoa farmers of southern Ghana,[29] until their farms were mapped in connection with swollen shoot disease. So it is entirely reckless to attempt to ascertain areas by oral enquiry.

All this would not matter so much were it not that many respondents are apt to be very unreliable when asked, as an alternative, to state the quantity of different crops which they have produced. Among the more general reasons for this are: first, the usual lack of any domestic incentive to measure and aggregate the output from several or many plots,[30] which are not necessarily harvested simultaneously – this second example of a disinclination to aggregate is the more comprehensible when one reflects that some of the output may be sold, some self-consumed; second is the fact that with many forest crops (such as plantain, banana, cassava, cocoyam) there is no particular time of harvest, but either cropping as and when required or when ripening happens to occur; third is the fact that in West Africa, unlike south India, grain is commonly stored in the household granaries on the stalk (see p.20 above), the bundles being extracted for threshing as required; fourth is the use of indigenous measures of quantity, which are not nearly as standard as non-villagers would like to suppose.

Perhaps it is partly because respondents are often so *evidently* baffled by questions relating to acreages and crop production that official questionnaires, such as those issued by the All-India National Sample Survey,[31] so commonly include questions on household income and maybe also expenditure, for these offer respondents and their interrogators better opportunities of work-

29. See Hill (1963) on the indigenous means of measuring, and dividing, blocks of land purchased for cocoa farming.
30. But as farmers are often capable of making reliable estimates of the yield of particular farm-plots under grains (such as millet, sorghum or paddy), more use should be made of their expertise even though they often quantify in terms of indigenous units, such as bundles of unthreshed grain.
31. The original initiative for establishing this extraordinary survey, which now runs into several hundred separate reports, was taken by mathematicians who probably became bored in the longer run by problems affecting the actual conduct of the work in the field, so that the series became petrified. (It is significant that no explanatory notes embellish the immense published questionnaires.) Such a survey is in the true Indian tradition: 'From the late nineteenth century the British rulers began counting things with extraordinary zeal and the resulting heap of statistical data is probably unequalled in the non-western world in this period. The quality is very variable' (Baker, 1984:16).

ing out 'plausible figures' collusively.[32] But yet I think that such statistics are generally of lower quality than any other material regularly collected from householders, except for that on indebtedness.

Let us see why respondents find questions about weekly, monthly[33] or yearly household income such a problem. Householders have no incentive to aggregate household income over time, even if it were computable. In a fundamental sense, it is because country people generally, like the Tallensi of northern Ghana studied by Fortes, 'do not think of the lapse of time as being associated with cumulative changes in their culture or social structure but rather as a periodical or cyclical rhythm of eternal repetition',[34] that they tend to conceive of economic events, of a day-to-day kind, such as the purchase of small quantities of food, as consisting of never-ending ebbs and flows. Time rolls on and on and is not divided into convenient accounting periods; and anyway there are no simple answers to enumerators' questions such as would satisfy a taxman in the West.[35] Rather do householders see their situation in terms of generalized assets and liabilities, and generalized (though maybe highly seasonal) ebbs and flows.[36] Nor is there *necessarily* a firm conceptual distinction between what the Western taxman would regard as income and capital – this being partly because many forms of the latter, such as houses, fall down or decay so rapidly in the cruel climate that they are in a constant state of dissolution and re-creation.[37]

But even if notions such as monthly or annual household income are not conceptualized by householders, surely it may be reasonable to expect questioners to be able to compute them from such evidence as they are able to gather? Unfortunately, it is not, unless the time and money are available for them to make daily

32. Also, there is no escaping the crying, though unreasonable, international demand for statistics of household income.
33. As with the All-India National Sample Survey, 'recollection' of income over the past month is often requested.   34. Fortes, 1945:x.
35. Apropos of frequent attempts which are made to assess household income in rural Sri Lanka, Vitebsky (1984:90) reports that 'the more of such information is uncovered, the more any procedure of double-checking will reveal much of it to be false'.
36. Thus, Indian farm labourers may receive a considerable proportion of their total annual cash income at harvest time: see p.111 below.
37. But sometimes the distinction may be very strict, as with the migrant cocoa farmers of southern Ghana: see pp.135–6 below.

enquiries from each earner in the household, such as most householders would never permit, even if their members were willing. It is wrong to assume that cramped living conditions are inconsistent with financial privacy, for West African and Indian wives are generally far more secretive within the household than their Western counterparts. Household members seldom receive regular wages or earnings, which can be conveniently aggregated over a period; certainly not daily-paid farm labourers whose work is usually quite irregular.

As for the notional income derived from the consumption of 'own produce', which must clearly be included, it is presumably usually the official investigator himself who calculates the value of such quantities as the householder estimates. But considering the usual lack of reliable village price quotations,[38] enumerators must surely be tempted to value the produce at 'ex-farm rates';[39] these, presumably, usually refer to prices in the larger market centres, which necessarily include such items as transport and handling charges, so that the putative income from the consumption of 'own produce' is liable to be considerably over-valued rather than under-valued, as is fairly commonly assumed in the literature. This is far from being a trivial consideration. Since in most tropical countries the geographical distribution of population is such that the great bulk of foodstuffs is consumed in the countryside (mainly the deep countryside), the over-valuation of the 'income' from self-consumption inflates official statistics of *per capita* income considerably. As the probable over-valuation of much produce that is marketed has the same effect, though to a lesser degree,[40] we can see that official figures may well seriously underestimate the extent of poverty and make nonsense of official 'league tables' of *per capita* income by country.

When dealing with his own income over a period from non-

---

38. Most south Indian villages lack markets, and the small village shops are apt not to handle basic grains, except in small quantities at certain seasons. (But for an unusual situation where everyone in a Nigerian village knew the local prices of basic grains at all times see Hill, 1972, Chapter 9.)

39. Certainly, All-India National Sample Survey No. 98, for instance, gave such instructions.

40. If enumerators rely on remembered figures of cash receipts from selling produce, these will be apt to be very inaccurate in those regions of West Africa where women do most of the marketing; but, in south India where specialized traders commonly collect produce from villages, statements of receipts might be more reliable.

farming, including farm-labouring, activities, the householder suffers from the same difficulties as 'his womenfolk': the ordinary man does not aggregate the daily pittances picked up here and there from numerous miscellaneous jobs. There are, also, definitional and accounting difficulties. If in the past month a man has sold a cow for $(x + p)$ rupees which he had bought for x rupees a year earlier – is this a *capital gain* of p rupees (minus expenditure on fodder etc.) or *yearly income* of the same sum? Endless similar examples of the logical difficulties of distinguishing capital from income could be provided.

Although villagers seldom conceptualize their standard of living in terms of aggregates such as monthly income, this does not imply that relative household living standards are not a matter of passionate concern to them or that judgments on this matter are apt to be seriously faulty. On the contrary, rural people (unless themselves too poor and disabled) are able to assess the relative wealth[41] of members of their community far more accurately than are townspeople, this being partly because of the close correlation between a householder's scale of farming, which can often be readily judged by all, and the profitability of his other occupations. *By paying far more attention to economic inequality, economists would be realistically reflecting village attitudes*: do they ever want to do this?

I conclude this discussion of householders' genuine ignorance with the assertion, justified in more detail below (p.93), that indebtedness is not a subject which can be reliably studied by means of statistical questionnaires, as it is so often by official investigators and others. The investigator expects a deadpan answer – 'My household owes x rupees' – from a respondent whose various household members are usually involved in nexuses of debt and/or credit relationships, of varying states of maturity, such that aggregation is both impossible and senseless. But as 'debt', even though it is the other face of credit, is invariably regarded as 'a problem', it is very commonly included in questionnaire enquiries of a 'budget survey' type.

Closely connected with householders' genuine ignorance is their deceptiveness – indeed, the two are often indistinguishable

---

41. I use this vague word as an indicator of general 'well-being' rather than the misleading 'income'. See pp.74–5 below.

owing to respondents' refusal to admit that they are obliged to guess. As an example of the straightforward intent to deceive, I take the apparent reluctance of many south Indian householders to admit the extent to which 'their womenfolk' work as paid farm labourers, so that official census statistics are apt vastly to under-estimate the extent of women's participation in agriculture.[42] Admittedly, as we shall see, this is partly the fault of the census organizers, whose definitions of farm labourers and other occupational groups are most unsatisfactory, but this defect cannot account for the fact that, as fieldwork suggests, the official census figures on women labourers may be but tiny fractions of the correct magnitudes.[43]

I now turn away from official statistics compiled with the help of householders to those collected by other means, starting with figures of the sizes of Indian farm-holdings.[44] Such figures usually derive from village land records, which again are of very variable quality; if experience in the state of Karnataka is any guide, they are liable to be very out-of-date, and to be showing rapid deterioration over time. The basic difficulty with these figures is that landowners are under no obligation to report ownership changes to the local *panchayat* secretary and may, indeed, be averse to doing so.

Another serious difficulty, which is never officially discussed, is that many farmers own plots situated outside their own village area,[45] so that if, as commonly happens, it is the *panchayat* secretary who is officially requested to provide statistics of farm-holdings by household he will necessarily exclude such plots, as being outside his records. It is suspicious that village survey reports, including

42. See also n.47 below.
43. It is entirely respectable to extrapolate from six ordinary villages only to a much wider area, on the basis of the ratios of female labourers to the total female population in the census reports, especially as official Indian surveys of other types invariably show much higher proportions of female labourers.
44. I am here ignoring West Africa since, owing to the lack of cadastral surveys there, householders ought to be unavoidably involved in identifying their various farm-plots for measurement – but, presumably, this is seldom practicable. Indeed, all official West African figures of the size distribution of farm-holdings, unless they relate to certain perennial crops, are suspect.
45. See Hill, 1982, Chapter 3, for evidence that, both in Hausaland and in south India, it is fallacious, as well as statistically misleading, to suppose that villages as corporate units usually own neatly demarcated tracts of arable land.

the official *Village Survey Monographs*,[46] never mention this
problem.

Another problem affecting the direct use of village land records
is that they necessarily omit the landless, who are not liable to tax.
So either landlessness is ignored or its incidence has to be ascer-
tained by enquiry from householders, who may be reluctant to
admit their plight, particularly if their farms are irrevocably
mortgaged. In general, it is certain that the effective incidence of
landlessness in south India is higher than the figures suggest, as
many small land-holders (and this affects Hausaland also) are too
poor to cultivate efficiently, perhaps having no manure or plough
animal, so that they prefer to let out their land to more competent
people. Since married sons who live with their father never own
land, even if their fathers are landless, we have here another reason
for finding the statistics misleadingly low.[47]

In India the procedures for ascertaining statistics of farm-
holdings differ from state to state: it must be remembered that
land matters, including Land Reform legislation, are generally not
the concern of the central government. So the quality of such land-
holding statistics as are not derived from existent land records
must be very variable – so variable that the unqualified word *farm*
may mean farm-holding in one state and farm-plot in another, for
explanatory notes are seldom provided.

The embarrassed tone of a report on agricultural statistics in the
southern state of Kerala[48] probably results from the fact that one
investigator only was assigned to each of 265 'villages'[49] in order to
conduct 'area enumeration and crop cutting experiments there'
for cassava (there known as tapioca), coconut, areca-nut, cashew-
nut and pepper. Whether 'area enumeration' meant some kind of

46. A few villages were selected for resurvey following the 1961 population census, each
being the subject of a separate monograph issued by the census authorities.
47. Married sons who cannot farm for themselves, because their father's holding is so
small that he can give them no land, ought logically to be added to the list of landless,
were this not statistically impracticable. (In this connection it is worth noting that
most dependent married sons, who work on their father's farms, are regarded as
'cultivators' in the Karnataka census, although hardly any dependent women workers
are so classified.)
48. *Report on the Timely Reporting Survey of Agricultural Statistics in Kerala 1977–78*, Government of Kerala, 1980.
49. One of the miserable investigator's difficulties is that in this exceptional area of
dispersed settlement, which often means ribbon development, there are two types of
'village area' which everyone tends to confuse.

estimation by the investigator is not stated. Of course, had farmers been asked for their acreages under each crop they would have been bound to have been very inaccurate, if only because of inter-planting, which is usual with all these crops, except where pure stands of coconut palms exist.

Estimates of crop yields per acre are often based on crop-cutting experiments, as in the Kerala case; always an exercise beset by appalling difficulties, these are worst where crop mixtures are common. In order to ascertain the total production of particular crops in any state the yield figures are then applied to estimates of total areas under different crops. Such publications as the *Indian Statistical Abstract*[50] are so uninformative on the procedures followed that no opinion on the general reliability of yield and production figures can be formed. But the history of these stat-istics is most disreputable as many contemporary historians, notably Dewey and Charlesworth,[51] constantly emphasize. Thus the 1928 *Report* on the Royal Commission on Agriculture in India (1928) stigmatized All-India agricultural statistics 'as not merely guesses "but frequently demonstrably absurd guesses" '.[52] With the best will in the world, such an inheritance is hard to repudiate.

I turn now to an entirely different subject, that of Indian livestock censuses. While such censuses are supposed to be conducted quin-quennially, in practice they are far less frequent.[53] So far as I can tell, the overworked village officials (now the *panchayat* secretaries) are allotted no extra assistants for this impossibly difficult exercise of livestock enumeration which is imposed on them. All economists, and many anthropologists, take these censuses very

50. Issued by the Central Statistical Organization, Government of India. (The long dis-cussion on 'measuring crop yield' in the FAO publication (Chapter 10, n.1) makes no special mention of third world problems.)
51. See, in particular, Dewey's chapter, 'Subordinate [village] Officials and the Reliability of India's Agricultural Statistics', in Dewey and Hopkins (eds.), 1978, and 'Trends in the Agricultural Performance of an Indian Province' by Charlesworth in Chaudhuri and Dewey (eds.), 1979.   52. Dewey and Hopkins, 1978:283.
53. According to the official *Statistical Abstract India, 1978*, the last census to have been carried out in most states was that of 1972; it was stated that the figures had been collected through 'village revenue agencies'. I have not yet found references to more recent censuses.

seriously, at least the cattle and buffalo figures; but among the many weighty articles, in Indian and other internationally renowned publications which are based on them, I can find none which throws serious doubt on their inherent reliability.[54] From my own experience,[55] I know that it is a general rule that cattle censuses are always unreliable, even if conducted by expert staff, unless they are associated with a practical purpose (other than taxation), such as inoculation against rinderpest; and even then, age-classification, for example heifers or cows, presents much difficulty.[56] But if the economists who manipulate these very important figures have any doubts about their reliability, they keep them to themselves.

The greatest statistical surprise which I experienced in south India related to the population of nucleated villages as recorded in the Karnataka census.[57] On my first day's fieldwork in 1976 I discovered that the population of the village of Hullahalli was about a half of that indicated by the 1971 census, after allowing for presumed growth meanwhile. The explanation was that the populations of two 'stranger-villages', which were not listed in the census, although they had been established about half a century earlier by migrants from some distance away, were included with that of the older village Hullahalli. These stranger-villages were

54. Perhaps the most famous of all such debates was that on 'The Cultural Ecology of India's Sacred Cattle', initiated in *Current Anthropology* by Harris (1966). To what extent, if at all, the bad statistics are responsible for the belief that most plough animals in south India are bullocks or buffaloes I cannot say; but so far as dry land ploughing was concerned, my suspicions were aroused by the fact that the great majority of plough animals in the six villages where I worked were observably cows. I am, also, most puzzled by the fact that my cattle count indicated that cows outnumbered bullocks by at least 3 to 1, a much higher ratio than earlier cattle censuses for the old state of Mysore (later Karnataka) had ever revealed (see Hill, 1982:162). Although I know that my count had its inaccuracies, it was likely to have been far superior, so far as the ratio of males to females was concerned, to an official census, owing to the time and care we spent on it. My contentious finding that all village cows were sold long before they had become useless owing to age fortunately corresponded with that of Epstein (1962).
55. This extends from attempts to count cattle myself with the aid of an official, to detailed analyses of published and unpublished official statistics. See Hill, 1970.
56. The very high rates of buying and selling of cattle, including cows, in south Indian villages, means that local officials cannot possibly keep pace, in their minds, with the changing ownership pattern, and also create other difficulties.
57. It is always stated that nucleated villages are the rule in south India, except in the state of Kerala.

each situated a mile or more from Hullahalli, *from which they had not emanated.*[58]

Later I discovered that Hullahalli was not anomalous, for the lists of villages in the 1971 Karnataka census volumes had remained unchanged since 1901 – and probably since 1871 when the first census was conducted, for many 'uninhabited villages' are in the list, having probably been destroyed by the terrible famine of 1876–8. Such stranger-villages being common, at least in south-eastern Karnataka, this practice of village grouping for census purposes makes nonsense of all statistical analyses of village size in that region, as presumably in many other regions, including entire states. So we see that, in India at least, it is often the sheer force of tradition which accounts for bad statistics.

Since I am sure that the widespread reliance on statistical questionnaires, directed at householders by minor officials, is one of the main causes of bad official statistics, I conclude this chapter with a further brief discussion of the attitude to statistical aggregation among ordinary rural people, followed by a defence of low-level officials, based on evidence provided by B.H. Farmer's *Green Revolution?* It is not the fault of these officials that, as my own experience has shown, they are apt to be far too gullible, uncritical, friendly, collusive and trustful in their dealings with respondents.[59]

Owing to shortages of staff and money, most questionnaires do not resemble population census schedules, which record the situation at a given point of time, but deal with occurrences over a period, such as a month. As we have seen, it is ignorant to assume that ordinary householders, who are not in weekly or monthly employment, have any occasion to think in terms of their own monthly income (including income from 'own produce') and

58. Whenever I have discussed this important subject in India I have invariably failed to convince my listeners that Hullahalli is not a peculiar place and that no concept of breakaway villages applies in south-eastern Karnataka. It is because the census grouping of villages and hamlets makes no sociological or administrative sense, and is entirely unnecessary, each unit actually being enumerated separately, that one's evidence is, unfortunately, disbelieved.

59. When in the field with my very intelligent assistants I have been constantly struck by their readiness to accept blatantly contradictory statements, which it was then my function to query; not to believe what is said, especially if the respondent is one's own countryman, is so embarrassingly rude that critical faculties are suspended.

expenditure, let alone that of the entire household. Certainly, when traders return to the market place to replenish their stock they are often well aware of the net profit made on their last purchase; but this does not imply that they will necessarily think in terms of the seven-day week, for visits to the market are apt to be irregular and most West African 'market weeks', outside the Muslim north, are shorter (see pp.46-7 below). Although the phases of the moon have so much religious and sociological significance, the flow of economic life is not conceptualized in regular cycles, despite the general awareness of market weeks, it being very common, for instance, for traders to postpone returning to market until they have sold their entire stock.

But 'the failure to aggregate', in a manner which seems natural to Westerners, is due not only to the attitude to time, but also to 'the inclination to differentiate'. Thus, if a polygynous father is asked for his number of children he is apt to hesitate briefly while he tots up the number by each wife (past and present), for he seldom has occasion to think in terms of the total. Again, if a south Indian farmer owns twelve widely dispersed plots, some being casuarina plantations, some being irrigated paddy land, others being planted with mixed basic crops, it is true to say that both the total number of plots and the (unknown) total acreage are uninteresting figures from his viewpoint – as the number of plots and the acreage under casuarina trees *only* are not.

Of course, high-ranking officials in charge of extension schemes are bound to express themselves, however unrealistically, in terms of aggregates. In North Arcot some research workers associated with *Green Revolution?* found that only 13% of a certain cultivated area was under High Yielding Varieties of paddy in 1972–3, the official figures for the same area, in the same year, having been between 39% and 48%. This is what the authors call 'top-down targetry in agricultural administration', the belief being that all concerned will work harder to achieve the target if '[aggregate] statistics derived from some senior imagination are disaggregated down the hierarchy with sufficient authority to induce those at the bottom to try, or try harder, to turn them into reality'.[60] The low-

---

60. Chambers and Wickremanayake in Farmer (ed.), 1977:162. Mencher (1978:265 *et seq.*) reports very similarly on the administrative use of 'targets' in Tamil Nadu.

ranking officials therefore find themselves under intolerable pressure to 'prove' the accuracy of targets invented by others who have not consulted them, and the achievement of targets becomes largely a 'book-keeping affair'. Such is the heavy burden on the local officials that it is often impossible for them to meet individual cultivators, their reports then being based (at best) on the quantity of seed distributed by official sources, the average seed rate per acre, and a factor to account for 'natural spread' from seed used from other sources. The overestimation of crop follows directly from the fact that the efficiency of the local officials in promoting production is judged by their reports on the targets achieved.[61]

In an earlier work[62] I reluctantly yielded, for the first time, to pressure from those who insisted that I ought to make some practical suggestions for the improvement of bad statistics. Since I am not a professional statistician, but only one who does her best to collect essential statistics in the field,[63] as well as to utilize published figures when writing up her material, I shall not repeat that argument here. I note only one of its points, which is that the fact that any statistical series shows consistent trends is no indication of reliability, since so much statistical 'cooking', much of which is unavoidable, is partly designed to provide such assurance. I also urge that statements such as 'although these figures are far from perfect at least they indicate the right orders of magnitude and the right trends' should always be treated sceptically.

It is not fanciful to insist that as the sophistication of 'data processing' increases, so the quality of the finished statistical product declines. Increasingly, so far as the rural third world is concerned, the power lies with those who have become so astoundingly proficient in manipulating the figures they receive 'from below' – with the eager people who derive so much enjoy-

---

61. For a persuasively expressed confession to this effect, see Mencher, 1978:265.
62. Hill, 1984, Appendix.
63. Which, if one is studying economic inequality, include (as a minimum): the estimated areas of farm-plots and farm-holdings, which involved the use of aerial photographs in Hausaland; the size and kin-composition of households; the estimates ages of householders; and some figures on migration.

ment from their advanced electronics. Infatuated by their technology, it is beneath their dignity to contemplate the *inherent unreliability* of their 'basic data' – and their resultant impotence is never contemplated. Consequently, all the commands come from above, and the less ambitious, and far less clever, 'data collectors' cower underneath. How can the international world be persuaded that the problems of collecting statistics, and allied material, at the ground level in the third world, are just as intellectually challenging, and far more important, than mere mathematical processing?

APPENDIX
The Berg Report

The World Bank report *Accelerated Development in Sub-Saharan Africa: An Agenda for Action* (1981), which is commonly known as the Berg report,[65] provides a good example of a recent tendency to base weighty discussions on official statistics which are simultaneously admitted to be of doubtful quality.

One of the main themes of the agricultural chapter of this report is that 'the growth rate of agricultural production began to decline [in the past two decades] and, in the 1970s, was less than the rate of population growth almost everywhere'; 'food production per capita was at best stagnant in the 1960s and fell in the 1970s' (p.45). Footnotes refer to a Statistical Appendix of astounding verbal brevity where hardly any of the 'statistical uncertainties' are mentioned, certainly not the common lack of demographic material (see p.64 below).

The three justifications for the acceptance of the figures which are presented in the following paragraph are all unconvincing:

While [agricultural] production statistics are highly tentative (particularly for subsistence foods) and must be regarded with caution, other evidence substantiates the poor performance in this sector: the mounting domestic food prices in most countries; the steep rise in cereal imports; and the export crop figures which . . . indicate a substantial decline (p.46).

First, food prices would have been bound to have risen substantially owing to the world-wide inflation, especially the rise in petrol prices which

---

65. After Elliot Berg, the economist, who was the co-ordinator of the group responsible for writing the report.

greatly affected marketing costs. Second, the rise in cereal imports mainly reflected rising consumer preferences for rice, which most African countries had never produced in quantity, and for wheat (for bread), which does not flourish in the tropics.[66] Third, the huge decline in exports of such crops as groundnuts and palm produce may be entirely due to increased domestic consumption,[67] a point which is mentioned, though not emphasized, on a later page.

The report uncritically endorses (p.47) the trends conveyed by the worst of all production 'guestimates', those for roots and tubers (see pp.33–4 above on cassava); it states that the annual growth rate for sub-Saharan Africa for these crops was 1.8% in 1969–79, compared with 2.0% for the previous decade!

Finally, the report adduces no evidence for its overall statement that returns to labour in agriculture are *generally* declining. 'Fallows are being shortened. . . Cassava. . . is more widely cultivated at the expense of other crops' (p.14).

66. In northern Nigeria, for example, where great efforts have been made to expand production, yields continue to be very low indeed. (Besides, the authors seem to have overlooked their own point (p.76) that, owing to the overvaluation of many African currencies, imported wheat and rice were growing steadily cheaper.)

67. A possibility which I noted as long ago as 1971–2 in Hausaland where farmers were refusing to accept the low price for groundnuts for export offered by the Marketing Board in favour of selling on the open market.

CHAPTER 4

THE VAIN SEARCH FOR
UNIVERSAL GENERALIZATIONS:
3. HISTORICIST FALLACIES

⟨✦⟩

Since, with rare exceptions,[1] development economists disdain the
work of anthropologists, they are, presumably, unaware that it was
as long ago as the last decades of the nineteenth century that the
notion of *development by stages in the growth of society* became outmoded. It is true that anthropologists subsequently had a hard
struggle to free themselves from historicist or even evolutionary
theories – thus Leach refers to: 'Malinowski's persistent struggle to
break out of the strait-jacket of nineteenth-century historicist
theory without getting hopelessly bogged in empirical detail.'[2]
Economists' similar dread of incomprehensible marshes of empirical
detail is doubtless one of the main reasons why so many of them
still cling to an historicist approach, though it is fairly commonly
believed that there is simply no alternative.

This latter belief has been bluntly expressed by Lewis,[3] who
claims that when economists pass through phases of dissatisfaction with deductivism and feel a need to appeal to history, they
find there are few relevant facts: 'It is only for a very few countries
and for very recent periods that any adequate quantity of historical
records exists; and even when there are plenty of records we
cannot always be certain exactly what happened.' So Lewis is
obliged to resort to such generalizations as that 'Economic growth
entails the slow penetration and eventual absorption of the
subsistence sector by the capitalistic sector.'[4] Such an ambiguous
statement seems to imply that capitalism is apt to creep into the
countryside from the cities (for what otherwise can the capitalistic
sector be?), almost as a kind of virus. This is a belief which takes no
account of the fact that in many tropical regions, *until quite recently*,
the countryside was the matrix within which most economic

1. Such as Chambers, Lipton, Myrdal, Schultz and others.
2. Leach, 1957:136.   3. Lewis, 1955:15.
4. This statement of views expressed in Lewis (1954) is drawn from Enke, 1964:168.

enterprise flourished,[5] most traders having been countrymen, and large cities having been rare and anomalous places; and it altogether underestimates the capacity of rural communities to innovate, both organizationally[6] and technically, on their own initiative. In localities such as northern Nigeria where, in the nineteenth century, most farm-slaves had been bought for cash by ordinary farmers, the institution of farm-slavery was indigenous rural capitalism *par excellence*, especially as much of the grain produced by the slaves was sold in the wider market.

Insofar as Lewis is thinking of the poor quality of official statistics in the rural tropical world, especially when they are time series, he is indeed justified in denigrating the 'historical records'. But there are other kinds of records, one of which may be denoted as 'anthropologists' experience', which nowadays, despite the rejection of old-fashioned historicist theories, usually has some time-depth.[7] Thus, we know from our own experience that the simplistic exposition of the three-stage 'transition from subsistence to specialised farming' in Todaro's extremely influential textbook[8] is dangerously misleading, and not only because it almost entirely overlooks the implications of innate rural inequality. We know, too, that until the Great Inflation gravely damaged West African rural economies, especially in Ghana, it was quite untrue that the agricultural sector was so inefficient that it could 'barely sustain the farm population, let alone the burgeoning urban population, even at a minimum level of subsistence' (p.231). Indeed, the amazing capacity of that sector to keep pace with the rising demand for farm produce from non-agriculturists ought to have excited favourable comment – as it never did.

5. See Hill, 1982, Chapter 12.
6. As, for example, West African migrant cocoa farmers, who were not unique but merely enterprising to an exceptional degree.
7. I think that economists are quite unaware of the possible reliability of historical enquiries based on both oral interview and archival or contemporary material, which may be statistical – such as the extensive work on the organization of farm-slavery in West Africa.
8. Todaro, 1977:241–5. It almost seems that economic textbooks like Todaro's, which specifically relate to the 'developing world', are even more unreliable guides to that world than general textbooks. Thus the huge textbook on 'developing economies' by the distinguished Nigerian economist Aboyade (1983) has very little to say on *peasant production (sic)* and asserts that 'while rural wage employment was not a dominant feature, a free market in rural land was even more rare' (p.372).

Astonishingly, in his summary of the 'stages of farm (*sic*) evolution' (p.245), Todaro concludes that 'Most Third World nations are in the process of transition from subsistence to mixed farming.'[9] Under subsistence farming 'output and consumption are identical' (p.242), presumably in terms of the individual household, not the village, but this is not stated; also, 'the law of diminishing returns is in operation', apparently for all farmers, and 'the peasant (*sic*) usually cultivates only as much land as his family can manage without the need for hired labour'. It is implied, though not stated, that virtually every household meets its 'minimum consumption requirement' – 'catastrophe' being the only alternative. One has to agree that the 'peasant's environment' is indeed 'static' (p.242), since he appears to have no cash income from farming and no occupation other than farming. I believe it to be unlikely that any such rural communities have ever existed in the tropical world.

As for the second stage, which Todaro unfortunately calls 'mixed farming',[10] this is a condition such that 'the staple crop no longer dominates output', so that the farmer may have a 'market-able surplus' of other crops (p.224). As it is 'unrealistic to think in terms of transforming a traditional agrarian system which has prevailed for many generations [stage one] into a highly special-ised commercial system', so it follows that this second stage has not yet been reached, communities being in transition. The most misleading feature of this second stage is that 'cash crops' are distinct from 'staple crops', the implication being that the latter are never sold for cash. In general, confusion about 'cash crops' does untold analytical damage: first, because there is no staple crop which is never sold; second, because most West African and Indian cultivators usually derive the bulk of their farming income from the sale of staple crops; third, because there are not many non-staple (non-plantation) crops, other than cocoa and coffee, which are produced on a significant scale and never self-consumed; and fourth because it is nowadays fashionable to

9. While he appropriately disregards plantations of the types which are commonly owned by expatriates or companies, he fails to note the existence of indigenous, and unmechanized, oil-palm, rubber, kola-nut, etc. plantations.
10. In West Africa this term has long connoted 'plough agriculture' which was first introduced, in a few savannah areas, in colonial times.

assume that the Western world distorts tropical agrarian economies by demanding a switch to cash crops, which are falsely equated with export crops.[11] Certainly, Todaro seems to regard cash crops as somehow exotic, for one of the unexpected advantages of his progression to stage two is that the degree of disguised unemployment is reduced, since these crops will grow during the 'slack season' – which is not here identified, as it ought to be, with the dry season.

It is, also, astounding that it is not until this second stage that 'simple animal husbandry' is introduced; did the stage one Indian cultivator own no small livestock and pull his plough himself?

In stage three, 'which may or may not be an ultimate national goal', 'the provision of food for the family with some marketable surplus no longer provides the basic motivational objective', for farmers now specialize in particular crops as in industrialized countries. Of course there is no mention of West African cocoa farming in 1900, which was already apt to be highly specialist; if there had been, the author could hardly have laid so much emphasis on the need for advanced technology at this stage.

Since stage one, from which no tropical country is supposed to have freed itself, involves no oxen-drawn ploughs and no large-scale irrigation works,[12] such as have existed in Sri Lanka for at least two millennia, one might feel that the author has Africa, rather than Asia, in mind. But as the logic of stages one to three is 'no market, some market and all market', and as rural periodic markets are such ancient institutions in many regions of West Africa (as in other continents), the idea of the inevitability of the persistence of stage one does not wash in Africa either. This is a process of idealization in which only stage two bears any relation to reality – and then with no analytical precision.

The second main group of historicist fallacies I wish to expose relates directly to indigenous market places and trade. Todaro

11. In northern Nigeria the early colonialists were subject to the same confusion; rather unsuccessfully, they did their utmost to encourage the growing of suitable cotton for export, and were taken aback when the cultivators preferred to concentrate their efforts on producing that staple crop, groundnuts, for export. See Hill (1972) and Hogendorn (1978).
12. I can find no reference to communal irrigation in Todaro's book, highly important though it has long been in Asia.

reflects much prevailing economic orthodoxy in assuming that village exchange, whether market exchange or not, was generally unimportant until quite recently, the implication being that *trade was necessarily urban-based*. But in many regions of pre-colonial West Africa, for instance, the numerous indigenous periodic market places, which handled a far greater volume of trade than the relatively very small number of city markets, were an essentially rural phenomenon, as we shall see. Furthermore, *pace* the substantivists in the recent Polanyi debate (see p.22 above), the function of these markets was basically economic.[13]

Before justifying these statements, I must dispute the common view that barter is an early 'stage' in rural economic development: a necessary forerunner of monetary exchange. Humphrey has recently drawn attention to the fact that it was Polanyi himself[14] who suggested that 'the evolutionary doctrine of the economists preoccupied with the emergence of markets might virtually be reversed', though (surprisingly) his views were largely ignored. He regarded 'the true starting point' as long-distance trade, not barter, arguing that such trade often engendered markets. Whether or not, as Polanyi assumed, market places often involved acts of barter, Humphrey herself wishes to escape from the notion of barter 'as a natural human propensity' (p.50). I must add that it had always been so inconvenient: Adam Smith referred to 'this power of exchanging' as 'very much clogged and embarrassed in its operations'.[15]

Many of the pre-colonial,[16] rural periodic market places of West

13. The useful, though over-influential, *Markets in Africa* (1962) is flawed by the unrealistic introduction by the two substantivist editors, Bohannan and Dalton, the one an anthropologist, the other an economist; so far as West (though not East) Africa was concerned, they showed a lack of time-depth in associating the growth of market places with colonialism (which in northern Nigeria, for instance, was a period of little more than half a century, ending in 1960) and they were wrong in asserting that 'the more pervasive the market principle, the less the economic importance of the market place' (p.25). (Fortunately, nearly all economists ignored their views; this was not surprising considering that *market place* is seldom an entry in the indexes of contemporary economic textbooks.)
14. Humphrey, 1985:49; Polanyi, 1957.
15. Smith, 1776:126. Nowadays, so far as I can ascertain, it usually involves no more than small-scale casual exchange among village women outside a market place.
16. In some regions market places are very old; there is evidence for the existence of considerable markets over a large area of the western Sudan in the mid-fourteenth century. Almost everywhere there was a standard market week varying in length from two to eight days; with the exception of the seven-day week, it was usual for individual markets to be open only once weekly. See Hill, 1966 and 1985.

Africa provided for the needs of local producers, consumers and
traders as well as serving as foci for long-distance traders. Certainly
there were a number of renowned city markets, among them
Katsina and Kano in Hausaland, but the volume of trade that they
handled in the early nineteenth century must have been quite
small relative to that passing though the thousands of rural
periodic markets which then existed, many of which must have
been very large indeed. The city markets were not the apices of an
hierarchical marketing structure such as Skinner, in his well-
known articles on marketing and social structure in rural China,
regarded as 'characteristic of the whole class of civilizations known
as "peasant" or "traditional agrarian" societies'.[17] And the long-
distance trading caravans which linked the savannah and forest
regions preferred rural market places, as they provided grazing for
their transport animals, which were mainly donkeys. Whereas the
great city markets of the savannah, such as Katsina and Kano, were
essentially entrepots for the trans-Saharan trade, some of the huge
rural periodic markets were basically entrepots linking the savannah
and the southern forest zone.[18] Summing up very simplistically,
West African market places were essentially rural phenomena,
both because the very great bulk of the indigenous population[19] of
consumers and local traders lived in the countryside and also
because high proportions of long-distance traders were themselves farmers who often travelled many hundreds of miles with
their transport animals in the dry season.

While it is well known that the nineteenth-century map of West
Africa was bespattered with rural periodic market places,[20] there
were, also, marketless areas about which much less is known. But
they should probably be regarded as anomalous, since there was,
for instance, no general tendency for non-centralized societies to
be marketless as is sometimes assumed: thus, the rural periodic
markets of the main acephalous societies (societies which lacked

17. Hill, 1966:297, n.11. The very serious point here may be that West African country
    people, unlike the Chinese, were not peasants!
18. They were often situated in villages or small towns, such as Jega in north-western
    Nigeria, one of the most noted markets of the western Sudan. *Ibid*: 300, n.32.
19. In the mid-nineteenth century a high proportion of the population of Kano, when it
    was at its seasonal peak, consisted of strangers, including many Arabs.
20. The locations of many of which are known from written sources unless, as was fairly
    often the case in some regions, they were situated in open country.

chiefs of any notable authority) of eastern Nigeria (Ibibio as well as Ibo), were among the most remarkable in West Africa. In this connection it should be noted that long-distance trading caravans did not depend on travelling through long chains of market places – that, indeed, they often avoided such centres. Even to this day, the long-distance trade in kola-nuts, which grow in the south and are more largely consumed in the north, operates independently of market places.[21]

In the market places of the West African forest zone, unlike the savannah, women usually far outnumber men both as traders and customers. For many centuries[22] it has presumably been usual for local women to transport and to market crops produced by their own and other households, to the degree that most market men were strangers. And when, after the second world war, most long-distance trade was conducted by lorry, southern women became prominent in this field as well. In savannah market places generally men traders predominate. And they alone are to be found in the great cattle markets, such as that at Kumasi in Ghana.

Finally, it must be emphasized that there is no reason to doubt that most market trade, in the past couple of centuries *at least*, involved cash transactions; among the countless forms of indigenous currency,[23] perhaps gold, gold dust and cowry shells had the widest circulation, the two former types having been very ancient.

The literature on African (particularly West African) markets is vast: thus, 406 works and other reference material of historical interest on markets are included in the bibliography of Fröhlich,[24] which considerably pre-dated the recent upsurge of interest in West African marketing which began in the late 1960s and particularly involved geographers. India is an astounding contrast. The very long bibliographies on world market places by Bromley[25] clearly reveal the essential triviality, until very recently, of nearly all the relatively scanty literature on Indian rural periodic market

21. Such marketless trade has long been facilitated by indigenous 'landlords' (*mai gida*), who provide the traders with lodging, helping them to sell their wares if need be. See Hill, 1966 and 1985.
22. In Wolfson (1958:50 *et seq.*) a Dutch description, dated 1602, of market women on the Gold Coast is cited.
23. See Hopkins, 1973:67 *et seq.*   24. Fröhlich, 1940.   25. Bromley, 1977 and 1979.

places. Not only that, but the whole subject of agricultural
marketing remained unstudied until fairly recently. Thus, Husain
notes that that subject was specifically mentioned in the terms of
reference of the Royal Commission on Agriculture in India, which
was appointed in 1926, and that 'never before' had it been given
any serious thought.[26] Contemporary historians agree. According
to Baker

Indian historiography has often been peculiarly antagonistic to the rural
market [place]; on the basis of rural-romantic or primitive-communistic
views of rural self-sufficiency, it has viewed the market as a specifically
alien institution. In particular it has often portrayed the denizens of the
market as low types who were able to steal the major part of the
peasant's produce.[27]

But such ignorance should afford no comfort to those who hold
that high proportions of third-world cultivators have not yet
attained Todaro's second stage of development (p.53 above), for
there is much evidence of coin having been used many centuries
ago in south Indian villages, for example, for the payment of land
revenue and rent. Such currency must have accrued from transactions conducted according to some market principle, if not
inside a market place: villagers were already part of the 'cash
economy'.

Did the obsessive British concern with Indian Land Revenue in
the last century account for the official lack of interest in market
places – for the resultant gaping holes in official archives? Or was it
rather that the rural periodic market places tended to be both few
and small? I think that while it is at last becoming evident that the
former explanation should be favoured, account should also be
taken of a grand inter-continental contrast between West Africa
and south India, which may explain the greater importance of
rural periodic markets in the former region. Perhaps mainly
because of their control over the means of transport, whether
human or animal, West African villagers commonly took their
own farm produce to market, whereas south Indian cultivators
were far more often dependent on transport provided by outside

26. Husain, 1937:71–2.   27. Baker, 1984:253.

traders.[28] West African farmers had a much greater need for nearby markets than their Indian counterparts.

Another distinction was, possibly, that large periodic markets in India tended to be an urban not a rural phenomenon as in West Africa. Thus the traveller Buchanan recorded the existence of at least two huge 'weekly fairs' in Mysore towns, one of which had 154 'shops', being 'frequented by merchants from great distances'.[29] But even if rural periodic markets tended to be small, they were certainly numerous in Mysore, for Buchanan recorded that

At different convenient places in every *Taluc*[30] there are weekly markets, which in good parts of the country may be about two or three miles from each other... At all these markets business is carried on by sale; no barter is customary, except among a few poor people, who exchange grain for the produce of the kitchen garden.

The most recent enquiry, which supports the belief that Indian systems of rural periodic market places commonly have much significance, as elsewhere in the world, is that by Wanmali,[31] which relates to the system of rural periodic markets in a single district of south Bihar. Lacking other authorities,[32] one is obliged to attach much importance to Wanmali's opinion that Skinner's hierarchical model (p.56 above) is not applicable to rural India, since such hierarchies as exist are 'of an extremely local nature' (p.205). 'The officially accepted models[33] of the provision of services in rural India are based on incorrect assumptions of the demographic, functional and spatial characteristics of the regional settlement

28. In south India, where most bullock carts probably had hopelessly ramshackle solid wheels until (say) a century ago, and where, owing to the lack of roads, carts were used mainly for local transport, the essential pack oxen were owned by non-cultivators, and farmers never participated in long-distance trade, certainly not in the manner of Hausa farmers who joined very long-distance trading caravans with their donkeys. Even today most south Indian householders own no cart, whereas it is a mark of extreme poverty for a Hausa household to own no donkey.
29. Buchanan provided long lists of wares which were handled. See Buchanan, 1807, vol.II:29 *et seq.*
30. He was referring to Mysore *taluks* – administrative divisions. *Ibid.*, vol.I:125.
31. Wanmali, 1981.
32. The failure to study systems of rural periodic markets is all the more surprising considering that the maps of the One-Inch Survey of India published in 1915–31 recorded the location of periodic markets and the day of the week.
33. Wanmali is particularly critical of the work done on regulated urban markets, which usually ignores rural periodic markets.

system' (p.208). The functions of rural periodic markets have been greatly underestimated.

The ordinary person in the street believes that two horrendous factors have transformed the world since the 1930s: the nuclear bomb and the third-world population explosion. It is because I believe that the notion of a *population explosion* has been mainly disseminated by economists (as well as politicians), and is quite unhelpful, that I include this brief discusion under the heading of economists' historicist fallacies.

The only undoubted fact about this explosion is that rates of population growth started to rise very rapidly in third-world countries generally after the second world war.[34] But the economic consequences of such growth have received little systematic study. Thus, writing about India, Cassen has reflected on the 'curious fact' that hardly any work has been done on the relations between population growth and land ownership: 'It would be interesting to know at what point in history villages in various regions ran out of unclaimed land to cultivate, when the squeeze of land shortage began and what manifold effects it has had.'[35] As for population pressure in the low-lying flood-prone areas in the Bay of Bengal – why that, he states, began in the eighteenth century.

Any idea of an explosion would seem to imply growing food shortages. But the economist A.K. Sen is satisfied that, even if the United States is excluded, 'there is as yet no indication that world population expansion has started gaining on the growth of world food supply'.[36] He has cogently questioned the view that famines, in particular the Bengal famine of 1943 which may have caused 3 million deaths, are necessarily caused by 'food availability decline'. His approach to starvation and famines concentrates on 'the

34. With the possible exception of parts of West Africa.   35. Cassen, 1978:276.
36. Sen, 1981:158. Here I find myself falling into the traps (see Chapter 2) of dealing in averages and quoting unreliable figures, but on the latter point at least one can say that'there is no real evidence'. Cassen (1978:25) asserts that foodgrain output has risen faster than population in the Indian post-Independence period. As for West Africa, the dubiousness of the Berg Report's pessimistic views has already been noted (pp.49–50). The report is in any case self-contradictory: on one page (92) it notes the deleterious effects of sparse population in many African countries, on another (p.15) it casually refers to 'the population explosion' as reducing per capita farm output.

entitlement approach' – 'on the ability of people to command food through the legal means available in the society, including the use of production possibilities, trade opportunities, entitlements *vis-à-vis* the state, and other methods of acquiring food' (p.45). Those who died were devoid of entitlement to commodity bundles, including food. Although such an idea is familiar enough to anthropologists, coming from an economist of great repute it created something of a sensation. There is now no excuse for causally associating famines and population explosions.

Since he concentrated on death (from lack of food) and not on hunger, Sen was scornful about the 'grossness' of 'the category of the poor', as giving no indication of the severity of deprivation: 'The category of the poor is not merely inadequate for evaluative exercises and a nuisance for causal analysis, it can also have distorting effects on policy matters' (p.157). Maybe, but such an argument should not deter those who are empirically concerned with the various causes of individual impoverishment – particularly with gross forms of rural impoverishment. It is partly because economists are so inclined, as we know, to deal in averages (average consumption of grain per head, average yields and so forth) that their work on the consequences of rapid population growth has proved so inadequate.

To contest the notion of population explosion is not to deny that Cassen may be right in believing (p.231) that per capita income in India would have risen more rapidly[37] in the twenty-five years after 1950 (or so) had population growth been slower. Nor does one doubt that increasing pressure on scarce farmland usually damages the poor much more than the relatively rich, especially in relation to scarcities of firewood (which are often critical) and of grazing. But the idea of an explosion ought to imply two things: that owing to *qualitative* changes nothing is the same as it was before and that an irreversible disaster has occurred.

There is little evidence of post-war qualitative changes in agrarian systems resulting directly from population growth. In the case of south India land had become a saleable factor in many

37. But here again 'there is no real evidence'.

districts in the nineteenth century. Thus, writing of the Tamilnad valleys (where the main crop was irrigated paddy), Baker states that they 'had been relatively crowded for many centuries and although the population did increase in this tract in the twentieth century, there was no sense in which population pressure was a novel factor.'[38] By the end of the nineteenth century in Tamilnad generally 'it was becoming difficult to find spare lands which were capable of cultivation'(p.136).[39]

In West Africa the localities where farm-selling was common in colonial times were either those where it had existed before the colonial conquest[40] or where the introduction of a new perennial crop, such as cocoa, had been responsible for changes in land-tenure systems. There is no evidence of increasing population pressure, as such, having resulted in new-fangled land-selling in the post-war years. Certainly, a causal connection between increasing population density and higher incidences of outward migration is *sometimes* evident, as in the case of the Tallensi of northern Ghana,[41] who still never sell farmland; but, as we shall see (Chapter 11), many other factors besides population density influence rates of outward migration, to the degree that the 'labour emitting areas' may be notably sparsely populated.

As for the question of the 'irreversibility' of the so-called explosion, one has to note the views of an expert like Cassen who, galled by continuous statements that the condition of India was 'hopeless', sought to persuade the world, including government officials and international relief agencies, that 'India's situation calls for, and repays, analysis, not alarmism':[42] he trusted that readers would 'derive a sense that, while the problems are great, they can be made less so'. The conclusion of his prolonged

38. Baker, 1984:168.
39. Baker sees the population expansion from 1881 onwards as extending back 'into medieval history' (pp.135–6).
40. Such as parts of Hausaland in northern Nigeria, where selling certainly went back to the beginning of the nineteenth century. See Hill, 1972:240.   41. See p.126.
42. Cassen, 1978:xi. I understand that Indian socio-economic conditions are considered so depressing in American academia as to have led to a marked decline in student interest. But are not, for example, the possibilities of such measures as land consolidation (see n.37 on p.105) really fascinating? See Etienne (1982:213) for the argument that international organizations are quite wrong in advocating 'drastic reforms' in India when very great advances could be effected by giving additional momentum to many improvements *which are already in train*, notably those involving irrigation and water control.

examination (Chapter 4) of 'Population and the Economy', in which he examined half a dozen types of evidence, was that

Aggregate income grows, some get better off; if any of the gains, other than those in 'overhead consumption', have benefited the poorer half of the population, it is not very often discernible. How long this state of affairs can continue is an open question. In many ways that question may prove to be largely political (p.256).

Like Cassen, Myrdal regarded pessimistic analysis of the effects of population growth on capital investment and output as being 'too mechanistic and schematic': 'it gives the appearance of knowledge where none exists and an illusory precision to this pretended knowledge.'[43] He placed considerable emphasis on the possibility of raising agricultural production in South Asia by means of increasing the cultivable area (pp.1261 *et seq.*); even in India there might be scope for such expansion.[44] He also considered (pp.1281 *et seq.*) that certain Indian cultivators made insufficient use of their irrigation facilities. Myrdal was writing before it had become politically conventional to deplore the Green Revolution on the grounds that the benefits of increased productivity were so commonly rendered nugatory by enhanced inequality.

The doom-mongers[45] refuse to distinguish between the effects of high population growth on well-populated regions, like the Indian sub-continent, and generally sparsely populated domains such as sub-Saharan Africa.[46] In 1981, when India's population was

43. Myrdal, 1968:2067.
44. He cited certain 1960 FAO statistics (how reliable?) indicating that there were some 22 million hectares of farmland in India which were 'cultivable but not cultivated', compared with 160 million hectares that were actually cultivated. (In south-eastern Karnataka, where overall population densities are high, I got the impression that the reluctance of farmers to cultivate farmland more than a few miles from the nucleated villages or hamlets, where they all live, led to the neglect of a fair proportion of cultivable land in some localities.)
45. See Postscript. It is also worth noting that a leader in *The Times* (11 March 1985) asserted that 'Africa's population is obviously growing too fast for the continent's capacity to sustain it'.
46. Hart (1982:133) rightly contended that West Africa 'is one of the most sparsely populated regions of the world'. But population density is apt to be very variable within small radii: see e.g. Forde (1946:71) on enormous local variations in eastern Nigeria. Although Ethiopia is not part of sub-Saharan Africa, I wish to draw attention to a remarkable letter in *The Times* of 24 January 1985 from J. Kelly who, having worked as a doctor in that country for fourteen years, asserts that it 'is a vast country with much fertile land which is under-populated': 'infertility is a much greater problem than any imagined over-population'; 'not only drought but war have pushed the situation well beyond self-help'.

recorded as 683 million, the average density was 541 persons per square mile; while this is a far more reliable figure than any available for Anglophone West Africa, except possibly for Sierra Leone, it is still certain that West African densities, which are some of the highest in sub-Saharan Africa, are generally far lower. Even if the present-day population of Nigeria is put as high as 100 million,[47] its population density is only 280 per square mile, compared with figures of the order of 120 per square mile for Ghana and Sierra Leone. Moreover, vast uninhabited areas, such as deserts or mountainous regions, which depress the Indian density figures, are lacking in West Africa south of the Sahel.

Indeed, the demographic situation in West Africa contrasts so strongly with that in South Asia that no socio-economic demographic generalizations can possibly relate to both regions. In the absence of up-to-date population censuses in Ghana and Nigeria,[48] it is difficult for a non-demographer to judge whether the universal presumption of very rapid population growth in Anglophone West Africa is well founded – presumably it is, though there is a surprising dearth of up-to-date vital statistics.[49] My reason for retaining slight doubts derives from very high infant and child mortality rates which apparently persist.

According to MacCormack, who cites Okoye, the infant mortality rate (deaths under one year) for Sierra Leone in 1974 was

47. The latest estimate from the Nigerian National Population Bureau of 94 million for July 1984 is much higher than all UN and other 'international estimates'. On the basis of a presumed figure of 85 million Nigerians for 1980, the Berg Report (Appendix to Chapter 3 above) estimated, on unstated presumptions, that it will rise to 172 million in the year 2000. (Nigeria is far more populous than any other sub-Saharan country.)
48. There has never been a reliable Nigerian census, not merely because of the well-known unreliability of the 1963 census (which replaced the even more hopeless count of 1962), but because all earlier censuses, including that of 1952–3, are certain to have been serious under-counts.
49. Given the very poor medical facilities in most rural areas, where some four-fifths of the population lives (according to MacCormack, 1984:199, 31 out of 146 Sierra Leonean chiefdoms in 1980 were without any health facility); and given, also, the high incidence of malaria (see below) and poor transport facilities – the 'considerable improvement' in the West African expectation of life which Rimmer reports (1984:69) on the basis of official figures, is hard to understand unless it is mainly due to rapidly falling mortality rates in urban areas and their surroundings. The Berg Report states point blank (no notes) that the African life expectancy is 47 years (p.87). See Dyson (1982:50–2) for a table showing infant mortality rates for 78 tropical countries; West African rates, which are not up-to-date, are generally much higher than for any other region, the highest of all having been 291 for Upper Volta (now Burkina Faso) in 1960–1, against 130 for India in 1972.

as high as 225 per thousand (and apt to be much higher in rural than in urban areas), compared with 60 per thousand in Sri Lanka in 1975.[50] A survey of a group of Sierra Leonean women over 40 showed that they had lost 508 children per 1,000 births. Most deaths of children under 5 years 'were from environmental diseases such as tetanus, malaria and diarrhoea with malnutrition as a contributing factor' (p.200). Sierra Leonean life expectancy at birth was only 36 to 40 years for females and 33 to 37 years for males, compared with a projected 53 years for the whole population of India in 1980.[51] Presumably endemic malaria, which according to one Sierra Leone survey afflicted over a third of all children between 3 months and 5 years old, was mainly responsible for the much higher death rates in Sierra Leone[52] than in India–for, owing to drastic mosquito control measures, death rates from malaria in India were down to very low levels by the mid-1960s.[53]

My attitude must not be misunderstood. Of course there is much evidence that in many regions, especially in India, increasing population density is one of the factors accounting for the slow growth in output per head and greater landlessness. The trouble is that 'in both academic and practical cultures, among both political economists and physical ecologists, most analyses and prescriptions are partial, concentrating on one or a few explanations and actions and ignoring others.'[54] In opposing a partial approach to the problem of rural poverty Chambers suggests (p.44) the need for 'a balanced pluralist approach, empirically based and with a wide span in both political economy and physical ecology', a view with which I concur.

50. MacCormack, 1984:200; Okoye, 1980.
51. Cassen, 1978:131.
52. According to Bruce-Chwatt (1980:287), mosquito control measures in sub-Saharan Africa generally have continued to be limited almost entirely to large towns, so that malaria remains as endemic as ever elsewhere.
53. Although it is widely believed that the incidence of malaria has risen since that date, mortality rates certainly remain extremely low compared to West Africa.
54. Chambers, 1983:40.

CHAPTER 5

PAUSE: HOW CAN
THE IMPASSE
BE RESOLVED?

❦

On the rare occasions when development economists work in the field they usually do so, in the manner of Bliss and Stern, without consulting any anthropological writings before they go there – or indeed when reporting their findings.[1] Nearly all economists have so little time for economic anthropologists that they scarcely acknowledge their existence, as even respectable textbooks show. On the other hand, I think that many anthropologists have a secret reverence for (perhaps combined with a fear of) economists,[2] a reverence which lay behind both the retreat from economics by the substantivists in the Polanyi debate (see p.22) and the still deeper subsequent withdrawal into the closed world of marxism with its anti-empirical bias. Anthropologists cannot avoid being overawed by a powerful academic discipline which commands financial resources vastly superior to their own, and which continues to exert so much authority in the world despite its inability to solve the problems of inflation and unemployment in industrialized countries. It is perhaps for this reason that their normally severe critical propensities are apt to be suspended when faced with such 'economic generalizers' as Boserup, whose work, did she happen to be an anthropologist, would be less highly regarded.

For many reasons the tiny discipline of economic anthropology is rapidly becoming obsolescent, especially in third-world countries themselves, this being in some degree due to its inability to persuade development economists, whether in academia or the international agencies, that its findings can be really useful. So it is partly to ensure our own survival that we must demonstrate our indispensability. The present book has both negative and positive purposes. As a polemical work it aims to expose both the

1. See Bliss and Stern, 1982.
2. Perhaps they are particularly envious of their mathematical approach?

66

unnecessary degree of unreality and the Western bias involved in most economic theorizing about the rural tropical world, as well as economists' gullibility in their use of official statistics; its positive contribution is that of demonstrating, in the chapters which follow, that economic anthropologists are well capable of generalizing about broad issues in a way which should seem highly relevant to development economists. Our predilection for study-ing the minutiae of how things work has been almost universally misunderstood: it would be as appropriate to blame cell biologists for their lack of concern for the whole organism.

It was in an attempt to advance matters that in my *Dry Grain Farming Families* (a comparison, based on much fieldwork, of certain rural economies in Hausaland and south India, which both mainly depended on the cultivation of dry, i.e. unirrigated, grain)[3] I presented a plea for 'the systematic categorization of broad types of rural under-development in the contemporary, tropical, third world – for a respectable typology of agrarian systems' (p.49). In so doing, I noted[4] the economist K.N. Raj's claim that economists are indifferent to the pervasiveness of socio-economic heterogeneity,[5] and also the economist Roxborough's assertion that if the plurality of agrarian systems were accepted, 'the Byzantine debates about the correct definition of a "peasant" would become irrelevant'.[6] So, as a start, I sought to identify one important type of agrarian system which appeared to exist in the two regions under comparison: a type which I carefully denoted *a* dry grain mode, since there were certainly a number of other dry grain modes elsewhere in the tropics.

In expressing my surprise that so little emphasis had been placed in the economic literature on the need for what may be called 'a socio-economic classification of tropical agrarian systems', I ventured to suggest that the number of important classes (import-ant in terms of the sizes of population involved) would not necessarily prove to be at all large, perhaps nearer twenty than a thousand. If that were so, it might be that the task of classification

3. While some unirrigated paddy was grown in the south Indian villages, the area under unirrigated millet was very much larger. More non-grain crops, notably groundnuts, were grown in Hausaland than in south India.   4. Hill, 1982:49, n.1.
5. Robinson and Kidron (eds.), 1970:31.   6. Roxborough, 1979:95.

could be undertaken reasonably rapidly by a group of experts drawn from various disciplines, provided sufficient agreement on the principles of classification (economic, demographic, social, agricultural, technical, etc.) were obtainable. Our persistent profound ignorance of the basic workings of the agrarian systems in many regions would mean that the classification would be provisional – but surely any respectable classification would be better than none?[7]

As for the particular dry grain mode which I tried to identify, I suggested that it exists in very densely populated tropical regions where unirrigated grains, such as millets and sorghums, are the basic crop; where grain yields are low by any standards; where land is sold for cash; and where certain other conditions are satisfied.[8] I was astonished to find that socio-economic generalizations that might be made about such a dry grain mode (applicable in all cases to each of the regions in the two continents) were very numerous and of wide scope. I was, however, not surprised to discover that many of these conclusions were at variance with 'contemporary prevailing orthodoxy',[9] such as is reflected in mainstream textbooks as well as in popular compilations such as *Peasants and Peasant Societies*.[10] It is my contention that we cannot escape from this orthodoxy unless our generalizations relate to particular agrarian systems which yet remain to be identified. The study of tropical agrarian systems must be regarded as in its infancy until such a taxonomy has been attempted. .

But what *can* I mean by 'contemporary prevailing orthodoxy'? I believe that it was as a result of the highly motivated enthusiasm of the supporters of some ahistorical versions of marxism, from about the end of the 1960s throughout the 1970s, that a kind of corpus of orthodox beliefs (or received doctrine) took partial expression; and that, most interestingly, this became in due course acceptable to people of greatly varying political persuasions owing

7. This is no exaggeration considering that economics textbooks never distinguish irrigated and dry crops when discussing 'subsistence farming'.
8. See Hill (1982:50) for the nine 'necessary conditions' which I tentatively suggested for the existence of this dry grain mode.
9. Some idea of the nature of prevailing orthodoxy may be gathered from Hill (1982:Chapter 17); see also Hill, 1985a:126–7 for a tentative summary list of aspects of prevailing orthodoxy which appeared *not* to apply to the particular dry grain mode which I had tried to identify.   10. Shanin (ed.), 1971.

to the lack of any serious or systematic alternative. The curious thing about this body of orthodox beliefs is that it both exists and does not exist. It *does not exist* because of the lack of any reliable expositor of especial renown who has presented it as a properly organized coherent system of wide application. It *exists* to fill the vacuum in our knowledge of the workings of tropical agrarian systems, which is such that any vaguely familiar set of plausible suppositions serves to relieve the anxieties of ignorance; one knows that it *does exist* because of the commotion that is caused if one unknowingly steps upon, appears to dismiss or question, any of these implicit suppositions, especially in the field of population studies.

This bridging chapter is not the place to elaborate my plea for an agrarian taxonomy, which I have already uttered at length elsewhere.[11] It heralds a further contribution to the resolution of the present impasse, as represented by the chapters which follow. These chapters relate to some important and practical subjects, which economic and other anthropologists (and also some economists and historians) have surely studied in a useful and general way, and which ought to be deemed relevant by development economists.[12]

11. Hill, 1982.
12. While it would have been quite possible to have written these chapters without including so much in the way of bibliographic material, I have provided this documentation in order to show that large numbers of anthropologists, many of whom would not count themselves 'economic', have done useful work in the past few decades.

CHAPTER 6

THE LOGICAL NECESSITY FOR ECONOMIC INEQUALITY WITHIN RURAL COMMUNITIES

࿇

Although every economist knows that any economic model relating to a village where all households enjoyed equal living standards would be preposterously unrealistic, the pressure exerted by the amorphous word *peasant* often enhances the belief in the appropriateness of the notion of an average (typical or modal) household which is, in any case, built into marginalist orthodoxy. So, as we saw in Chapter 2, the search for universal generalizations about individual rural communities is normally expressed in terms of 'ordinary households'. It is considered entirely respectable to search for *general motivations*, such as 'risk-aversion' or 'profit-maximization', without any regard for the fact that the motivations of cultivators with one acre are bound to be very different from those with five, twenty or forty acres.

Behind the presumption of uniform motivations lies a largely unconscious Golden Age fallacy, which is shared by marxists and non-marxists alike: the sentimental belief that there was a time, often not long ago, when egalitarianism reigned in the village, possibly being associated with communal farming – a meaningless expression, which no one ever attempts to define. The false presumption of what may be called 'equality at the base date' then accounts for the very common idea that outside influences must always have been responsible for disturbing the 'aboriginal equilibrium'.[1] If that is so, it is then regarded as necessary to look beyond the village for the basic causes of economic inequality within it.

My two purposes in this brief chapter are first to argue, on general principles, that '*inequality* at the base date' ought to be our

1. See Long (1984:2) for an important plea for 'an actor-oriented analysis of social process'. 'Although it is undoubtedly true that much important structural change has resulted from the impact of outside forces. . . it is, I believe, theoretically unsatisfactory to base one's analysis on the notion of external determination.'

starting point, such village inequality being perpetuated indefinitely; and second to insist that the findings of economic anthropologists invariably show that village inequality is pronounced. In this chapter I am not concerned with *qualitative differentiation*, a matter which is appropriately deferred until Chapter 15, but, as it were, with the mere arithmetic of inequality. However 'wealth' may be defined, it is invariably found that some households are much better off than others and that the graph relating the number of households to wealth (defined, say, in terms of the sizes of farm-holdings) is fairly smooth along its middle length.

Since economic historians are seldom able to push their analyses of village household structure right back to the days before cash circulated,[2] it is a matter of little significance that, for convenience, I prefer to confine the concept of inequality at the base date (innate inegalitarianism) to cash economies. Why in cash economies is the concept of general application? I address myself to this question in very brief and simple terms, under six headings, re-emphasizing some points I have already made.

First is the fact that villagers are highly competitive people. Every householder is basically concerned with bettering his household's economic situation by legitimate means (which would preclude him, for example, from seizing his neighbour's land), without regard to the effect that this has on other households. This does not mean that the village feels no corporate responsibility to assist those who are starving or that all the customary mechanisms for rendering communal assistance[3] have fallen into desuetude; but it does imply that *no egalitarian ethos is put into practice in villages*. The rich are admired, feared and envied; and the gravely impoverished are pitied, despised and helped by some people. But as no villager ever explicitly presumes that total equality is either a natural condition or a desirable political aim, it would be extraordinary if it happened to be attained by chance.

2. Little is known about the relative wealth of the general run of farming households in rural economies before cash circulated, this having been many centuries ago in south India and at least two centuries ago in Hausaland.
3. Such as collective farmwork performed free or for small reward for reasons of pity, obligation, friendship, kinship, enjoyment, etc. See, for example, Hill, 1972:251.

Second is the fact that the riskiness of economic life in the rural tropics is so great, in terms of such adverse general factors as climatic uncertainty, crop diseases and insect attack, that for reasons of chance alone some households are bound to suffer more than others. When we add to this the fact that some individual households are naturally much more vulnerable than others owing, for instance, to ill health or the lack of working sons and daughters, or to political disfavourment, we can see that it is inevitable that even if everyone happened to cultivate five acres (as is inconceivable), some households would be bound to get lower yields, and so to be poorer, than others.

Third is the well-known fact that cash economies always tend to operate in a manner which raises the rich and depresses the poor. As other less general considerations also have to be taken into account, this does not necessarily mean that the gap between rich and poor constantly widens, or that there is no individual upward mobility; but it does imply that certain dice are always heavily weighted in favour of the rich. Thus, to repeat my significant example, the rich are those who store grain for a seasonal price rise, while the poor are apt to sell much-needed grain immediately after harvest when prices are lowest.[4] Then (see Chapter 8) the poor have much worse access to credit than the rich and pay more for it. Again, poor men do not necessarily benefit, as the rich do, if they happen to have several sons, for these sons will be forced to work as ill-paid farm labourers (Chapter 10) and cannot afford to migrate as farmers. In general, as we know, the poor are always under duress and cannot seize economic opportunities which are open to richer people. It is universally true that the poor get lower returns per unit of effort than the rich.[5]

Fourth is the fact that the rich are better able to meet the expenses associated with efficient crop production, such as the purchase of

4. Since the staple crops of the West African forest zone, other than maize and to a limited degree yams, are unstorable (this applies to bananas, plantain, cassava and cocoyam), crop speculation by farmers is far less important there than in the savannah where the staple crops, millet and sorghum, are eminently storable – much more so than maize, which is stored on the cob in open barns. See Hill (1972) on granaries.

5. Since formulating this *a priori* statement I have learnt of the empirical evidence provided by Longhurst (1984), that poor workers in Hausaland produce 'a smaller quantity of available energy from farm produce per unit of their energy input' (p.i).

plough animals or organic manure (dung).[6] It is partly for this reason that I am unable to accept the validity of the famous inverse relationship between yield per acre and the size of farm-holdings, which used to be widely current in India. Besides, it would seem to be quite peculiar that there should be such a very important exception to the general rule that the poor are necessarily less efficient than the rich in all their self-financed economic activities.[7]

Fifth is the fact that most cultivators, particularly in West Africa, have non-farming occupations which may do much to reduce the risks of farming. As common sense would suggest, and as detailed observation invariably confirms, the richest farmers are those who pursue the most lucrative non-farming occupations so that they are better insured than the poor against crop deficiencies. As it is usually impossible for any man to enjoy high status within

6. The case of manurial dung is especially relevant here since by the act of purchasing it within the village community, richer farmers deprive poorer farmers of its use. In south India and Hausaland much dung is apt to be applied to the land by richer farmers, whether or not they buy chemical fertilizers. As my argument is a general one, I am not here dealing with the effects of the introduction of chemical fertilizers, modern technology, etc., which are still unavailable in many regions.

7. Until fairly recently it was generally accepted that in Indian agriculture there was an inverse relationship between yield per acre and the size of the farm-holding. While there are still some who believe that the empirical evidence for this relationship is unassailable, others consider that the whole question of size and productivity relations is highly debatable: see Rudra and Sen (1980) for a useful and sophisticated summary of the state of play up to that date by two of the key participants. In this very brief note (see also Hill, 1982:Chapter 8) I seek to argue on *a priori* grounds that the likelihood is that the smallest farmers, say those who cultivate no more than 2 or 3 acres of dry farmland, obtain notably poor yields. The reason I confine my argument to dry farmland is that in districts where both irrigated and dry farmland exists, richer farmers may well cultivate tiny holdings of highly productive irrigated land, so that there is not necessarily a close relationship between 'wealth' and size of irrigated holding such as we know exists for dry land. Assuming, then, that the smallest cultivators are the most impoverished, 'the inverse relationship' implies that the poor farm more efficiently than the rich. But throughout this book the general argument is that the poorest farming households are necessarily so ill-organized and lacking in finance that they are bound to be the least efficient; it is not true, as so commonly assumed, that they are apt to benefit from having more family labour per acre on which to call, for each household member is likely to lead an independent hand-to-mouth existence, hurrying to pick up odd jobs when they happen to become available – in which case no organized family labour force exists. It is the rich farmers who benefit from the superior efficiency of the large groups of farm workers, both family and hired, which are employed only on large farms.

Additionally, being crippled by the lack of finance, the poorest farmers are those who cannot afford to buy organic manure (let alone chemical fertilizers), and who are all too apt to sell any supplies they have available. Very often they own no plough animals, being obliged to hire at high cost. Finally, there is the ambiguity attaching to the world *yield*. If yield is expressed in terms of value not quantity, then account must be taken of the lower than average prices received for basic crops by poorer farmers, who are so often forced to sell when seasonal prices are lowest, and whose bargaining position is generally weak.

his community unless he is seen to prosper as a farmer, so hardly anyone deliberately opts out of farming to devote himself to other work.

Sixth is the greater prevalence of under-employment among poorer people in these highly seasonal tropical economies, this being another reason why life for the impoverished is so much more risky than for the rich, as Myrdal cogently argues.[8]

This list of six inter-related reasons for the innateness of inequality could be made very much longer; but I hope that it is sufficiently persuasive and provides adequate introduction to the empirical material which follows. The point is that inequality is socially institutionalized, in terms (say) of headmanship (the right to collect taxes) or the relationship between marriage payments and status – the latter being a particularly useful example since anthropologists are far more competent than economists to examine and discuss it.

In the Hausa village of Batagarawa, where no land-holding class existed, there were 171 'farming households',[9] of whom 8 were landless,[10] and 39 (23%) cultivated 2 acres or less;[11] the largest holding was 56 acres, the next largest 30 acres and 11 households cultivated 20 acres or more. Given this dispersion, it is hardly relevant that the average holding was 6½ acres.

I classified the households there into four 'wealth groups', ranging from 'rich' (on village standards) to very poor, by secretly asking three prominent and perspicacious local farmers (of whom one was 'rich', two in the next group below) to undertake such a grouping, each one making his judgments independently. Although none of us then knew the acreage figures, I later found that in terms of the size of farm-holdings there was hardly any overlap between the groups, so that nearly everyone in Group 1

8. Myrdal, 1968.
9. Hill, 1972. Owing to the importance of the system of *gandu*, under which married sons work on their father's farms although they may live in separate houses and do some farming for themselves, in this earlier publication I used the term 'farming unit', not farming household, to cover both fathers and their married sons.
10. I regarded them as 'farming households' since they were aspirant farmers, unlike my next-door neighbour, who was a professional drummer, and a few other men, mainly newcomers.
11. These statistics relate only to the manured farmland, around the village, which was cultivated every year; there were also some 'bush farms' which had to be fallowed.

('rich') had a larger holding than nearly everyone in Group 2 and so
on down the scale. This proved two important points: first, as was
corroborated by much other evidence, that the extent of landownership closely reflected a household's living standards, and
second that ordinary intelligent farmers *think in terms of inequality*.
Indeed, it soon became clear that within the local community each
man's standard of living is considered to be one of his most important attributes.[12] In ignoring inequality, economists are overlook-
ing the very economic matter which the local populace considers
of paramount importance.

I lack the space to list more than a very few of the 'economic
indicators' which confirmed our original classification. Rich
farmers had bought about 27% of their farmland (the poorest but
3%); rich farmers had seldom sold farmland; rich farmers had more
(usually much more) of everything, such as livestock, which was
readily countable; rich farmers invariably had far more lucrative
non-farming occupations than poor farmers – and their sons were
never farm labourers; rich farmers bought manure (dung) while
poor farmers sold it; rich farmers much more often retained the
farming services of their married sons (in *gandu*) than poorer
farmers. The rich farmers being better off in every way, and so on
down the wealth groups, it was no wonder that the village assistants found the classification so straightforward: *there were so many
infallible indicators of relative wealth and poverty*. Most significantly,
poor farmers were often forced to sell their whole crop at low post-
harvest prices: grain sales are not necessarily surpluses.

Turning to the Indian sub-continent, the author of an
impressive recent book on rural Bangladesh[13] classified households in four categories according to the number of months' maintenance provided by each source of income which, wisely, he did
not express in monetary terms. In one small village (p.91), 16% of
75 households were in the top category, being able to enjoy a
comfortable living for at least fifteen months on one year's

12. The important Hausa concept of *arziki*, a word which is on everyone's lips, represents
a philosophical and fatalistic theory of classlessness in a milieu of admitted inequality.
Having the double sense of prosperity and good luck, *arziki* represents life as a game of
chance, which some are more likely to win than others – though they, too, may lose.
See Hill, 1977:155–6.   13. Schendel, 1981.

harvest, against 20% in the lowest category which regularly went
hungry. He obtained similar results in other villages. The villagers
themselves took a keen interest in economic inequality; in one
group of villages both the poorest and the richest people viewed
village society 'as a dichotomy based on landownership' (p.174).
For one village (p.162) the author was so fortunate as to be able to
compare his own statistics of the distribution of landownership in
1978 with comparable figures for 1922 and 1955. Between 1922
and 1978 the proportion of landless households had risen from
26% to 38% compared with figures of 21% and 48% for those
landowners who had one acre or less; this meant that 53% of
householders owned more than one acre in 1922 compared with
only 14% in 1978, a change which was only partly due to population increase. In one of his villages about 60% of all households
could not survive on their income from land alone (p.86); and 35%
of all households derived most of their income from non-
agricultural sources.

The deeper cash penetrates into the 'recesses' of village
economies the more competitive they are likely to become, thus
increasing the riskiness of life for the most impoverished.
Therefore, a high incidence of land-selling, such as was common in
Hausaland until recently (see Chapter 13), certainly enhanced
inequality. Most writers on village economies in the Indian sub-
continent play down land-selling,[14] which presumably always
occurs to some degree, Schendel being no exception. In his
important book on agrarian structure and ideology in northern
Tamil Nadu, J. Harriss mentions the rigidity of the land market,
the reasons for which he scarcely analyses.

Although it is unfortunate that Harriss does not distinguish
irrigated and dry land, for they are very different categories, he
provides excellent statistics (p.116) on the distribution of land of
all types for 275 households in one village. As many as 44% of these
households were landless and 18% of landholders owned no more
than 1½ acres; at the other end of the scale 5% of householders
owned 15 acres or more, only three farmers (1%) owning more
than 30 acres. Such inequality was very marked, for the 'top 6.5%'

14. Though Bailey (1957) was primarily concerned with the question of why so much land
      in a highland village of Orissa was sold.

of households owned nearly a half (47%) of the total cultivated area, and somewhat over half of all the landholders owned insufficient land to provide for their own consumption needs.

In much of the Indian sub-continent land distribution is to such a high degree a function of caste that undifferentiated multi-caste figures of landownership provide poor evidence for the universal innateness of economic inequality (irrespective of the nature of qualitative differentiation) which is the subject of this chapter. Unfortunately, as we shall see (Chapter 14), few publications provide reliable land-holding statistics for particular castes.

As all Indian village surveys unavoidably expose inequality (though they seldom analyse it), little purpose would be served by providing additional empirical evidence in support of my *a priori* insistence that village economies are fundamentally inegalitarian. As I have said, my consideration of socio-economic differentiation is deferred until Chapter 15, it being necessary to examine many other relevant matters meanwhile.

CHAPTER 7

THE FARMING HOUSEHOLD:
ITS DEFECTS AS
A STATISTICAL UNIT

For many practical reasons there is no escape from expressing economic inequality in terms of households, or farming households, as in Chapter 5. This is more unfortunate than is generally recognized, since so many households in the rural tropical world do not conform to the Western stereotype of the integrated nuclear group that necessarily dictates our statistical approach, inappropriate though it may be. The main purpose of this brief chapter, which further develops some of the arguments previously made, is to look at a few of the 'defects' of this statistical unit in terms of the departure from the stereotype, and to suggest the need for a degree of sub-classification of households in certain circumstances.

So that our definition may relate to the varying circumstances in different regions it is best to regard the farming household as being, in vague general principle, a group of kin and affines, which eats from the same cooking pot, lives under the same roof and cultivates the same land, and is commonly based on at least one conjugal unit. But, as we shall see, there are so many variants on this norm, especially in West Africa, and so many reasons why a person's individuality (rather than his/her position as X's spouse) requires emphasis, that one often wishes that the individual adult (such as the mother with her children, the father or the married son) might be the basic statistical unit – though this would not obviate the need for sub-classification.

In West Africa the 'dynamics of the conjugal relationship'[1] may involve little more than sexual, child-rearing, cooking, load-carrying (water, firewood etc.) and marketing services on the part of the wife and sexual and food-providing services on the part of the husband. In the course of their daily lives people mainly

---

1. To borrow a useful phrase from Abu's excellent article (1983) on the separateness of spouses in an Ashanti town.

associate with members of their own sex who satisfy their need for friendship; and men and women (with their children) almost always eat separately. So it is not surprising that in some West African societies, notably urban Ashanti,[2] husbands and wives may live in separate houses with members of their own lineage for at least some part of their married lives, in which case cooked meals may be delivered to the husband from the wife's household if it is nearby.

In very general terms one may say that West African husbands and wives seldom perform the same task simultaneously: if they are on the farm together, division of labour is usual.[3] In some societies wives have their own farms, which they cultivate without their husband's help, except that he may clear the land; such wives may well expect to be renumerated in cash and/or in kind if they work on their husband's farms. However, in many societies, especially those in which land is individually owned, most of the farming is the responsibility of the husband who in the savannah zone always has charge of the household granaries; the wife is then dependent on him for the 'issue' of basic foodstuffs, just as she normally expects to receive periodic (even daily) cash allowances for the purchase of essential additional requirements, such as meat and vegetables.[4]

In some West African societies, notably in the forest zone where most of the food-crop marketing is the responsibility of women, husbands usually reward their wives for handling produce from their farms. In general, West African wives, even those in Muslim seclusion, enjoy a high degree of economic independence of their husbands – or, one could even emphasize husbands' independence of their wives! The wives are as much traders on their own account as are their husbands. And if, for example, a Hausa wife wishes to buy groundnuts from her husband in order to produce groundnut oil for sale, she will be apt to do so at, or near, the market price.

In south India the farming household is more closely integrated. Even though husbands and wives may tend to specialize in

2. See Abu (1983), in particular for the discussion of the symbolic relationship between food and sex (p.161).   3. See Hill (1975) on West African farming households.
4. See Abu, 1983:160 *et seq.*

different tasks, they and their older children may still be rightly
regarded as working as a team on the family land, under the
husband's authority. Indian wives do not enjoy a degree of
economic autonomy comparable to that of their West African
counterparts, a fact which is connected with the rarity of polygyny,
which is virtually universal in West Africa, in the sense that most
men aspire to have more than one wife as they grow older.

Who, then, are the 'household heads' with whom the whole
household tends to become so closely identified when we are
studying economic inequality? In West African patrilineal,
matrilineal, or non-unilineal societies,[5] the household head when
the spouses are co-resident is always a man, the same being true of
south India. As for widows, in south India they are often household
heads,[6] even of extended households including married sons, for it
is generally of the nature of Indian marriage that wives are
transferred permanently to their affines, so that there is no question of their returning to their own kin in a dependent capacity in
the event of widowhood. In Hausaland, on the other hand, women
household heads are very rare, although they often live as dependants in their married sons' houses. West Africa is so ethnically
heterogeneous that one may make only very broad generalizations, such as that women are usually not household heads when
men of their own generation are in the household – but even then
much may depend on who, if anybody, owns the actual house.

Although it is widely believed that three-generational households which include married sons, which are commonly known as
joint households in India,[7] are everywhere on the decline, there is
little firm evidence that this is actually so, except from the state of
Kerala in south-west India, where everything is always 'different'.
Indeed, as population densities and the prices of farmland
increase, married sons may be increasingly obliged to continue
working on their father's farms because they are unable to acquire

5. Corporate lineages are lacking in both Hausaland and south India.
6. In the six Karnataka villages about a fifth of all farming households were headed
   by widows.
7. Households composed of two or more parentless married brothers are also joint
   households; as in Hausaland, such households show rapidly decreasing survival
   expectations.

land for themselves and lack the means to migrate constructively.[8] My own and other people's very limited findings have shown that the institution of *gandu* in Hausaland, under which married sons continue to work indefinitely on their father's farms in return for various rewards,[9] generally continues to flourish; and there were very few parents in the six Karnataka villages who had been abandoned by all their married sons.[10] We should all keep an open mind on future developments, both because the modern desire for independence from parental control, which is often not as strong as is commonly supposed, is liable to conflict with decreasing economic opportunities, including the stagnation of the land market (Chapter 13); and because the advantages of larger family work forces are well recognized by householders.[11] But again, owing to ethnic heterogeneity, and very varying population densities, it is difficult to generalize about West Africa: thus, there are many lineage-organized societies such that sons always part from their fathers on marriage, if not before, being then entitled to claim their personal usufructural rights over land.

Following the lead of Fortes,[12] much (perhaps too much) has been written about the standard development or life-cycle of the domestic group, with its three stages of: (1) expansion (the period of procreation); (2) 'dispersion or fission' (the departure of sons on marriage); and (3) decay (death, followed by replacement by the next generation). As Fortes himself of course realized,[13] this theoretical model is far from being of universal application: thus, in a society where married sons tend to remain with their fathers indefinitely the third stage will never be reached. Comparative empirical studies relevant to economic inequality which are based on concepts of the life-cycle remain at an early stage. The same is

8. The very big houses, inhabited by a hundred people or more, which are found in very densely populated countryside near Kano city in Hausaland, represent one type of response to increasing population density; it is not only that rates of outward migration (particularly from such houses) are remarkably low, but that married brothers always remain co-resident, though farming separately. See Hill, 1977: Chapter 11.   9. See Hill, 1972.
10. The sons often consult together as to which of them should remain living with their parent(s). (The main reason for the fairly low incidence of joint households in all rural communities is that many parents die before their sons marry. See Hill, 1982.)
11. Maclachlan (1983:140) has actually demonstrated that south Indian households containing more than one *man* have higher crop yields per acre.
12. See Goody, 1958.   13. See Fortes, 1978:18.

true of the more recent and much more broadly based work on the 'biological cycle of family life' which, following the translation (1966) of Chayanov's much earlier work on Russian peasantry, assumed enormous theoretical importance.

The practical statistical conclusion of this brief discussion is that while we are all obliged to use the farming household as our basic unit when studying economic inequality, it is often desirable to distinguish several household types, even though this may involve taking a larger sample. In my own work I always avoid sampling[14] and examine whole populations, owing to the much greater advantages of analysing the *relationships* between all the households in the community than of studying a number of unconnected households. Thus, according to circumstances, one might find it necessary to break up the category *household* into several subcategories selected from the following: ordinary conjugal households (parents and children); 'joint households'; households headed by widows (with or without other members); households headed by sons with living fathers; conjugally split households – and so forth. Failing some degree of sub-division, empirical findings on equality are sometimes as defective as the multi-caste statistics on the sizes of farm-holdings (criticized on p.77 above), collections of figures having no structure or innate logic.

14. It may surprise statisticians and economists to learn that anthropologists are always aware, without being told, when any author has used mathematical sampling procedures.

CHAPTER 8

THE NEED
TO BE
INDEBTED

❧

Because rural and tropical communities in which cash circulates are innately inegalitarian, so it is inevitable that the impoverished (in particular) need to borrow and that richer people should wish to put their surplus funds to work. It is mistaken to assume that such borrowing and lending as takes place within a village community necessarily enhances inequality (it may, indeed, reduce it), or is bound to be 'bad' for some other reason. As Baker has put it in relation to the history of rural Tamilnad, credit-granting reflected the fundamental inequalities of local societies but did not create them,[1] borrowing between cultivators being best considered as part of the hierarchically ordered system of distribution within the village, big men being expected or even obliged to provide credit. 'Just as the village leader was expected to distribute grain to keep the village alive, so he was expected to distribute capital resources to keep the village lands under culti-vation'.[2] Those impoverished people who are too poor to borrow have, as it were, fallen beneath the community and are therefore without hope.[3] Borrowing and lending are necessary for the health of any rural community, 'an intrinsic part of the system of pro-duction'[4] – hence the provocative title of this chapter. To cite Baker again, the expansion of local debt may well be evidence of the 'rapid growth of a commercial economy' (p.258), rather than of any submission to rapacious creditors.

With certain notable exceptions,[5] the literature on the subject under discussion tends either to be very crude or very sophis-ticated. When crude, it is commonly strongly tainted with the two

1. Baker, 1984:332. 2. *Ibid.*: 154–5.
3. My local assistants in Batagarawa (see p.74 above), constantly spoke of the inability to borrow as a significant indicator of gross impoverishment.
4. Baker, 1984:332.
5. Such as a number of historians of India (notably Baker, 1984) and also Firth and Yamey, eds., 1964.

colonial prejudices that the impoverished should be protected from their helplessness, foolishness, fecklessness (and the slippery slope of increasing indebtedness) and that most creditors are wicked, rapacious scoundrels; when sophisticated, it is apt to be largely involved with the intricate personal relationships uniting the parties and with the interesting long-term sequences of alternate borrowing and lending which sometimes develop. This chapter is not sophisticated: it is another attempt to 'decolonialize the attitude to debt'[6] in the knowledge that local borrowing and lending are as inevitable as buying and selling, involving no inherent moral overtones. Throughout the colonial empire rural indebtedness was ignorantly and priggishly regarded as a moral problem, a sign that 'natives' lacked the virtues of thrift, self reliance and so forth. Village credit-granting was never seen as the converse of stultification – the sign of a lively economy.

The colonial attitude to debt was as moral as that of missionaries to adultery or polygyny. This was partly a matter of semantics. In the home country the general attitude was that 'debt was bad' – so bad that at one time it had even led to transportation; so, of course, it followed that it was even worse in the colonies. But had the colonialists employed *borrowing* rather than *debt*, they might have reflected that it was the richer and more secure members of their own society who were able to borrow from the bank or otherwise, and that something similar might apply in a colony. Also, as pointed out by Charlesworth,[7] a complex and massive network of agrarian credit had been 'routine' in England before the industrial revolution. But as *debt* was the word, there was a strong tendency which, as we have seen, has persisted until the present day, to regard borrowing as a problem, almost as a kind of illness, for which a cure should be found.

Another semantic obstacle was the colonial tendency to identify creditors with moneylenders – a word with many unpleasant associations, which were fully exploited by 'the man from the CPC' (see the Preamble above). But in West Africa a moneylender

---

6. The obsessive attitude of British officials to the problems of Indian indebtedness in the second half of the nineteenth century is indicated by the fact that the subject was 'at the core of a large proportion of official correspondence in the Revenue Department' Kolff (1979:53).   7. Charlesworth, 1985:84.

proper is a man who makes a regular profession of lending money at cash interest, perhaps relying on personal surety rather than physical security; and the colonialists sought, how successfully one cannot say, to control his activities by means of legislation, some of which still exists. But the point here is that all the licensed moneylenders were in the cities and really large towns; there were none in the countryside, where virtually all the local creditors were themselves richer farmers, who might also be traders, and whose lending was a supplementary activity. Such local men were not much given to lending out cash on interest;[8] their loans took multifarious forms, one of the most interesting of which involved the mortgaging of farmland. Of course a mortgagee (a creditor) may impose wicked, crippling terms on his helpless mortgagor (the debtor) and be all too inclined to foreclose; on the other hand he may not (see the Preamble above), a possibility which is in no wise conveyed by the emotive *moneylender*.

Before going to south India in 1977, I had heard so much about moneylenders in that continent that I was greatly surprised to find that, as in West Africa, the main village lenders were farmers. But since that date several historians of India,[9] most notably Baker, have revolutionized thinking on the entire subject of credit-granting, and all are agreed that most local creditors were cultivators in the nineteenth century, as they still are today. According to Charlesworth, in rural Maharashtra 'almost everyone with any funds dabbled in lending' and the key to the relative economic position of cultivators depended on their degree of independence and autonomy in the credit relationship as well as on their command of resources.[10] Several of the contributors to Dewey and Hopkins's volume (1978) were concerned to decry the significance of the notorious small trader/creditor known as a *bania*, partly on the grounds that he was a semi-urban creature, and most people lived in the countryside.

8. Unless they lend outside the village to (say) wage earners in a nearby city, as sometimes happens in rural Hausaland.
9. See several chapters, some of which are not cited here, in Dewey and Hopkins (eds., 1978) and in Chaudhuri and Dewey (eds., 1979), as well as the works of C.J. Baker.
10. See Charlesworth, 1978:102. In his excellent chapter Charlesworth lays much stress on the significance and innateness of economic inequality. 'There was never . . . an egalitarian golden age in Maharashtra' (p.103).

By examining the role of credit-granting 'against the background of the local society and economy', Baker has emphasized many reasons, additional to those already cited, why it was no accident that most Tamilnad creditors were village cultivators in the nineteenth century and earlier. Ordinary cultivators were 'the only people who were really capable of assessing a villager's creditworthiness'.[11] Richer men were *expected* to provide credit to poorer men, and were sometimes under virtual obligation to do so, even though there was often 'no real computation of interest payments and no real expectation of repayment'. The point was that cash, like grain, had to be redistributed. Village creditors gave out 'loans' in order to secure dependants who could not repay. 'Anyone who made a cash profit from agriculture immediately set about lending some of this to his neighbours' (p.156); and as lending became more competitive, debtors were sometimes able to switch their patrons. While town merchants were often too nervous to extend credit to villagers, village creditors sometimes extended their operations into the towns. In such a countryside it made 'no sense to view agriculture through the theoretical retina of the individual, independent peasant, toiling away in the fields and wrestling hopelessly with the *external* forces of trade and money-lending' (p.331).

A recent report from rural Bangladesh is similar. Many cultivators there regarded loan granting as essentially a 'social service' even though they might make 'inordinate profits';[12] and many of their clients agreed with them. Although they charged much higher rates than the banks, at least they did not demand bribes and their protective attitude of patronage might have been welcome to the borrower.

The terms and conditions involved in credit-granting vary on a continuum from very harsh to lenient, and it is only by studying the type of credit involved that we can begin to assess the situation. But before turning to consider some particular categories of credit-granting, I make some general points.

Although the prevailing moral condemnation of village-

<hr />

11. Baker, 1984:154.   12. Schendel, 1981:172.

generated credit often stems from the colonial past, one must remember that other ideologies also may be involved, notably the official Muslim attitude to usury. The Hausa case is interesting as demonstrating the unavoidability of widespread borrowing in highly seasonal rural tropical economies, particularly those where there is one short rainy season[13] and where grain is readily storable. Most Hausa country people are sincere and active Muslims who would wish to avoid usury, as defined by legal texts and scholars, were this remotely practicable. But even if they have a vague understanding of the highly obscure recent texts on the subject, they find themselves faced by a quite impossible ideal.[14] There, as elsewhere, very high proportions of viable householders are indebted, and many creditors are also debtors, for *debt* is not a homogeneous category.[15]

It being universally agreed that everyone with idle money does well to lend it out,[16] the number of farmer-creditors in any community must always be considerable, though such is the coyness of creditors that it is never ascertainable. As for the number of debtors, this is invariably very high, both because *debt is a natural condition* and because, as I have just said, people often borrow with one hand (for one purpose) and lend with another.[17] For all sorts of good practical reasons people do not think in terms of the *net balance* of debt or credit. Here again (see p.47 above), the tendency to differentiate negates any urge to aggregate in order to arrive at *net* indebtedness, which means that the bald terms *debtor* and *creditor* are often meaningless, especially as the biggest creditors are often the biggest debtors, as in the industrialized West. This is one of many reasons (three others being the secretiveness of creditors, the short-term nature of much credit

13. In dry grain areas of south India there is only one annual crop despite the occurrence of two monsoons.
14. On the absurdity of any attempt at the strict application of concepts of usury to the Hausa countryside see Hill, 1972:329–31.
15. An idea reflected in a Hausa proverb: 'Hoarding your money won't pay your debts.'
16. Even if there are banks in the general vicinity few villagers, other than bank-borrowers, visit them.
17. Baker (1984:279 *et seq.*) notes that it was not unusual for wealthy landlords to receive cash deposits from poor people, such as widows, who required some trustworthy person to look after their money.

and the likelihood of default)[18] why, as I have earlier insisted, the incidence of that non-existent 'disease' known as 'indebtedness' cannot be measured by any questionnaire approach.

Nor can such an approach be used to ascertain terms and conditions which are often unclear, unstatable, unfulfillable, if not unknown. It is very often inappropriate for outsiders to think in terms of interest *rates*, both because borrowing is apt to be timeless (interest rates are never computed) and, again, because of the attitude to default. From the creditor's angle the important question is not how long the debt has been outstanding but the prospects of repayment; as for the debtor, his usual concern is to repay as slowly as possible without incurring his creditor's final displeasure, and maybe to borrow more when his debt has diminished sufficiently.

Written documents recording the transaction and the terms involved are, I think, fairly rare unless mortgaging of farmland is involved, and even then they are often lacking in some regions. But as neither party may have understood the document when it was drawn up by the local letter-writer or 'petty lawyer', and as conformity to the agreed terms (which may be self-contradictory) cannot anyway be taken for granted, such agreements are often less useful than might be supposed. But, owing to the extreme bashfulness of creditors and (to a lesser degree) of their loyal clients the debtors, they are often not proffered in evidence.

This bashfulness, which is often nearly universal, is liable to misinterpretation for secrecy is commonly as much associated with selling as with lending. Thus in Hausaland the sale of grain by one householder to another is commonly wrapped in secrecy, either because the seller is frightened of taunts that he is neglecting his family by selling grain they require for themselves or because he is ashamed of appearing to be 'too rich' by village standards. But as the act of borrowing *is* somewhat less embarrassing than the act of lending, creditors may occasionally be identified by their debtors, though it is usually necessary to appeal to third parties. Although some creditors have bad reputations in their village because, for

18. One may surmise that partial default and/or late repayment are so common as to be 'usual', which is an aspect of the continuing personal relationship that so often obtains between creditor and debtor.

example, they are apt to foreclose on mortgagors in cruel fashion, the general view of creditors is that they are helpful people, so that the moral stance of ignorant outsiders does not reflect general village attitudes. To be a rich man and not to help anybody by lend-ing – and people do use 'help' in such a context – is to be miserly and to indulge in conspicuous waste.[19] Money is expected, by all concerned, to work as hard as possible, and to deserve a reward for so doing.

Another reason why credit-granting is so hard to study in the field is that it does not occur to either party that loans in kind come into the category of *debt*. Such loans are common both because pre-harvest 'assistance', by means of 'grants' of grain etc. (which may or may not be repaid in full or in part), is often necessary and because one of the main ways in which richer people help the poorer is by granting them non-cash loans which *enable them to set themselves to work*. Thus, in Hausaland traders may receive produce which they pay for after selling it; transport donkeys may be borrowed and paid for when the labour is over; grain may be granted to farm labourers who repay, over a period, in terms of work; pay-ment for the use of a temporarily borrowed farm may be made after harvest. And, just to take two examples from south India, rich men there may lend cows to poorer people, who are then rewarded with the first calf; and the owners of 'silk egg factories' (graineurs) may supply eggs on credit to village silkworm rearers (sericulturists) who need this help because they lack funds.[20]

There are, also, other categories of debt which official surveys overlook. Such, for instance, are very short-term 'bridging loans' to finance a trading expedition; loans made by wives to their husbands, which are often said to be common in many regions where wives are active traders;[21] and loans which big village creditors often receive from the outside world for relending locally.

I turn now to one of the most interesting and important forms of borrowing, namely the mortgaging or pledging of farmland, and I

---

19. It is because villagers generally have a very good idea of 'who has money', that idle money is so conspicuous. 20. See Charsley, 1982:153–4.
21. Nadel (1942:371) states that in Nupe country, in northern Nigeria, the most usual kind of borrowing involved 'close relations', most frequently husbands borrowing from their wives.

start with the pledging of Gold Coast (Ghanaian) cocoa farms. In the Gold Coast the practice of mortgaging or pledging[22] land, rivers, creeks, persons, property (cloth, gold, gold ornaments, etc.), and the more permanent economic trees (oil palm, coconut, and kola) goes back to time immemorial, as in many parts of the world; and cocoa farms were pledged in the earliest years of cocoa growing. We know about early cocoa farm pledging because officialdom was far more interested in the dangers of indebtedness than in the encouragement of production; thus, in evidence before the West African Lands Committee, which sat from 1912 to 1914, one witness actually suggested that the government should decide the terms on which cocoa farms should be pledged![23]

This type of pledging is relatively easy to study since Promissory Notes, which are fairly readily available to research workers, usually record the sum purported to have been borrowed and the various terms and conditions agreed. After examining several thousand Promissory Notes, which were made available to me by the Cocoa Purchasing Company,[24] I found that there were three main types of agreement involving creditors who were cocoa farmers,[25] and that moneylenders (proper) were seldom involved; I concluded that, if only because there was so much competition between creditors, terms and conditions were generally reasonable, within the West African context.

I had earlier analysed applications made by co-operators to the Gold Coast Co-operative Bank Ltd for loans for the redemption of

---

22. The same word in the Twi language – *awowa* – was used for all these transactions.
23. Hill, 1956:59.   24. See the Preamble above.
25. First was a tripartite type of agreement, such that equal parts of the cocoa from the pledged farm went respectively to the labourer (or whoever was in charge of the farm), to the creditor as interest, and to the creditor as debt repayment. As the farm would be automatically redeemed; as the debtor might very well act as the labourer and thus get one-third of the crop himself; and as the debtor would usually have had other farms which were not pledged – it can be seen that this type of pledging was not necessarily harsh. The second type of agreement involved automatic redemption of the farm after it had been cultivated by the creditor for a fixed term of years, which in about a half of the 108 cases analysed was as long as six years or more. But many of the Promissory Notes contained serious ambiguities. I concluded that the sum which was recorded as having been borrowed often, or perhaps usually, included timeless interest of 50%. Some documents explicitly stated that the debtor could redeem his farm at any time by repaying the net sum outstanding. With the third main type of agreement, which was usual in Ashanti, the debtor was supposed to repay the sum borrowed by a fixed date, failing which the farm would either be sold or appropriated by the creditor, or 50% would be added to the original sum borrowed and a fresh agreement drawn up. The formal period of the loan was often very short, most commonly a year or less.

pledged farms.[26] From this material I learnt that many of the debtors were related to their creditors, who were not uncommonly their wives; and that the number of creditors seemed to be nearly as large as the number of debtors, so that it was not a case of the wealthy few lending to 'the impoverished many'. As for the stated causes of pledging, it is worth noting (rather unreliable though this material may be) that such 'negative' causes as 'inherited indebted uncle'[27] were more commonly mentioned than 'positive' causes, such as the cost of extending a cocoa farm: some of the negative causes were so explicit as to be quite plausible.[28]

Given this evidence as well as that in the Preamble, and taking account, also, of the high reputation of the important creditor-farmers of Akwapim, the home of the earliest migrant cocoa farmers of southern Ghana, it is clear that the common practice of mortgaging cocoa farms cannot be summed up as generally deplorable: that, indeed, it had, and has, many positive features.

In the southern Gold Coast and Ashanti where, until the advent of cocoa, most farmers exerted usufructural rights only over their land, as most non-cocoa farmers still do today, there had traditionally been no right of foreclosure over pledged land[29] – 'Debt dies but never rots' was an old proverb. But in regions such as Hausaland, which lack perennial crops and where land is commonly bought and sold, it is possible that nowadays, though not formerly, a great proportion of land transfers, other than those involving fathers and sons, results from the failure of mortgagors to redeem their land, for the incidence of voluntary land-selling is much reduced, as we shall see. Neither in Hausaland nor in south India, if Karnataka be reasonably representative, do documents record the transactions, and it seems very likely[30] that nowadays in

26. See Hill, 1956:77–83.
27. This formula might have meant that, on the death of a relative, often a mother's brother, the farmer had either found himself with certain obligations of inheritance which he was unable to meet without pledging a farm, or that a pledged farm had been inherited.
28. For example: 'grand-daughter's debts because of adultery'; 'labour costs on maize farm that failed'; 'adultery fee for boy and death of uncle'; 'death of sister and litigation *re* my niece bewitched'; 'fined for not taking my expectant wife to the clinic before her delivery on the way'; 'borrowed to pay debts of truant grandson now in Police'; 'house destroyed by storm'.   29. See Meek, 1946:182.
30. Though I myself found no way of collecting hard evidence, since none was forthcoming from creditors. For historical material relating to farm mortgaging in India see Musgrave, 1978:222 *et seq.* See also Baker, 1984:211 and Schendel, 1981:324 *et seq.* and 329 *et seq.*

both regions this is a most undesirable, even a desperate, way of raising money, creditors (in this case) being so eager to foreclose.[31] This contrast between Ghanaian cocoa farmers and grain farmers shows the need for a general awareness of the facts of the case before any type of borrowing is praised or condemned.

As already noted, the method of borrowing often depends on the purpose of the loan: thus, in Highland Orissa in India 'different kinds of loans are kept in separate compartments and governed by different conceptions of behaviour'.[32] This especially affects loans in kind, and I have already mentioned those which enable penurious men to set themselves to work; but pre-harvest loans of grain are probably the most common transaction of this type. In Hausaland one bundle of grain (millet or sorghum) is commonly given in return for the promise to return two bundles after harvest; since grain prices always fall abruptly, though very variably, after harvest, one can only say that the timeless 'rate' of interest is certainly much less than 100%. Bailey reports on the lending of paddy (unhusked rice) at a timeless interest 'rate' of 50%, such loans being granted to paddy farmers only.

Should any discussion of loans in kind include the loan of land – and, if so, should land-borrowing proper[33] be distinguished from tenancy and share-cropping? On balance I have decided to postpone consideration of share-cropping to Chapter 14, even though in India it involves the loan of plough animals and other inputs in addition to land. I am also postponing dealing, until Chapter 10 in this case, with the kinds of indebtedness which involve bonded labouring in India.

In any discussion of indebtedness one should include, at first sight curiously, the rotating credit associations which abound, with many variations of detail, in many world regions. These are such that each member of a group, formed for the purpose, makes a periodic (perhaps weekly or monthly) cash contribution, one

---

31. Is it curious that renting, though not mortgaging, is sometimes (or usually?) prohibited by Indian Land Reform legislation – certainly in the Karnataka case?
32. Bailey, 1964:113.   33. Such as *aro* in Hausaland (see p.158 below).

member taking the whole kitty on each occasion until all have received a share. Such systems involve debt, for those who are lucky enough to receive their share early in the cycle are indebted to those who have to wait; indeed, the whole art of management is to ensure that the fortunate members, the creditors, continue to maintain their regular contributions. Such savings groups enable their members to accumulate funds for such purposes as buying a bicycle or a goat or extending a house; but they are not usually of much use in emergencies. They are found in south India – and also in many regions of West Africa, including Hausaland, where they flourish particularly among women.

In this brief survey we have certainly seen that the debt associated with village-generated credit takes a variety of forms. It is because, as a result, the nexus of personal relationships involving borrowing and lending is complex, exists on so many levels, has so many functions and entangles nearly everyone[34] – that even this outline, which omits many types of indebtedness, and is a deliberate over-simplification, must seem to lose itself in its own subject matter. But this does not matter if I have achieved my two polemical purposes: these are to show that no necessary moral connotations attach to indebtedness in general; and that '*the* debt' which is supposed to adhere to so many households is an illusory, ever-changing, at the best of times elusive concept,[35] which cannot possibly be caught by a questionnaire or any other form of quantitative butterfly net. Only qualitative enquiry, suggesting general magnitudes, will do. And, as for the criteria which would enable one to judge whether, from the debtor's viewpoint, any particular debt-relationship is 'good, bad or indifferent', they are almost as numerous as the types of debt.

As a concluding point, I note that by concentrating in this chapter on the conventional and redistributive concept of *household debt*,

34. Most debtors are certainly indebted to numerous people and in numerous ways. But Bliss and Stern (1982:109) stated, on the basis of a survey that they undertook, that only in a few cases did households have 'more than one loan'!
35. If this seems like exaggeration, it must be remembered, for example, that many debts are incurred with no intention of repaying in full and that many creditors are kind-hearted. There is often a continuum running between the selling, the lending and the giving-out-free of grain, such that the real nature of any transaction may ultimately prove to be any one of these possibilities.

based on village-generated credit, I have largely ignored the pump-priming function of credit-granting, for instance in relation to West African trade. Because it is possible for market women to borrow farm produce or craft goods from others, repaying after selling is completed, lack of starting capital is no hindrance and very high proportions of all able-bodied women in the West African forest zone, notably in Ghana and Yorubaland, are very active traders, many of them travelling long distances to buy and to sell. The same ability to borrow the raw materials enables any secluded Hausa woman, for example, to produce such processed foodstuffs as groundnut oil for sale.

The most notable credit financed enterprise of all, in my experience, was the migration of Gold Coast cocoa farmers (see Chapter 11, Appendix A) which, starting from virtually nothing in the late 1890s, led to the creation of the world's largest cocoa exporting industry within some fifteen years. Land was bought on credit from chiefs, who received a small down payment, the balance being paid in instalments usually over many decades, though seldom or never in full, from the proceeds of selling the cocoa; then, richer cocoa farmers resold land to poorer men on easy terms; and one way and another, with the help of credit, no man from Akwapim, the main homeland, was ever prevented by poverty from acquiring land. Most amazing of all, these 'peasants' raised their own capital of many thousands of pounds, by subscription from individual richer farmers, to finance the construction by European contractors of bridges[36] and roads facilitating access to their distant cocoa farms. Officialdom failed to notice what was going on at the time (thus, the three contractor-built bridges never featured on any published map) and I have yet to come across any discussion on 'peasants' which mentioned these 'public works', this *indigenous economic development*.

36. According to the original accounts, to which the successor farmers gave me access, the cost of one of the three bridges had been about £2,000; it had been opened to walkers in 1914, when a 3d toll was charged. Between about 1916 and 1926, it may be that the farmers raised nearly £50,000 for the construction of contractor-built lorry roads. See Hill, 1963:Appendix VIII(3).

CHAPTER 9

THE FLEXIBILITY
OF INHERITANCE
SYSTEMS

ᠭᠬᠵ᠊ᠣ

'There is no evidence at all that the inheritance
system as such tends to excessive fragmentation.'

Leach, 1961:143.

In this chapter, in which I discuss briefly and simply various
aspects of systems of inheritance of farmland, my main concerns
are to show that these do not operate nearly as rigidly as is
commonly supposed, and to link inheritance with considerations
regarding inequality, already discussed in Chapters 2 and 6.
Cultivators 'do not operate their inheritance rules in such a way as
to make the whole system uneconomic';[1] and just as in Britain,
much uncertainty often attaches to the detailed arrangements for
transmission of property between the generations. Among other
diverse matters to be discussed are: first, the fact that in
polygynous societies the sons of richer fathers may inherit no
more farmland than the average man; second, that in the forest
zone of West Africa land rights are not necessarily heritable at all;
and third, that the scattered nature of the ordinary farmholding
does not necessarily impede inheritance processes.

In patrilineal societies, or in non-unilineal societies, such as the
Hausa or the Hindu, where the sons are in practice their fathers'
main inheritors,[2] there are usually many imperfections or uncertainties attached to systems which are supposed, in firm principle,
to assure equal division between male heirs.[3] Thus 'rules', where
they have been formalized, are apt to be bent if not broken; written
wills are everywhere very rare; no formal provision is made for
sons who are unmarried when their father dies, though they may
be provided for, in due course, especially if there is an adminis-

---

1. Leach, 1961:143.   2. I shall later deal with the position of daughters.
3. I discuss the 'indivisibility' of family property in patrilineal societies below.

trator of the estate; 'equal division' is often entirely impracticable for numerous reasons; much property is apt to be casually dissipated at the time of the father's death; fathers may casually sell much of their farmland during their lifetimes, despite the protestations of their sons; and sons who have migrated, or who have been taken away by their divorced mothers when young,[4] may or may not receive a share – probably, they usually do not. Finally, bargains may have to be struck between the sons over different forms of property, such as land, houses and livestock. There is nothing odd about the fact that one brother may give cash compensation to another whose share seems too small, for brothers do often sell property, including land, to each other; but the agreed valuation of land and houses often presents much difficulty.

In Hausaland it is commonly stated, and sometimes believed, by town and country dwellers alike, that the matter of the division of property on death is invariably referred to the court of the *alkali*, the Muslim judge. But normally such reference only occurs in the event of a dispute or serious doubt.[5] The number of courts relative to the size of the population is remarkably small, and they would be overwhelmed by work were more than a tiny minority of inheritance cases to be referred to them or their agents. Also, as individual families naturally want to avoid court costs, they are inclined to do their best to sort out their own affairs – sensibly but not defiantly.

I have said that in polygynous societies the sons of rich fathers cannot depend on receiving sizeable inheritances;[6] this is because rich men tend to have more wives, and so more sons, than poorer men.[7] In extremely densely populated localities, such as Dorayi in

---

4. Although fathers usually endeavour to retain their young sons, they are some-times unsuccessful.
5. Inheritance is a very sensitive subject there. The only time I got into trouble during more than two years in rural Hausaland was when I was overheard discussing inheritance with a blacksmith and was commanded to explain myself to the District Head.
6. See Hill, 1977:141. As Lloyd puts it for Yorubaland, 'a high degree of polygyny, together with the inheritance laws, renders it impossible for a man to perpetuate his status in most of his children' (Lloyd, 1974:54).
7. While it is true that Muslim men may have no more than four wives simultaneously, polygyny in Hausaland is associated with very high divorce rates, so that a man may have had many wives in the course of his life. (For statistical evidence that richer husbands tend to have more wives than poorer men see Hill, 1972 and 1977.)

Hausaland,[8] there is nowadays very little upward mobility, and few sons of poor men stand any chance of becoming rich themselves. There and elsewhere the lucky inheritors are the brotherless sons of rich fathers, a fact which has also been observed in monogamous Hindu India.[9]

Luck also features largely in a type of inheritance system, found in parts of southern Ghana and Nigeria, which is legally known as division *per stirpes*,[10] and colloquially as 'division between wives'. Under this system the sons, taken together, of each wife receive equal shares, so that if one wife has an only son, he will receive four times as much property as his half brothers whose mother has four sons. Lloyd refers to this system in Yorubaland as 'a most rigidly followed rule'.[11] But I think he means that the courts interpret the rules rigidly, while accepting the difficulty of dividing two houses into three parts; for a son may be denied his share if he refuses to participate in his father's funeral celebrations – but may, even so, be responsible for his portion of his father's debts.[12]

If we regard *inter vivos* (lifetime) distribution as being usually, though by no means invariably,[13] equivalent to inheritance on death then, I suppose, no society lacks fairly well-formulated ideas about how property ought to be distributed between the heirs – maybe over the longer run with the help of a trustee or administrator, who is not a beneficiary. But, as I have said, it is the observers rather than the actors themselves who tend to idealize common practices, to regard them as rigid rules. Having standardized the rules, these observers then commonly criticize the actors for following them – not realizing that they have often done nothing of the kind, hard commonsense having actually prevailed.[14]

At the same time, it is because many local communities have strong general ideas about the principles involved that heavy-

---

8. Hill, 1977.
9. Bailey, 1957:90.   10. See Derrett, ed., 1965:18.   11. Lloyd, 1962:296.
12. On the inheritance of debts see Derrett (1965:13) and p.91 above.
13. Thus, when it comes to division of farmland on death in Hausaland, no account is taken of the farms which have previously been given to sons in return for work (in *gandu*) on their father's farms.
14. In the Appendix to this chapter I deal with some questions relating to the division of farm plots (fields) between sons; this is often commonsensical, involving no unnecessary sacrifices on the altar of equality.

handed legislation designed to ride roughshod over prevailing conventions stands no chance of success. In Karnataka, so far as I could tell, no one paid the faintest attention to the absurdly impracticable Prevention of Fragmentation Act of 1966, which sought to prevent the partitioning of plots of less than three acres on death, declaring that they should pass, by lottery if necessary, to one son.

In both Hausaland and south India the law states that daughters should receive a share of property on death: in Muslim Hausaland half as much as their brothers, in India equal shares. But unless male heirs are lacking, it seems[15] that daughters seldom receive their due in either continent unless they appeal to the courts, as they occasionally do, often with some success. Whereas male chauvinism must be a large part of the explanation for this defiance, the wish to reduce the degree of division on death must also have an influence. 'Joint households' in the broad sense (see p.36 above), may also be seen as an attempt to postpone the evil day of partition, one which is certain to fail in the longer run unless all but one of the sons migrate.

I turn now to consider West African matrilineal societies, as represented by the Akan, a broad socio-linguistic group which includes many Ghanaian and Ivory Coast cocoa farmers. In these societies *matrilineal* does not, of course, imply anything about the relative status of individual men and women, for it is certainly not a synonym for *matriarchal*; nor does it mean that women are apt to be the heirs or successors of men; they are rather societies in which everyone belongs, by birth, to his mother's lineage – it being believed that 'one lineage is one blood' or a lineage is 'one person'.[16] A man's heir is not normally a son, for he belongs to his mother's not his father's matrilineage; while it is often baldly stated that a man's heir is a sister's son (a maternal nephew), this is to overlook the fact that his younger brother (or younger brothers taken successively, in order of age) takes priority, so that a sister's

15. There has to be some doubt, as in both continents farms inherited by women often appear to be owned by their husbands or brothers, or are actually given to them.
16. The best introduction to Akan matriliny is Fortes (1950). A useful source on cocoa farming and land rights is Okali (1983); she states that sisters' sons may 'feel even less economically secure than offspring' (p.177).

son inherits only when the line of brothers by the same mother is exhausted. Although in theory, according to Fortes, a 'senior nephew' should inherit, his claims may be set aside in favour of a more junior man who is considered of 'better character'.

So under this 'one-heir system' inheritance is apt to be both extraordinarily unequal, as between members of any matrilineage, and subject to an enormous element of chance. On the one hand, a popular or well-educated man may be the heir of several of his mother's brothers, and if they happen to be successful migrant farmers who own a lot of widely dispersed cocoa land, he may find himself overwhelmed with responsibilities, which he either has to neglect or to pass on to others;[17] on the other hand, there are unlucky men who may happen to inherit nothing, a situation which is not as serious as appears at first sight, as usufructural rights would never be denied to them. Indeed, the right of any member of a matrilineage to cultivate portions of lineage land is itself an aspect of inheritance; this 'social security system' justifies the apparent unfairness of the sole heir system.

Also commonsense may again come to the rescue. Although, in general, sons do not inherit from their fathers, members of the father's matrilineage often waive any claim over his self-acquired property; so cocoa farmers often buy cocoa lands for the very purpose of providing for their sons.[18]

Although I have inadvertently implied the existence of a single inheritance system in these matrilineal societies, this is because, like everyone else, I have for the moment overlooked the position of women farmers. In localities where the cocoa farmers are not migrants, but indigenes whose forebears were food farmers, it seems that nearly a half of them are women farmers in their own right. Under the women's inheritance system, which is entirely distinct from the men's, property normally passes to a daughter; it would not pass to a man unless there were no suitable woman heir, for instance a sister or (lacking a daughter) a sister's daughter.

17. Which may have very deleterious effects on the efficiency of farming, especially as educated absentees may be preferred as inheritors. However, the trustful attitudes of inheritors to those they put in charge of their farm is often very impressive; the latter commonly appear to be owners proper.
18. This often meant that individuals bought far more land than they required, so that it might 'lie down', uncultivated, for many decades. See Hill, 1963.

I turn now to contemplate the rather common West African circumstances in which land may not, in the usual sense, be 'heritable' at all. As we know, the food-farming system known as 'bush fallow' is usual in the forest zone.[19] Owing to the prevalence of trypanosomiasis and the consequent lack of organic manure (and maybe, also, for other reasons), farms have to be 'rested' after being cultivated, perhaps after one year only; the length of the fallow period is never standard but always depends on the particular circumstances. Whether individual cultivators exert permanent or long-term rights over the plots they had once cleared and cultivated, and then fallowed, is often unclear, though it is known to be common in some societies; insofar as no permanent rights exist, it is obvious that they lack the power to transmit farmland to their heirs.

Meek asserts that the principle 'that he who clears land establishes rights of a permanent character' has existed all over the world from 'ancient times'.[20] I doubt both this axiom and the obvious corollary that such rights would be transmittable to a man's heirs. Lloyd explicitly states that in Yorubaland it may not be possible to speak of land rights being inherited by individuals. A man may have definite legal rights over the land while he uses it, but as soon as it is fallowed 'it reverts to the community, whose members will re-allocate it whenever the bush has regenerated sufficiently to permit cultivation'.[21]

The societies in which such doubts over inheritance exist may or may not be those where land is held by descent groups or corporate lineages.[22] In lineage organized food-farming societies no individual 'owns' land, in the usual Western sense, for he or she cannot sell it, and exerts usufructural rights only; however, by established custom, it may sometimes be that these rights are heritable. In this connection it must be noted that land cannot necessarily be permanently extricated from a system of corporate ownership by means of purchase where, exceptionally, that is

19. In many societies self-acquired land is treated differently from lineage property – see Derret, ed., 1965:26 and Lloyd, 1962.
20. Meek, 1946:23.   21. Lloyd, 1962:74.
22. Although such land is 'corporately owned' it is always farmed by individuals; communal cultivation is not only unknown, but formed no part of 'traditional memories'.

allowed; in other words, the act of purchase does not necessarily produce a new category of 'individualized land', as is often supposed. Thus, with the migrant cocoa farmers of southern Ghana, as well as with certain other peoples, purchased land was invariably dragged back into the 'family system' by means of a process which was necessarily complete by the time of the third generation, whose members exerted usufructural rights only.

Owing to the difficulty of mapping farmland, other than cocoa land, in the West African forest zone, where aerial photographs fail to reveal the farm boundaries and where the pattern of farm ownership under systems of bush fallow is bound to undergo continual and rapid change, statistics relating to the sizes and composition of farm-holdings are extremely scanty.[23] Failing evidence to the contrary, we can only presume that most farmers cultivate several scattered plots, as they do in the West African savannah and in south India.[24] Such dispersal does not necessarily impede the transmission of farmland between the generations, for ideas about the need for equality between inheriting sons, for instance, are not so strict that each separate plot has to be divided between them – it may rather be convenient to share out the plots, as though dealing a pack of cards. In Batagarawa I found that division between brothers did not account for the fairly large pro- portion of plots of one acre or less: that, in fact, plots of this size were not often divided on death, unless the father owned but one plot.[25]

But where population densities are grossly high, so that many holdings consist of small numbers of tiny plots, these plots (see Appendix) may suffer further serious fragmentation, as in Dorayi, where many of these 'particles' were too small to be distinguish- able on a large-scale aerial photograph or to be worth cultivating properly.[26] Turning to south-west India, unpublished figures which I collected in 1982 in an exceedingly densely populated farming locality in southern Kerala showed that in 1968 37% of all

23. Nor are there any maps showing the boundaries of clan lands. (The fact that, in any locality, some clans apparently own much more land than others in relation to their population must be a common cause of household inequality.)
24. See the Appendix to this chapter.
25. See Hill, 1972:34. Morris (1981:53) also found that small farms in Hausaland were often not divided.   26. Hill, 1977.

'dry plots', an expression which includes house sites in this area of dispersed settlement, were less than one-tenth of an acre compared with 10% in 1904; the corresponding proportions for plots under half an acre were 88% and 45%.

My general conclusion is therefore that, except where population densities are so unusually high that the situation is anyway desperate,[27] the commonsense attitude of farming populations usually ensures that inheritance processes in themselves seldom lead to inefficient farming, this being particularly true in those parts of the West African forest zone where no proper 'inheritance processes' exist! In most localities where high and increasing population densities are the main causes of advancing poverty (and the Karnataka villages are in this category), rural populations certainly do their best to alleviate the situation pragmatically by adapting any inheritance 'rules' to meet their needs.

But yet, looking over my shoulder as I write, must be those who know that the Japanese 'sole-heir system',[28] which is such that it is very rare for two married brothers to reside in the same farming household for any length of time, has proved immensely advantageous. Unfortunately, however, this does not help us over India for, as the anthropologist Nakane states (p.7), if Japanese farmers today 'had to divide their property among all brothers and sisters it would become impossible to live on most farms'. Japanese land reform measures, which extended over a long period when the population was far less dense than today, have no relevance to modern India and owing to the dearth of modern industries in the Indian countryside it is inconceivable that non-successors would happily relinquish their father's farm-holding to a brother. Inheritance systems reflect socio-economic realities, not *vice versa*.

27. Thus Dorayi, with its population of c. 1,500 per sq. mile, is highly anomalous, manurial cattle dung having to be *brought in* from Kano city (see Hill, 1977:77).
28. According to Nakane (1967:6), although the 1947 Civil Code gave equal inheritance rights in the father's property to all sons and daughters, among agriculturalists non-successors hardly ever demand this right.

APPENDIX

Farm-Plots and Inheritance

As we have seen, in both West Africa and south India the ordinary farm-holding – the total area cultivated by the individual household –usually consists of a set (a 'portfolio') of scattered farm-plots or fields. This often leads to much confusion, as published statistical tables commonly employ the unqualified word *farm*; and there are no words for *holding* in the local languages.

Contrary to much common belief, the basic reason for this dispersal of plots is in no wise connected with inheritance (indeed such dispersal may be seen in newly settled localities); it is that in most societies permanent rights over land are normally established, in the first instance, by the acts of clearing, cultivation and manuring,[29] the migrant cocoa farmers of southern Ghana who, for peculiar reasons, were able to buy their land outright, having been a highly anomalous case. It therefore follows that any farmer who needs to expand his holding commonly finds that his neighbours have already appropriated all the land near his existent property, so that he has to remove further away from this and maybe further away, also, from the village site (if any), for land near a village is usually especially coveted. In the inner ring of the very densely populated Kano Close Settled Zone, where land has long been bought and sold, and where the population lives dispersedly, it may easily come about over the passage of years that none of the farmland surrounding a particular home-stead is owned by its residents.

Before discussing the size of plots, I must make an attempt to define that emotive word *fragmentation*. It is often supposed that the very fact that a holding consists of a set of farms, many of which are apt to have areas of one or two acres only, is evidence that fragmentation has occurred. This is an error, for many farm-plots when first established are quite small, representing an area which could conveniently be cleared and cultivated by one man in a single season. We should distinguish between *subdivision* – the concept that each individual's total holding of land tends to diminish as population increases – and *fragmentation*, the cutting up of tiny plots into

---

29. However, in some societies, such as the Afikpo of south-eastern Nigeria (see Ottenberg, 1965:55), the ordinary holding consists of various plots because they have been acquired by different means.

even smaller portions.[30] Fragmentation can result from farm-selling (plot-*portions* are often sold); from division on death; from gifts (especially to sons); and from renting or mortgaging of portions. So even when the figures suggest that fragmentation, as distinct from subdivision, has occurred, one must not jump to the conclusion that 'inheritance is at fault' – especially as it is, unfortunately, very unusual for any statistical time series to exist.

In West Africa generally where, as we know, cadastral surveys are lacking, there is a very great dearth of reliable statistics relating to plot size, except in cocoa-growing areas and in Hausaland where a fair number of investigators have measured plots.[31] For seventeen different Hausa localities average plot size, for what such figures are worth, was under 2 acres in six cases, and between 2 and 3 acres in another six cases. For six localities where size distribution figures were available the very great majority of plots was under 3 acres; in no case was the proportion lower than two-thirds. In all cases a third, or more, of all plots were between 1 and 3 acres. An important distinction had to be made between the three very densely populated localities where over a half of all plots were under one acre (the proportion must have been at least two-thirds in Dorayi, which was not surveyed until later)[32] and the other four places where proportions were much lower; I would see fragmentation as having occurred in the former but not the latter localities – from which it does not, of course, follow that inheritance was necessarily the cause.

As for Ghanaian cocoa-plots, the sole-heir rule followed by their matrilineal owners ensures that any fragmentation is not due to inheritance. The agricultural economist Beckett found that in the southern Ghanaian village of Akokoaso a negligible proportion of plots was under one acre, two-thirds having been between 1 and 3 acres.[33] For cocoa-plots owned by non-migratory women farmers in four villages in Akim country, in the 1950s, I found that between a half and two-thirds were under one acre – and that plots over 3 acres were very rare[34]. (Neither in Akokoaso nor in Akim country did any significant amount of farm-selling occur.)

In India published statistics are not as plentiful as might be expected considering the existence of village land records based on plots, and there is unfortunately a very strong tendency for irrigated and dry plots to be

30. See Charlesworth (1978) for an interesting discussion of the distinction. He noted the case of one Deccan village where enormous numbers of tiny irrigated vegetable plots had been sold in the 1920s for vegetable growing.
31. See Hill (1972:232) for a list.   32. See Hill, 1977:130.   33. Beckett (1944:67).
34. Unpublished material extracted from official records. (Interestingly, plots owned by men invariably tended on average to be somewhat larger.)

bulked in published statistical tables, although the two very different categories of farmland *are* distinguished in the village records. One notably reliable, though old, source is H.H. Mann,[35] who found that in a village near Poona more than a half of all plots were under an acre – about a quarter having been between 1 and 2 acres. In one of the Karnataka villages I studied it seemed that more than a half of the unirrigated plots were under 2 acres. A very thorough survey of a South Gujarat village by Mukhtyar showed that about a third of *holdings* were less than one acre, implying the existence of many very small plots.[36] From the scanty material available, from which I have drawn but a few specimen figures, I think that we are justified in concluding that in many densely populated, long-settled localities in India a high proportion of plots is under an acre.

With existent technology, especially in Ghana among cocoa farmers, a one-acre plot is not necessarily inconveniently small – not even for ploughing, considering the extreme simplicity of the ordinary Indian plough. But the farmers are much inconvenienced by the widespread dispersal of plots which, in India, are often situated up to three to four miles away in other village areas.[37] It is obviously impossible to set a limit, such as half an acre, below which severe fragmentation exists, for much depends on the circumstances, especially as half an acre of good irrigated land may be a most desirable property.

35. Mann, 1917.   36. Mukhtyar, 1930:121.
37. I am grateful to Dr Philip Oldenburg for drawing my attention to a very large-scale programme of land consolidation which, he states, has literally redrawn the map of the gigantic north Indian state of Uttar Pradesh in the last twenty-five years. Land consolidation means that each farmer in a village exchanges all the scattered, irregularly shaped plots in his holding for a single plot with straight boundaries. Following detailed enquiries, Oldenburg contends that, to his own surprise, the consolidation programme has been carried out efficiently and fairly, providing hope that other rural development schemes might be similarly well administered and beneficial.

CHAPTER 10

THE NEGLECT
OF FARM-LABOURING
SYSTEMS

❧

> 'It seldom happens that the person who tills the
> ground has wherewithal to maintain himself till
> he reaps the harvest.'
> Adam Smith (1776: 168)

In this chapter, which deals with both free and bonded (attached)
farm-labouring, I endeavour to show how variable, and well-
adapted to the labourers' functions, the numerous farm-labouring
systems are apt to be. In West Africa, in particular, the notion of a
homogeneous labour force (*hired labour* – unqualified) is apt to be
nearly as misleading as that of the amorphous peasantry; and it is
equally common.

Unless they happened to be economic historians like Adam
Smith, British writers on economic principles have traditionally
ignored agricultural labourers completely,[1] both because they
invariably dealt in terms of *labour* (*labourer* does not occur in their
indexes), and because the matters of labour and wages implicitly
relate to industrial production. Partly for this reason, and also
because, as we have seen, official third world statistics usually
underestimate the numbers of farm labourers, the significance of
free farm-labouring systems continues to be played down by
development economists, though the question of bonded labouring, which is relatively insignificant statistically, has excited much
more interest. The prolonged and hopeless obsession with defining
tropical *peasants* has even induced the neglect of the free labourer,
and has led to many absurd attempts to define peasants as non-

1. Although there is much straightforward factual material in Marshall's immense
Principles (1890), the index includes only two minor references to agricultural
labourers one of which asserts, in typically Victorian manner, that they have 'less than
an average share of natural abilities' (p.711). (Modern official publications also tend to
ignore labourers. Thus in *Collecting Statistics on Agricultural Population and Employment*
(FAO, Rome, 1978), there is no mention of labourers in the main text although the
'agricultural population is formally defined as consisting of all those who derive their
main income from agriculture'.)

labour employing *cultivators*. Considering the common and regret-table tendency to equate *labourers* and *landless labourers*, it is presumably often thought, though never stated, that labourers are not peasants. What then becomes of the concept *peasantry*?

In regions such as south India and Hausaland, where most hired agricultural labour is daily-paid, many labourers are also cultivators on their own account – men or women who supplement their household farming income by working on the farms of others. As noted by Myrdal, an official Indian enquiry of 1950–1 found that some one-half of agricultural labourers also cultivated land on their own behalves.[2] Myrdal estimated that, roughly speak-ing, agricultural labourers in south Asia accounted for at least a third of the rural population,[3] a figure officially estimated as having been as high as 63% in south India in the 1950s. So it follows that for a large proportion of the rural population it is 'frequently impossible to draw a tidy line of demarcation between the small resident landowner and lesser members of the village hierarchy'.[4] Lumped together with the weakest elements (the landless) are large numbers of better-off men and women whose households may cultivate several acres.[5]

Despite this overlapping, Myrdal (p.1056) considered that the fact that rigorous enquiries on the agrarian hierarchy had not been sponsored officially 'must be partly ascribed to the vested interests in concealment among the upper strata, both in rural and urban areas... The numerical strength of the various social groups in the village, and the area of land each commands, may well be said to be among the best guarded secrets of the South Asian economies.'

Soon after Indian Independence two massive official enquiries on agricultural labour (1952 and 1956–7) collected vast quantities of material on wages, other earnings, time devoted to different tasks, 'unemployment', and so on. Myrdal was scornful about the value of the results, though he considered the second enquiry an improvement on the first. He concluded that 'The heavy invest-

2. Myrdal (1968:1055). As in this Indian Agricultural Labour Enquiry labourers were defined as deriving *at least* 50% of their income from agricultural labouring, the total number of people who did some labouring must be considerably underestimated.
3. *Ibid*: 1056. (This estimate is hedged about with reservations.)   4. *Ibid*: 1055.
5. For Randam, in Tamil Nadu, J. Harriss has recorded (1982) that the number of cultivating households which were partly dependent on labouring was 37, against 65 households which were solely dependent.

ment of energies in the preparation of measures of "employment" and "unemployment" among agricultural labourers' had created a 'mass of data, *none of which can sustain a firm judgment about the direction of changes in the magnitudes being investigated.*'[6] In general, he insisted, 'these studies have been led to ask the kinds of questions Western economists would wish to investigate in their own countries'. Those responsible had 'been reluctant to scrap received doctrine and to begin afresh by formulating a new conceptual kit appropriate to their economic conditions' (p.2221).

While such monumental enquiries are no longer in fashion, there has, of course, been no falling off of interest in the plight of the appallingly badly paid Indian 'landless labourer'. It is, indeed, most unfortunate that it is so difficult in practice, or with the aid of official statistics, to distinguish him/her from the labourer-cum-cultivator.

We know from the works of Buchanan,[7] for instance, that in south India daily-paid farm-labouring systems are very old, so that Chayanov was much more than a century behind the times in including India in the long list of countries which were 'unacquainted with the categories of wage-labour and wages'.[8] But in West Africa such systems were not introduced until this century: thus, in Hausaland farm-slavery did not begin to be gradually replaced by day-labouring until some sixty-five years ago;[9] and in the early days of cocoa farming in southern Ghana there were no day-labourers, other systems of labouring having been preferred ever since.

As day-labouring, involving local men and women labourers, is nowadays much the most widespread farm-labouring system in both south India and in some populous West African savannah regions, I start this discussion by simply listing the many features which, interestingly, it has in common in both continents:[10]

6. Myrdal, 1968:2200; my italics.
7. Buchanan, 1807; wage rates were recorded in cash in this remarkably detailed work. See, also, Kumar (1965), who emphasizes the importance of agricultural labourers in south India at the beginning of last century.
8. See Kerblay, 1971:152.   9. See Hill, 1977:208 and 218–9.
10. The main features of Indian day-labouring systems have been recorded by a great many writers. But, as the corresponding literature for West Africa is relatively scanty, I am here relying on findings in Hausaland by myself, in particular (Hill, 1972:Chapter 8), and others.

(a)   as work is everywhere spasmodic,[11] labourers are usually recruited for very short periods (sometimes only a day or two), at short notice, often only the previous evening;

(b)   most labourers work for many different employers during the course of the season;

(c)   the labourers' work is always supervised by the employer or his family representative;

(d)   for the foregoing reason, and also because labourers much prefer to work in company, several hired men usually work together, maybe alongside the farmer and/or his sons; there are few cultivators, other than Indian Brahmins, who disdain farmwork, so that labourers should usually be regarded as supplementing the family workforce.

Turning to the nature of the labour force:

(e)   labourers are usually both men and women, except in Muslim Hausaland where women are in purdah;

(f)   men and women may either work alongside each other or perform different tasks;

(g)   as we have seen, many labourers are farmers on their own account, or their dependants;

(h)   a fairly high proportion of the labour force consists of younger people;

(j)   older men are sometimes ashamed to be seen working locally, so that they take employment in neighbouring villages;

(k)   labourers are usually drawn from poorer households, even if they be dependants;

(m)   in any locality there are apt to be some popular, especially efficient, labourers, who work more regularly than the rest, many of whom consider themselves under-employed;

(n)   many men and women prefer to work only occasionally as labourers, even though they be poor.

---

11.   The unfortunate terms *rainy* or *monsoon seasons* may give the impression that rain is then regular and predictable; but in both continents most days are dry during these seasons and the unpredictable rain is often such a heavy downpour as to stop work. Cultivators are greatly inconvenienced by their inability to plan work in advance, being always at the mercy of the climate. (Rainy seasons are periods when rain *may* fall; dry seasons are entirely rainless.)

On the matter of daily wages:

(p)   in any locality these tend to be standard throughout the
      farming season, except at the end when they may fall
      somewhat, but they are not fixed by any village
      authority;[12]

(q)   minimum wage legislation, where it exists, tends to be
      ignored – which may usually be just as well, as observance
      would tend to increase under-employment;

(r)   women's wages are always lower than men's for the same task,
      but their *earnings* are sometimes higher if they specialize in
      certain arduous work;

(s)   employers sometimes pay wages in advance, in cash or in
      kind, but the wage rate may then turn out to be lower than it
      would have been otherwise;

(t)   cooked food is usually served on the farm, but some labourers
      prefer to take higher wages instead;

(u)   in most localities, wage rates, which vary with the nature of
      the work in India,[13] are very low by any standard, though as
      they are unrelated to the prices of basic food-crops, their real
      value is apt to fluctuate considerably,[14] as is evident enough if
      the worker elects to receive grain rather than cash.

Turning to employers:

(v)   although most employers are richer farmers, poor men and
      women are sometimes obliged to employ labourers
      occasionally, owing to their physical inability to do the work
      themselves or because of the exigencies of the harvest

12. Although everyone says they are standard, there is probably more variation than is
    admitted. Also, particularly in India, some workers prefer to be paid in grain, not
    cash.
13. For a table showing daily wage rates for five different paddy cultivation operations in
    twelve villages in 1973–4, see Farmer (ed., 1977:319); it was found that wages were
    higher in villages which were classified as 'quasi-industrial', because there was fairly
    continuous irrigation and labour demand throughout the year there. See Gough
    (1983:289) for various wage rates (for males?) in Tamil Nadu in 1975–6; rates varied
    between Rs 8–11 per day for ploughing and carting with the worker's own cattle and
    Rs 2–3 for weeding. See, also, Mencher (1978) and Harriss (1982). Only in the state of
    Kerala, in 1982, did I come across daily wage rates for men which seemed 'reasonable'
    – I exclude payment for threshing and harvesting (see below).
14. This is especially true in Hausaland where it is often said that seasonal prices are apt to
    double in the inter-harvest period. But much depends on annual crop fluctuations. In
    Batagarawa in June 1967 the standard daily wage of 2s 6d would have purchased about
    7 lbs of grain; in June 1968, when the standard wage was 2s and grain prices had fallen

season;[15] this particularly applies to Indian cultivators who own no ploughs or plough animals, and to widows without sons, who do not operate them.

So much for the numerous features which daily-paid farm-labouring systems tend to have in savannah West Africa and south India – and certainly, also, in many other world regions. But owing to caste, south India is to a small degree a special case. Although it is not unknown for employers to belong to lower castes than their workers, as a fairly general rule most labourers are drawn from the lowest caste or castes, especially if Harijans happen to be numerous. In many localities very high proportions of all able-bodied adult Harijans and their older sons and daughters do some labouring work.

In dry grain areas, south India is also 'different' because of the high degree of activity during the threshing period, when nearly all the grain is threshed on specially prepared yards, and when labourers are likely to earn far more than at other times. As the grains have to dry out in stacks before they are threshed, this period of high activity occurs some two or three months after harvest. There is no corresponding period in West Africa where, as we know, grain other than maize is stored on the stalk, and where threshing, mainly by women, not with the use of cattle as in India, proceeds gradually throughout the year.

Those localities which are largely dependent on irrigated paddy farming have a particularly high demand for labour at the harvesting-cum-threshing season, the latter rapidly succeeding the former in the case of this crop. This period is an exciting time, from which every labourer expects to benefit, and a considerable proportion of total annual earnings may then be received,[16] the generosity of employers being enhanced by the sight of the grain

owing to a glut, about 24 lbs of grain could have been bought. See Hill, 1972:Chapter 9 and 164. See J. Harriss (1982:121) on the relationship between wages and paddy prices; and, also, Keatinge (1912:69) for a splendid graph showing the relationship between real and money wages from 1873 to 1910. The idea that the individual's wage is related to his/her marginal product is entirely without foundation.

15. It is quite common for men to be labourers at one time and employers at another.

16. See Mencher (1978:208), who claims that, even though harvesting dates in any locality vary considerably from farm to farm in Tamil Nadu, there is, throughout the harvesting season, a very heavy demand for labour, even from smaller landholders who are labourers themselves at other times.

with which the workers are rewarded. For a locality in Kerala, Mencher has recorded that the harvesting labourers, who are men who work in large groups, might be rewarded with a sixth or a seventh of the total crop.[17]

So it may be that in south India most people have some work during the main paddy harvest following the north-east monsoon and during the later period when dry grain is threshed.[18] But I doubt if there are corresponding periods of 'full employment' in the savannah region of West Africa. In particular, I am sure that the extraordinarily widespread belief in a labour shortage at sowing-time is a myth, which is used as a stick with which to beat farmers who are wrongly supposed to delay groundnut sowing unnecessarily.[19] I also think that, among economists, the nearly universal belief in labour bottlenecks at one season or another is based on an implicit assumption of equilibrium, such tnat the hired labour cannot be more than adequate to meet the maximum demand, for otherwise men would migrate!

Ought the share-cropper (proper) – he who receives other inputs besides the loan of land – to be regarded as a labourer in this context? I think that primarily owing to his status he should not be, despite Baker's occasional tendency to bracket the *waramdar* in Tamil Nadu, who received a certain proportion of the grain harvest from his landlord, with either the bonded or the daily labourer.[20] So, having deferred consideration of share-cropping to Chapter 14, I turn now to the difficult problem of bonded labouring in south India, on which there is some literature.

One of the problems about bonded (or attached) labouring is to distinguish the circumstances in which it is, and is not, a special problem. As the numerous synonyms in various languages imply, systems vary, the only common feature being that they involve a contract between the employer and the labourer such that the latter undertakes to work full-time for the former for a specified or

17. Mencher, 1983:279–80.
18. See Farmer (ed., 1977:213) for statistics of monthly variations in labour employment.
19. Having been in Batagarawa on 15 June 1967, when the overdue planting rains fell, I could see for myself that grain-sowing was undertaken so quickly that no hired labourers were required. As for misapprehensions about unnecessary delays over groundnut sowing, see Hill, 1972:261.
20. See Baker, 1984:172, 174.

unspecified period. While it is often assumed that the labourer inevitably becomes to such a degree indebted to his master that he is unable to escape from his shackles and is a 'debt slave', systems and circumstances vary greatly and *some* bonded labourers positively enjoy the security provided and are envied by day-labourers. The situation has been made the more confusing by the fact that the legislation making bonded labouring illegal, which followed Mrs Gandhi's Twenty Point Programme of 1975, actually defined employer and labourer as creditor and debtor respectively, although it was certainly intended to abolish all types of 'contract labouring', whether they involved debt or not. As villagers know about this legislation, and suppose it to be all-embracing, one has to get to know them very well before they stop concealing the facts.

Before bonded labouring became technically illegal in 1975 (of course this did not lead, except in some localities for a few weeks, to its entire suppression), it is unlikely to have been a serious problem in many south Indian districts, owing to the relatively small number of labourers apparently involved. Since the legal abolition of the hereditary estate-holders,[21] most employers[22] had insufficient farmland to justify the engagement of full-time labourers, even though they were commonly 'household servants', who could be called upon to undertake any type of work. In Randam, before 1975, J. Harriss counted thirty-seven 'attached labourers'[23] (there usually known as *padials*), a very small number compared with that for free labourers, in a village with 275 households, of which 121 were landless. Although the relationship sometimes involved debt, he got no evidence of any resultant 'stigmas'. In any case, some *padials* were temporary employees, since a number of employers preferred to change their men every year or even every season.

Gough provides much detail for *panniyals* (a synonym for *padial*) in Tanjore District in Tamil Nadu,[24] which makes it clear that they were not usually bonded labourers in the conventional sense. In

---

21. Widely known as *zamindars* (see Baker, 1984); certain other words, e.g. *jodidar* in Karnataka, were employed in some regions. (The abolition preceded Land Reform proper.)
22. Other than those with coffee, tea, etc. *plantations* in mountainous areas.
23. J. Harriss, 1982:123.   24. Gough, 1983:279–80.

1952 these labourers were normally engaged by the year, though some were re-engaged for several years; married couples, together with mature children, might have been hired jointly; payment was in grain plus a little daily cash, harvest rates being double the normal; men worked for periods varying between 180 and 300 days annually.[25] The annual earnings, in cash and in kind, of a couple varied between the equivalent of about 2,300 and 2,700 lbs of husked rice[26] – and were later found to be much the same in 1976; and various perquisites, such as a house site, were provided.

Mencher found that *padials* accounted for only a small proportion of landless labourers in certain villages in Chingleput, Tamil Nadu, where paddy was the main crop, and that they were usually employed either for one year only or for periods between three and six years.[27] The situation bore no resemblance to the semi-feudalism which formerly existed in Gujarat in north India.[28]

In the Karnataka villages, where bonded labouring had been rare before its 'abolition' in 1975, the institution was rapidly rising again by 1977, perhaps in a somewhat modified form. All the cases of which I heard involved unmarried Harijans who had, as it were, been pledged to their employers for periods of two or three years, in return for a loan to their father which would be automatically liquidated by their service.[29] Having seen some of these young men at work, and lounging about in their employer's house, I certainly got the impression that they were better off than they would have been if living semi-starved at home.

Perhaps there were some ordinary farming districts in south India where bonded labouring was still common in 1975; if so, one does not know where they were.[30] I think that the vague belief that it had been both common and iniquitous stems from the

---

25. Considering that housework as well as farmwork was involved, and that Tanjore was primarily a paddy-growing area, this indicated that the incidence of underemployment among day-labourers in dry grain areas, where the demand for labour is lower, is likely to be tremendous.
26. Compared with estimated requirements of c. 800 lbs for a male labourer.
27. Mencher, 1978:189.   28. Breman, 1974.   29. See Hill, 1982:240–7 and 253.
30. Which may, of course be accidental; though the argument that few cultivators nowadays own enough land to justify employing full-time labourers is generally powerful.

knowledge that this may once have been so in some districts,[31] and from the fact that qualitative study of this institution is much easier and more intellectually attractive than the statistical study demanded by free farm-labouring.[32] Certainly, the dire poverty of many free labourers in south India is a much graver problem than that of bonded labouring.

So far this exposition has been relatively plain sailing, but when one turns to consider other types of farm-labouring in West Africa one immediately finds oneself in the kind of deep water which economists abhor because of all the intricacies that lie beneath. West African systems are so various and, in some respects, so surprising, that for those who are unfamiliar with the main ethnic groups involved the detail may seem tedious and confusing. Who would expect, for example, that considerations of land tenure loom nearly as importantly as the grand distinction between the relatively impoverished (labour exporting) northern savannah (and Sahel) zones and the southern forest zone? Before the imposition of the cruel immigration restrictions and expulsions under the Ghana Aliens Compliance Order of 1969,[33] it is likely that at least 12% (probably considerably more) of the total Ghanaian population of some ten million was of 'foreign origin',[34] and that a large proportion of the 1.2 million (or so) people who might have been thus classified were stranger-labourers from 'the north' or their dependants.[35] As many as ninety-two so-called 'tribes' were

31. See Baker (1984: e.g. 172–3 and 209), particularly for his account of how the *pannaiyal* (*sic*) was apt to get indebted in the nineteenth century. See also Hill (1982:241) for a citation from Buchanan (1807); and Djurfeldt and Lindberg (1975:65) for a citation dated 1879.
32. Such work can be very tedious and time-consuming. (When trying to cut a corner, I once asked each member of a group of Ghanaian cocoa farmers if they were employing a daily labourer on that particular day; surprised that each of them said 'No', I realized that they couldn't supervise the labourers when they were attending a meeting!)
33. 'Aliens' were given a fortnight to obtain the necessary immigration papers (which most of them had never possessed, especially if they had been born in Ghana), without which they would face expulsion.
34. An incomprehensibly difficult concept, which might even involve the country of birth of grandparents. See the uniquely detailed *Special Report 'E': Tribes in Ghana, 1960*, Ghana Population Census, 1964.
35. In order of the numbers of persons involved, the main countries were: Togo, Upper Volta (now Burkina Faso), Nigeria, Ivory Coast and Dahomey (now Benin). According to the census there were five non-Ghanaian ethnic groups, more than half of whose 'occupied males' in Ghana were farm labourers.

distinguished in the 1960 Ghana census[36] of whom, making an
extremely reckless guess, a third or more might have been peoples
who would have regarded their own or their forebears' 'homeland'
(a difficult concept in many instances) as a country other than
Ghana. As, according to Addo,[37] about half of the 'permanent'
employees in cocoa farms were of foreign origin before the expulsion of the aliens, a proportion which fell to about a quarter as a
result of the Compliance Order; and as the cocoa industry was
much the largest employer of stranger-labourers – I start by
examining the different systems of employment that were
involved in it.

With more vigour than precision, Hart states that cocoa farming
'is still an industry contained within the matrix of indigenous
family life. The development cycle of domestic groups combines
with the life cycle of cocoa trees to generate a constant flux, a
rhythm of growth and decay.'[38] The first half of this statement has
some truth if the principal type of 'labourer', he who is rewarded
with a share (usually a third, *abusa*) of the crop, is included within
the concept of 'indigenous family life'. Owing to an error of
classification in the otherwise excellent 1960 Ghana census, the
number of such 'labourers' has never been known at all accurately,
but I have estimated it at nearly a half of the number of cocoa
farmers in that year.[39] As we shall see, many of them were permanent 'pseudo-farmers' – almost the equivalent of indigenes,
although often strangers.

In Ghana[40] the '*abusa*-man', as I prefer to call him, is very
commonly denoted a *caretaker*; but since, at least in my experience,
he seldom manages his farms in the absence of his 'master', who
usually places a working relative in charge if he is not there working himself,[41] this word is misleading, as is *share-cropper*. The man is
a pseudo-farmer because he brings his wife and children with him
to work on the cocoa farms and is allotted a house, or house site, by

36. Some of the smaller 'tribes' were combined with others, so that the total number of
ethnic groups identified in Ghana was well in excess of a hundred.
37. Addo, 1974.   38. Hart, 1982:62.   39. Hill, 1972:74.
40. *Abusa*-men, known as such, are also common in the cocoa and coffee growing industries of the Ivory Coast; see, in particular, Köbben (1956) and Dupire (1960).
41. Many migrant cocoa farmers own land in several, some in many, widely-flung areas, so
absence from any particular farm does not, as is often thought, imply residence in
the city.

his master, as well as farmland on which he may grow food for self-consumption or sale. Food-crops also grow on any young cocoa farms in his charge. Besides, he is permitted to work as and when he wishes at his primary tasks of plucking, fermenting, drying and carrying the cocoa beans and may employ labourers to help him. If he dies, his job may be taken over by a son; and he sometimes evolves into a cocoa farmer himself. While members of many West African ethnic groups refuse to work as 'hired labourers' in any conventional sense, the position of *abusa*-man may be thoroughly congenial.

The astonishingly rapid growth of the Gold Coast cocoa industry in the twenty years (or so) after 1895, when exports were negligible, had always been regarded as a 'miracle'[42] until it was belatedly realized that *migrant* farmers who bought large areas of forest land were initially responsible.[43] But the migration could not have been sustained had not northern labourers, many of them from hundreds of miles away, been so responsive to the possibilities of a crop which they had never seen, the southern forests being approachable only by long journeys on foot. However, in the very early days, say before 1900, very few labourers were employed, since the farmers were adamant that any spare cash should be invested in land purchase. Immediately the trees started bearing cocoa, labour employment, *financed by the proceeds of selling the crop*, began; the *abusa*-men, virtually all of whom were strangers, began to trickle in, and when messages were sent back home, the flow soon became a flood.

In my preliminary work on cocoa farming,[44] I identified four other types of cocoa 'labourer' besides the *abusa*-man, two of whom were labourers proper. One was the '*nkotokuano*-man',[45] who superficially resembled the *abusa*-man in that he was primarily concerned with cocoa plucking, fermenting, carrying and so on, and was apt to be a stranger. But he was paid a fixed sum per load

---

42. Thus Hancock in his profound, though neglected, survey of the evolution of the West African 'traders' frontier' (1940) seemed to have no inkling that the migration had occurred, for he was advised to rely on Beckett's work on the village of Akokoaso (see Beckett, 1944).   43. See Chapter 11, Appendix A.   44. See Hill, 1956.
45. Much poorer than the *abusa*-man, he was found in a few districts only. See Hill, 1956:Chapter 2.

(of 60 lbs) of cocoa and, as a foot-loose man, whose poverty led to distrust, he usually worked simultaneously and temporarily with a number of different farmers, some of whom would not have been able to afford an *abusa*-man. He usually received no special perquisites and was certainly not a pseudo-farmer, but a genuine worker.

The other labourer proper was daily paid; he was probably usually a young local man, employed mainly for weeding, but he has been little studied. I think he was more common in Ashanti, particularly where most cocoa farmers lived in towns, than in the sparsely populated southern forests. In 1954 his daily wage varied between about 2s and 3s. His function was so peripheral that he hardly resembled the type of day-labourer already discussed above.

The other two types were, first, the 'contract labourer' (who is found in India as well as in many parts of West Africa), who is paid an agreed sum to clear, and maybe to plant, a certain plot of land in his own time, payment being delayed until the work is completed; such men, who never seem to be numerous, are usually farmers on their own account and resent being called *labourers*.[46] Finally, there was the interesting case of the 'annual labourer' – the farm-servant *par excellence*.

The members of most West African ethnic groups are too proud to be recruited as annual labourers, who are similar (except in the duration of their employment) to the Indian bonded labourer. So they used to be drawn from a tiny number of such groups, notably the Gurma from Upper Volta and Togo, who were sometimes recruited by an agent resident in the south, but including also the Krobo and the Ewe of the southern forest zone. On the cocoa farms of southern Ghana and Ashanti in the 1950s the annual labourer[47] was employed for a fixed period, commonly a year

46. The preference for contract work rather than day-labouring is very well illustrated in a fascinating article by Van Hear (1984), relating to large-scale rice farming in northern Ghana from the 1970s which involved several hundred 'entrepreneurs' – i.e. civil servants, high-ranking officers and bureaucrats, as well as local farmers. When the male day-labourers, who were usually transported daily from long distances away, began to express their dissatisfaction with their wages and conditions the employers were obliged to switch to contract labouring. (The word *dariga* in the title of the article means 'cheat', '*dariga*-men' being farmers who reneged on agreements made at labour recruiting markets.)
47. The findings of Addo (1974), which are more up-to-date than my own, suggest that the terms of employment of annual labourers have evolved over time.

(seldom, I think, longer), for particular tasks allotted to him, especially for clearing forest land, but also for planting and weeding[48] and any odd jobs. He travelled without his family and commonly lodged with his employer, who provided him with all his needs, maybe including a small cash advance, for he preferred to receive most of his money in a final lump sum with which he returned home. Only richer farmers with capital to 'squander' on wages, when it 'ought' to have been invested in physical assets such as land or houses, were prepared to employ such labourers for extending their farms; in Ashanti they often worked in gangs. Poorer farmers were obliged to do the clearing and planting themselves or to offer their *abusa*-men some special incentive to undertake work additional to their normal duties. Annual labourers possessed a superiority all their own; it is not surprising that they were often difficult to recruit in localities where *abusa*-men were plentiful – a further indication of the heterogeneity of the factor 'farm labour'.

Apart from the reluctance of many southern Ghanaian men to work as labourers as well as in many other capacities which they consider 'menial',[49] there was a need to attract strangers to the cocoa-growing areas, which were necessarily sparsely inhabited, cocoa being a low-yielding crop in quantity terms. Also, in districts where the cocoa farmers were indigenes, no man or woman suffered from landlessness since it was always possible to claim rights over land from their matrilineages.[50]

Cocoa cultivation demands much labour in the early stages of establishing a farm, but only spasmodic work when the trees are bearing, since there is only one main crop annually and the orchards require little weeding under their leafy canopies. So this perennial crop, like coffee in the Ivory Coast, attracted many semi-

48. See Beckett, 1944:90.
49. Southern Ghanaian men, with the notable exception of the Ewe of south-eastern Ghana, tend to disdain many types of work: thus, they leave most of the market trading to women, or male strangers, and much of the detailed farming, such as weeding, to women – a fact which explained the ability of many of them to take up migrant cocoa farming with such carefree alacrity in the early days. Certain southern Nigerians think similarly. For the Ivory Coast, Köbben (1956:56) reported that no Agni man will work with another Agni.
50. Thus, Beckett (1944:68) stated that no farmer owned less than one acre of cocoa, and that large number of new farms were still being established. But land scarcity may well have developed since.

permanent[51] or even permanent pseudo-labourers, as we have
seen, people who were well content with their new way of life,
especially perhaps in localities where there were prospects of
evolving into cocoa farmers on their own account.[52] They were
quite indispensable and often very numerous: Köbben reported
the existence of an Ivory Coast village with 700 farmers and about
2,000 labourers. The *abusa*-men had opportunities of supplement
ing their income by other work besides growing food for themselves; Boutillier noted that, when other duties permitted, they
sometimes worked in groups as contract labourers (*contractuels*).[53]

That farm labouring systems are well adapted to the functions and
circumstances of labourers is shown by the existence of '*abusa*-
type', daily, contract and 'annual' labourers among Yoruba cocoa
farmers. Although the proper development of cocoa farming
there came considerably later than in southern Ghana, and also
involved some migration of farmers and much migration of
labourers, the farm labouring systems developed independently in
response, as I have said, to the needs of the parties involved. The
main authorities, Berry and Galletti *et al.*, who are all economists,
fail to emphasize the significance of the relationship of the system
of employment to the nature of the work, but the working conditions of Galletti's quaintly named 'permanent labourers' so
closely resembled those of Ghana's annual labourers that their
functions are bound to have been similar.[54] Such labourers also
worked on the kola plantations of Yorubaland.[55]

West African farm-labouring and labour migration being such
closely related matters, I shall develop the present discussion
further in the next chapter. But meanwhile I must emphasize the
significance of much seasonal migration of labourers to both the
'emitting' and the receiving communities. Seasonal migration
during the long dry season in the savannah may be as necessary to

51. Probably most *abusa*-men were apt to make periodical visits to their homeland–'to go on leave'.
52. Dupire contrasts the position of *abusa*-men with that of casual labourers, who were mainly Mossi from Upper Volta, whom she called *sous-proletaires*.
53. Köbben, 1956; Boutillier, 1960:180.   54. Berry, 1975; Galletti *et al.*, 1956:211.
55. The kola-nut is an important stimulant in West Africa; in western Nigeria it is grown as an orchard crop.

the community as it is to the individual; which has, also, long been true of parts of densely populated Iboland in south-eastern Nigeria, which paid for its necessary imports of salt and bulk foodstuffs by seasonal labour exporting. Such labourers, who often travel in groups, commonly undertake seasonal tasks such as yam-mounding,[56] which are particularly arduous or disagreeable to the cultivator, who is often a woman.

I should also emphasize how fine the line between a migrant labourer and cultivator may be. Udo has described the so-called 'tenant farmers' of eastern Nigeria who flow in their thousands into certain areas;[57] they both grow crops on land which is notionally 'rented' and collect palm fruit from existing plantations, this being work which local people are reluctant to undertake. Then, there are the famous 'strange-farmers', or *navétanes*, who have for long migrated seasonally from Senegal to the Gambia to cultivate groundnuts there.[58]

Finally, I cannot forebear mentioning the Fulani pastoralists on the Accra Plains as another fascinating intermediate case.[59] Individual Fulani travel from many hundreds of miles away to take up 'employment' with local cattle owners who usually know little of the art of cattle rearing. As expert pastoralists many of these men soon gain much independence, acquiring cattle and even kraals of their own, and commonly employing Fulani assistants whom they reward with wages and board and lodging.

One of the most important implications of the existence of so much variation in the types and functions of employment systems, particularly in West Africa, is that it is unwise to *assume* destitution, insecurity or exploitation from the fact of farm-labouring. Thus, many inhabitants of the parched lands to the north of the savannah zone found a New World in the lush southern forests, where large-scale, rapid development of cocoa-growing occurred in sparsely populated regions.

56. The yam is a huge tuber which grows inside an earth mound.
57. Udo, 1964.
58. See Morgan and Pugh, 1969: 462:3, and Hart 1982:168, n.15.
59. Although this book is not concerned with pastoralists as such, these Fulani resemble other migrant 'labourers'. The Fulani are, of course, the great pastoralists of West Africa.

CHAPTER 11

MISCONCEPTIONS ABOUT MIGRATION

For one who has spent the equivalent of five years in the field studying many aspects of migration, the writing of this brief chapter presents especial difficulty, for so many different disconnected facets of such a vast and *emotive* subject keep intruding into one's consciousness. Besides, many of the misconceptions one is concerned to expose represent what Hart has called 'diffuse opinion': while 'it is hard to find such an opinion documented in print by reputable scholars, ... its popular currency is palpable enough'.[1]

One might say that the gulf between economists and economic anthropologists was especially wide on this topic, were it not for the notable and iconoclastic work by economists emanating from the Institute of Development Studies.[2] When the outstanding and well-appreciated work of the anthropologist Hart is added to this,[3] what need can there be to go on protesting? The answer lies partly in the very emotiveness of the subject;[4] in the universal fear that the growth of urbanization is 'an index of rural malaise' – whereas, in fact, it is neither novel nor dysfunctional, for 'migration and movement were intrinsic to the indigenous population's way of life even before the concentration of economic opportunities on the coast set up today's asymmetrical drift from savannah villages to forest plantations and city slums'.[5] It is also necessary to emphasize that, for all we know, many long-established flows have recently become reversed, especially in Ghana, owing to the very high inflation rates and the difficulty of procuring foodstuffs in cities.[6]

1. Hart, 1982:172, n.1 and 173, n.20.
2. Notably Connell *et al.*, 1976; Lipton, 1977, Chapter 9 and 1980.
3. E.g. Hart, 1974 and 1982.
4. The attitude of anthropologists is apt to be tempered by their own migratory experiences!   5. Hart, 1982:123.
6. Lipton has claimed (1977:224), on the basis of world-wide statistics, that urbanization rates in the third world countries began to decline in the 1960s.

Another reason for persistence is that the significance of rural/ rural as against rural/urban migration is still insufficiently appreciated.[7] Whereas the latter type of migration is only too visible in the slums and squatters' settlements, the former is largely invisible unless it involves the migration of farmers or labourers to the export-crop-producing forest zones of West Africa – the migration of southern Ghanaian cocoa farmers is dealt with in Appendix A below. Especially in south India, it is impossible to offer any opinion on whether the volume of intra-rural migration, omitting the very common migration of wives on marriage,[8] vastly exceeds that of rural/urban migration – *as may well be the case.*

But this common statistical dichotomy is not so useful as seems at first sight, first because many of those who venture into the cities do so temporarily and never become urbanized. Despite the excellent statements of Lipton and Hart on this matter, it is still possible for Rimmer to cite estimates for the annual growth rates of the West African urban population (6.9% in 1950–60 and 6.2% in 1960–70), without mentioning that the composition of the migrant population undergoes perpetual change.[9]

Two inter-connected reasons account for this West African ebb and flow: first, the importance of *intentional* 'circulatory migration',[10] by those who, whether they migrate seasonally, annually or for a longer term, automatically envisage their future in terms of resuming farming at home; and second the fact that

7. From the fascinating work by the geographer Pelissier (1966) on rural Senegal we learn (p.178) that over the past three generations rural Wolof people have moved about adjusting themselves to the changing natural potentialities of the soil with remarkable efficiency.
8. Insofar as it creates networks of kin over areas much wider than the single village, this kind of migration may be bound up with the migration of men who may, fairly commonly, remove to join their relatives (see Hill, 1982:198.)
9. Rimmer, 1984:69. On p.87 Rimmer claims, without providing evidence, that 'permanent or long-term settlement', particularly in the largest towns, has expanded relative to other types of migration since the 1940s. (For India, Cassen (1978:122) emphasizes the phenomenon of urban 'turnover migration'.)
10. See Hart, 1982:123. I find this term somewhat unsatisfactory since many such migrants make but one expedition, away from and back to their homelands; *not* the circulation of the blood! Since Hart distinguishes two types of long-distance migration, respectively circulatory and permanent (by 'settlers'), this is perhaps the place to mention the concept of 'permanent strangerhood'; thus, after nearly a century of migration, the migrant cocoa farmers of southern Ghana persist in regarding themselves as strangers, sociologically linked to their various homelands, which remain well populated.

'none but a few securely employed and affluent city dwellers' can expect to find the 'long-term life-support system' they need there.[11]

Lipton's concept of *pseudo-urbanization* also covers both the 'demographic illusion' of the growth of cities which is in large part due to the engulfment of neighbouring villages; and the statistical anomalies resulting from the reclassification of villages as towns when, as a result of natural increase, they pass a certain size.[12]

Hart and Lipton hold differing views on the desirability of encouraging flows, whether temporary or permanent, of villagers to cities. Hart believes that West African urban economies are 'very vital and capable of evolutionary growth' and is opposed to the general development policy of the international aid institutes which would reduce migration to the cities, 'which are thought of as centres of social pathology, material deprivation and political danger' (p.164). Lipton, on the other hand, advances many reasons for supposing that the urbanization of villagers enhances urban bias. Before examining some of his arguments, I must escape from the implicit intellectual trap of equating migration with movement to cities.

The phenomenon of migration is usually studied at the receiving end by non-anthropologists: both in West Africa and in south India, relatively little information has been collected from the emitting communities. One must, therefore, welcome the book edited by Connell and others[13] which is based on numerous village studies carried out in many tropical countries and, in particular, on a detailed statistical analysis of material from some forty Indian village studies, which unfortunately had at least six 'important limitations' (p.157), of which one was the understandable failure to record the migration of whole households. The editors were surprised – as I am not – by one of their main findings, which was that in any village the incidence of migration was greatest among 'the rather poor and the rather rich', the poorest people being unable to afford the delays, costs and risks of migration (p.197).

11. Hart, 1982:123.
12. Thus Lipton (1977:226): a 'statistical illusion' of 8,000 townward migrants may be produced if two villages of 3,000 each expand by natural increase to 4,000 and amalgamate. (Towns are usually defined as having populations of 5,000 or more.)
13. Connell *et al.*, 1976.

They were unimpressed by the usefulness of 'the Todaro hypothesis'[14] (which, interestingly, they refer to as 'mainstream analysis'), to the effect that urban income prospects explain most migration. Among their other general conclusions, which they modestly call 'hypotheses', are: first, that 'more and more migration is rural-rural'; second, that Indian migrants' remittances are of little significance; third, that motivations are generally economic, migration being *a form of investment*; fourth, that 'colonising migration' to promising new lands involves rich farmers only; fifth, that, as is well known, well-educated villagers have a high propensity to migrate – mere *literacy* being irrelevant; and sixth, that decisions are often taken by parents, not by the younger migrants themselves. But, partly because I am dubious of the quality of the Indian village survey material on which this essentially statistical analysis is based;[15] and also because a statistical approach underplays the gross variation in social factors and, possibly, lays too much stress on the 'typicality' of India, I must turn to more qualitative matters.

However, before doing so I must emphasize that in my experience the statistical incidence of outward migration is among the most difficult of all subjects to study, mainly because of the deliberate unhelpfulness, vagueness and lack of memory of informants (some of those who have departed tend to be forgotten), but also because of time-span definitions, the migration of whole households and so forth. The situation was so tricky in Dorayi that I was obliged to get all my information from migrants' non-kin, after having compiled household genealogies on which to hang it.[16] It is partly because these difficulties, which *are* surprising, are never discussed that any questionnaire approach is bound to yield lamentably inaccurate results.

As many scholars have realized, it is necessary to attempt some kind of typology of migration before we can make much intellectual progress. There are two main difficulties here: that each continent, or grand region, might require its own typology;[17] and that typologies are sometimes better based on conditions in the emit-

14. Todaro, 1969; see also Todaro, 1970.
15. These surveys were conducted under the auspices of Agro-Economic Research Centres on a more or less common methodology.   16. Hill, 1977.
17. To my great inconvenience in this chapter, systems of rural/rural migration in south India and West Africa seem to have little in common.

ting than the receiving areas. Apropos of the latter point, I start by considering West African systems of circulatory migration, *excluding seasonal migration*.

Circulatory migration is such an interesting phenomenon, and takes so many forms, that it is worth emphasizing that it is unknown to many societies. Thus, to the best of my belief,[18] when Hausa men leave their rural communities to take up work elsewhere, they almost always intend to sever their economic links with their homeland, to the degree that virtually all returned-migrants feel abject failures. As I see it, the extreme reluctance to return home, except perhaps on visits to relatives, derives from the lack of permanent rights over farmland in this society where corporate land-holding lineages are lacking. While it is true that a migrant's kinsmen would never deny him all access to land (if they had any) on his return, he would be only too well aware of their charity, for sons who are 'abroad', except in Mecca, when their fathers die, do not inherit. It is because the decision to migrate is regarded as so momentous that parents are often opposed to their sons' departures, which forces a fair number of sons to vanish over-night without saying a word to anyone – and they may never be seen again.[19] My hypothesis is that circulatory migration is a phenomenon of lineage-organized societies, resembling the Tallensi (or Frafra) studied by Hart.

In the case of the Tallensi it is because population density is so high that a considerable proportion of the adult male population *must* be absent at any one time, if standards of living are not to fall drastically: so far as the individual is concerned, circulatory migration, which is encouraged by the whole community, is regarded as preferable to the permanent migration, albeit involving fewer men, which would otherwise be necessary. But one must not conclude that circulatory migration occurs only in densely popu-lated localities: indeed, I inadvertently came upon a district where such migration seemed almost to be a consequence of the sparsity of the population. As this case presents so many contrasts to the Tallensi, and has analogies in a fair number of other Ghanaian regions, I provide a few facts.

18. See Hill, 1972 and 1977.　19. See Hill, 1977:143–5.

In certain food-farming villages in rural Fanteland,[20] a coastal region west of Accra, virtually every unmarried young man and woman migrates, with the support of their parents, on the grounds that 'there is no *work* here'. Cultivation, which is generally ill-organized and unenthusiastically pursued, partly *because* the labour of the young people is lacking, is not regarded as *work*. Whereas formerly a fair proportion of the migrants sought work in gold-mining communities up-country, nowadays they migrate in many capacities and to many places – as cocoa labourers, carpenters, clerks, traders, etc., partly to the cities and partly to the country-side. While most of the migration, more especially in the case of women, appears to be circulatory both in intention and fact, for it is common to return home for farming when middle-aged or younger, some people never come back to farm, though even then they are apt to return briefly at Easter or on ceremonial occasions.

This leads me to state that in West Africa it would be idle to attempt to establish any statistical relationship between the propensity to migrate and population density, there being too many other variables. One of these variables is the availability of non-farming occupations, notably craftwork and trade, which was certainly very poor in the Fante villages. Where the opportunities for craftwork and trade in the receiving area are notably good, then people may migrate from a less to a more densely populated locality, as happened on a large scale in the last century in the densely populated farming zone around Kano city. Certainly the main occupation of all these migrants was farming, even though the splendid opportunities of engaging in cloth production and long-distance trade were the prime incentives.

Reverting to the need for typologies of migration, one common category is, of course, migration for food farming, usually, but not invariably, from more to less densely populated localities. The incidence of such migration in contemporary Nigeria is quite unknown, although it remains certain, despite the lack of popu-lation censuses, that very great variations in population density still persist, especially in the savannah zone where migrants are

20. See Hill, 1978, which reports the outline results of a quick attempt to study (for once) a few non-cocoa-farming communities in the forest zone.

unlikely to have to buy land. The presumption must be that the migratory flow within the savannah remains (as ever) important, but it may not do so much to even out population densities as might be presumed, considering the very low incidence of migration for farming from the most densely populated localities, which is largely, though not entirely, due to poverty.[21] Very few impoverished households, unless involved in mass migration (see below), are ever able to afford to invest in the future by migrating for farming. As for migration for farm-labouring, which cannot necessarily be distinguished from migration for farming if the labourers sometimes evolve into farmers, one has to presume that the north/south flow, particularly to cocoa farms (see Chapter 10), remains reduced, for the currently reported labour shortage is presumably connected with the contemporary need for immigration papers. It is probable that the volume of non-seasonal migration by labourers to grow annual crops has never been large, owing to the lack of work in the dry season.

In referring to the migration of farmers, I have ignored the long-term 'seeping migration' of large communities, notably the Konkomba and the Lobi of Ghana;[22] the former people had pressed fast westwards out of an area of severe soil exhaustion into a more fertile zone, but continued on the move; the latter crossed into Ghana from the Ivory Coast, where they continued their eastward flow, whole compounds or households removing or sections hiving off. Perhaps this category should be omitted from any typology of individual or household migration?

The wide dispersal of many ethnic groups which was clearly revealed by the 1960 Ghana population census (see Appendix B) is, of course, to be explained by migration. From the census material relating to occupations[23] we can see, for example, that many peoples migrated in the capacity of traders. About a third of all the Hausa men recorded as 'occupied' in Ghana, many of whom had been born there, were traders or butchers; they were very widely dispersed geographically. Amazingly, the geographical

21. Reported by other observers as well as myself.
22. See Hill, 1970 and Appendix B below.
23. The internal consistency of the statistics in terms of ethnic group gives me confidence, for once, in this much criticized type of demographic material.

distribution of the total Yoruba population in Ghana, many of whom were immigrants from Nigeria, bore a considerable resemblance to that of the total Ghanaian population, the main reason being that about a half of all Yoruba males, and many females, were traders who had sought out occupational 'niches', for instance collecting such produce as maize or *gari* (cassava meal) in the countryside. Just as the Yoruba migrant had a marked reluctance to work in wage employment of any type, so members of other migratory ethnic groups had definite dislikes or preferences, most Hausa, for instance, resolutely refusing to work as farm labourers. The plain fact is that any typology of West African migration which wholly ignored ethnicity would lack all realism.

It is dubious whether any typology should distinguish those in Hart's 'informal sector', defined as people who, not being in 'formalized' wage employment, or having a regular 'own account occupation' such as market trading, pick up a living in an urbanized environment by means of 'odd jobs' such as portering, lorry loading and street vending. The main reason for this is, perhaps, that many of them are 'fringe traders' who are better classified under that rubric, another difficulty being the multiplicity of jobs taken by many individuals.

While this crude West African typology, based on occupation, is quite incomplete (it omits, for example, migrant fishermen, artisans, seamen, pastoralists, miners, clerks[24] and professional workers), it is possibly of some assistance in enabling us to escape from the urbanization obsession and from the belief expressed by Lipton that migration 'is chiefly a response to imbalances in the communities of origin',[25] when it is often an expression of individual enterprise. I now turn to deal briefly with the vast topic of seasonal migration.

Amin's general discussion[26] is unsatisfactory since, for example, it betrays far too much trust in official statistics; underestimates the general degree of intra-rural flow; uses such mechanistic terms as 'optimum density of settled population on the land'; and tends

---

24. For instance, the migration of literate Ibo from south-eastern Nigeria to man the offices, shops etc. of the generally illiterate north – most of whom fled, if they did not perish, during the Nigerian civil war.
25. Lipton, 1980:15.   26. Amin, 1974:73 *et seq.*

to forget its own distinction between those short-term migrants who do and do not participate in agricultural work in their homeland. I think it is most appropriate to define a seasonal migrant in the Hausa manner as one who 'ekes out the dry season' by working away from home.[27] Such a migrant may either work on farms in localities where seasonal rainfall patterns differ from his own or seek non-farming work, from a list of many conceivable varieties, in town or countryside.

The volume of seasonal migration is wholly inestimable, all the evidence being that the propensity to migrate in this manner is very variable both within and between societies and from year to year.[28] Nor is it possible to make any well-founded statements about its direction, except to note the existence of some southern societies where migratory groups of farm labourers are important. However I am prepared to hazard the guess that as: first, such a high proportion of the total population resides in the countryside; second, there are always many foot-loose labourers and much under-used skill in the cities; third, the nearest city may be far away; fourth, it is easier to find 'trade-niches' in the countryside, where there are many huge markets, than in the city – that, therefore, most seasonal migration is intra-rural, especially when it involves experienced men such as artisans, traders or butchers. I was much interested to find that marketless Batagarawa village was a reception area for seasonal migrants who came in from some distance east to produce, and trade in grindstones there.

Turning away from West Africa to India, one is at once struck by the extraordinary lack of literature on migration generally, as distinct from that on urbanization which is enormous. The general matter of intra-rural migration[29] (except, of course, of wives on marriage), seems to be virtually a non-subject, except to *some* of those who undertake village surveys; yet it is well known from the work of certain anthropologists that it is common in some regions,

27. In Hausaland the shorthand expression *ya tafi cin rani* means to spend the dry season (*rani*) in another place in order to conserve grain stocks; the head of an extended farming group (*gandu*) may even be expected to close the main granaries during that period. See Hill, 1972:217–18.
28. For the evidence on Hausaland see Hill, 1972 and 1977.
29. But see Chapter 7 of Vitebsky (1984) on intra-rural migration in Sri Lanka.

an example being a village in Highland Orissa where Bailey reported that newcomers held 39% of the farmland in the 1950s, having bought it from members of the Warrior caste who had held all the land before 1885.[30] The historian Bayly has referred to the 'mobile peasants' and mobile labourers[31] of pre-colonial days and to the enticements offered to cultivators to bring areas of jungle under the plough. But the silence of most contemporary writers on such subjects might almost suggest that the British land revenue settlements of the last century had frozen the pattern of landownership for ever!

Nor have generations of Indian demographers apparently done much to help, especially as the type of migration which involves groups of households, maybe of a single caste, in establishing new hamlets on uncultivated land, has been expunged from the records, as we know, by means of attaching them to pre-existent villages for census purposes (see p.45 above). While it is true that the census volumes record whether people were born inside or outside the State or the place of enumeration; and while such material would enable the population-receiving village areas to be statistically identified in bald terms – it is, of course, silent on the matter of outward migration. Cassen states that 'many dozens' of 'items on migration' were published during 1951–71,[32] but hardly any of those few which relate to intra-rural migration are included in his extensive bibliography;[33] and his discussion in that chapter is largely confined to the phenomenon of urbanization, though he mentions that 'in a country of tremendous movement', intra-rural migration is 'constantly in progress' (p.119), as one would expect where population densities are so variable.

For the sole purpose of indicating the kinds of conclusions which meticulous enquiries may reveal, I briefly summarize my own findings on male migration from and into the six rather densely populated Karnataka villages.[34] First, about a half of all outward migrants went to Bangalore city, which was within a twenty-mile radius, the proportion being lower for Harijans than

30. Bailey, 1957.   31. Bayly, 1983:297 and 44.   32. Cassen, 1978:119.
33. But see Gosal, ed., 1967, which records that there is considerable migration into, as well as out of, the *rural* Punjab.   34. Hill, 1982:Chapter 10.

for other castes;[35] second, Harijan migrants to other villages frequently married women there; third, most of those who migrated to the countryside journeyed no more than about twenty miles; fourth, the incidence of outward migration was about 20% – that is to say, about 20% of the adult male population was living elsewhere, a figure which showed little variation with caste; fifth, very few potential joint households[36] were broken by migration; and sixth, partly owing to lack of qualifications, there were very few who migrated for professional or clerical work. As for inward migration to the villages, about a fifth of all household heads were men who (themselves or their fathers) had removed from elsewhere, a fair proportion of whom were small shopkeepers. These 'strangers' were not a meaningful aggregate, not only because of the numerous castes and occupations involved, but also because so much depended on whether they married into the village – as more than half of them had done, thus confirming the finding on outward migration. Of course, this account omits all mention of the foundation, by associated immigrants, of nearby hamlets, which were then so incongruously enumerated with the old village.[37]

Turning, even more briefly, to Indian urbanization, it is worth noting that Cassen regards its volume as 'astonishingly small' compared with Africa and Latin America.[38] He was puzzled by the fact that, despite the rapid acceleration of industrial expansion, urban population growth was slower in 1951–61 than in the previous or subsequent decade. Nowhere is rural/urban migration so high as to lead to falling populations in the countryside – indeed, the rural trend is markedly upwards almost everywhere. Between the 1951 and 1971 censuses the proportion of the total population resident in urban areas rose by only 2% per decade to about 20% – and most of the c. 300 million 'additional people' India acquired between 1941 and 1976 were in the villages. Cassen is very much concerned to dispute ideas of 'cataclysmic' city growth arguing,

35. In Bangalore District, according to the 1971 census, the proportion of Harijans in the total population of the city and of towns generally was about half that found in rural areas – the respective proportions for all urban and rural areas in the district having been 10% and 21%.

36. In other words, most potential joint households evolved into actual joint households unless the father died when the sons were still unmarried.

37. See Hill, 1982:Appendix X(3), and p.45 above.   38. Cassen, 1978:120.

for example, that urban employment opportunities, especially for the educated, increase very slowly relative to the supply of labour. He believes that when urban densities reach intolerable levels inward migration ceases and people move out, this being borne out by the recent history of Calcutta. Even so, he is able to imagine a situation such that the Indian population will grow to 2 billion over the next hundred years, with an urban population roughly seven times the present one at 800 million –40% of the total.

I conclude by reverting to Lipton's argument that rural/urban migration tends to enhance 'urban bias', which he defines in terms of two 'gaps': namely that separating urban and rural income (and output per person) on the one hand, and the lesser endowment and efficiency of capital in agricultural then in non-agricultural economies on the other.[39]

Lipton's main concern is to dispute the neo-classical economists' argument that the process of migration from the countryside goes on until a position of equilibrium is reached, such that 'both villager and townsman know that nothing is to be gained by moving'. He argues that information and resources are lacking, especially among the poorest people, so that 'equilibriating urbanization' acts very slowly; leaves the poorest elements unaffected; and leads to a most undesirable brain-drain from the villages. He also affirms that 'migrant streams in Asia and Africa are overwhelmingly male',[40] which seems to me most unlikely to be true as a general statement, though it is certainly very difficult to interpret such reliable demographic material as exists.[41] Cassen refers to the 'increasing share of females among migrants' as tending to bring the urban sex ratio into balance.[42]

39. Lipton, 1977:145 and 1980.   40. Lipton, 1980:6.
41. Though this is not the place to examine the serious statistical complexities, I need to emphasize the puzzling fact that it is very difficult to pinpoint *rural* localities in either Ghana (using the superior 1960 census) or south India, where sex ratios are noticeably imbalanced. Although Bangalore is among the seven largest cities in India, the ratios of males per 100 females in urban and rural Bangalore District in 1971 were 109 and 103 respectively. The corresponding ratios for urban and rural Ghana in 1960 were 106 and 101. For those familiar with conditions in mining areas in eastern and southern Africa the very word *migration* is apt to conjure up ideas of male movement for wage employment proper, such as commonly precludes the inclusion of wives; in both West Africa and south India other modes of migration are far more important.   42. Cassen, 1978:124.

But while I find the deplorably influential marginalist orthodoxy ridiculous, and agree that, so far as the evidence goes, the poorest people have the lowest urbanization rates, I am yet worried by Lipton's implicit assumption that the better educated migrants are brighter or more skilled than those who remain behind. Of course, as a result of their migratory experiences successful men from the city are apt to enjoy high status when they confidently revisit their villages. But the higher educational system is so haphazardly selective, and so many poorer parents are unable to afford to maintain their sons at secondary schools[43] even if they happen to be within easy reach, that educated villagers should be seen as the lucky rather than the clever people. Certainly, most of the richest farmers in a village are likely to aim at higher education for at least one of their sons, but they seldom wish to part with all of them and are apt to be as haphazardly selective as the educational system itself. Fortunately, therefore, there is no validity in the argument that most bright men migrate to the city, leaving the unenterprising behind, so that everyone in the village suffers even more than they did before.

APPENDIX A
The Migrant Cocoa Farmers of Southern Ghana

The very rapid development of cocoa and coffee growing in West Africa has always involved the migration of both farmers and labourers into very thinly populated forest country. From the discussion of farm labouring systems in Chapter 10 it is already clear that the migrations for cocoa-growing in Ghana, Nigeria and the Ivory Coast had some common features.[44] But it was the migration from the Akwapim scarp, near Accra in Ghana,[45] in the years between, say, 1895 and 1914, which was the most astounding. In terms of scale, vigour, timing, enterprise, panache, socio-economic organization, political tactfulness, drive, self-confidence ...

---

43. While in many rural communities, especially in West Africa, it is unusual to find men with secondary school qualifications who have never migrated, primary school qualifications are so common that they bestow little competitive advantage in the job market.
44. Apart from the migration in southern Ghana there were also later migrations in Ashanti and Brong Ahafo; these seldom involved land purchase.
45. While this scarp was the homeland of the majority of migrants, and was the source of supply of cocoa seed, other ethnic groups were also involved.

this migration was an event unique in the economic history of the whole of sub-Saharan (Black) Africa.

My book on the history of this migration was sub-titled *A Study in Rural Capitalism*,[46] by which I meant to convey that the 'migratory process' *as such* had many capitalistic features, not that each individual participant was 'a capitalist'. While I now partly regret the use of this terminology, which has led to some misunderstanding, I still try to justify its employment as an expository device when referring to the mass movements that occurred.

Before listing some of the salient capitalistic aspects of the migratory process, I must distinguish the two basic modes of migration. The patrilineal migrants,[47] those whose property passed from a father to his sons, formed themselves into land-buying *companies*, as they were always called, which bought blocks of forest land for division among their members (who were usually friends, not kinsmen), in accordance with the sum of money each proposed to subscribe; although the members clubbed together for land-buying purposes,[48] their economic association ceased once the land had been divided, each man farming his strip of land independently.[49] The matrilineal migrants, on the other hand, being those whose property passed to a sole heir through the female line (see p.98 above), bought land individually or in association with a very small number of kinsmen; unlike the patrilineal farmers, they were prepared to grant usufructural rights over portions of their land to those male and female lineage members who required them. The richest companies and matrilineal groups sometimes bought very large 'lands', running into several square miles in extent.

The 'capitalistic features' of the migration included the following:

First, the concept of *investing* money in purchased land was clearly developed; such funds as the farmers had available at the outset were not, for example, to be 'squandered' on labour employment, but were strictly regarded as development capital.[50] The initial and heavy work of clearing

46. Hill, 1963.
47. The inhabitants of the towns on the Akwapim scarp are ethnically very diverse; as some were patrilineal and others matrilineal, I benefited from 'laboratory conditions' for the study of the effects of this variable.
48. There is definite evidence that land was cheaper the larger the area bought; thus, certain companies which bought 2,000 acres or more paid an average price of only 6s per acre, compared with 10s, 13s, 24s and 32s for smaller purchases, in declining order of the size of the land purchased. See Hill, 1963:58.
49. The width of each strip was proportionate to the sum deposited by each farmer. (These strips could conveniently be divided between sons on inheritance.)
50. The success of the migration owed much to the Basel missionaries who had established schools and experimented with cocoa-growing on the salubrious Akwapim scarp before the middle of the last century; many educated Akwapim men had accumulated money by migrating as craftsmen to other West African countries. Prominent Christians were among those most sensitive to the possibilities of the new

and planting had to be undertaken by the farmers themselves, since it was not until the trees came into bearing that funds were available for financing labourers.

Second, the farmers took a very long view. Not only did they contrive to pay for the land *in instalments* over many decades,[51] thus mainly financing their business investment from the proceeds of selling their cocoa, for the initial deposit had been small; but they fairly commonly bought far more land than they could conceivably cultivate for many years to come. This compulsion to reinvest their profits from cocoa-growing in the purchase of additional land arose from their knowledge that land fit for cocoa[52] was bound to become scarce and represented a reliable 'savings bank'. Another motive for buying additional lands was the fact that 'self-acquired property' (property which had not been inherited) could be passed by matrilineal farmers to their sons.

Third, the ordinary migrant was interested in working simultaneously on a number of different lands, which even in the early stages might have been separated by a day's walking distance: having started one enterprise he was desirous, as it were, of establishing 'branches'. A man with cocoa land in several widely dispersed localities regarded himself as a travelling manager; he usually placed a relative or a wife in charge at each place, affording them much independence.[53] At the same time, many lands lay neglected for many decades (they might even get lost), partly because the terrible outbreak of swollen shoot disease, which killed many millions of trees in the historic southern cocoa-growing area after about 1939, ruined many farmers financially, so impairing their financial capacity to migrate further to their uncultivated lands and forcing them to revert to food farming.

Fourth, as we have seen (p.94 above), the farmers invested money in public works, such as contractor-built roads and bridges; they also built modern houses in their homelands, some of them most capacious and imposing – to which their descendants have remained permanently attached to this day, for the migration was not 'emigration'.[54] They also

crop, provided they could move off their overcrowded scarp into unoccupied forest country.

51. In the 1950s the chiefs were still endeavouring to claim instalments on land which had been bought more than forty years earlier.

52. The list of tropical countries which grow cocoa on any scale is so short because this crop demands such special soil and other ecological conditions. (In the event, the southern Ghanaian farmers bought much land that ultimately proved unfit for cocoa.)

53. Cultivation commonly proceeded slowly at each place so that, for example, many lands bought in the early 1900s had still not been completely planted when swollen shoot disease developed during the second world war.

54. How should this form of sociological attachment to the homeland be classified by those concerned with 'modes of migration'? Certainly, the descendants of the original

invested in transport: in the 1920s it was the cocoa farmers who owned most of those new-fangled lorries in southern Ghana.

Fifth, patrilineal primary land buyers, those who had bought vacant forest land through companies directly from the vendor chiefs, were often prepared to re-sell portions of land, though seldom whole strips, to fellow townsmen at a profit. Known as 'second-hand land', these portions were clearly distinguishable on the farm maps.[55]

Sixth, the inheritance rules of both matrilineal and patrilineal farmers were modified, but not fundamentally changed, owing to the migration. Contrary to much uninformed belief, matriliny and private enterprise did not collide; indeed, the richer and more enterprising members of a matrilineage were egged on by poorer members who knew that they, too, might benefit.

Seventh, many cocoa farmers, as we have seen, became greatly dependent on labour 'employment'. The migration of 'northeners' to assist in cultivating this new crop resembled a gold rush; the farmers adapted themselves accordingly, modifying an already existent *abusa* system, already discussed above.

Eighth was the role of the large creditor-farmers, the 'farmer-financiers', who often assisted many other farmers[56] by buying, or otherwise acquiring, rights over their farmland, on which they might have paid few instalments.[57]

Such an enthusiastic, though necessarily brief, account of the migratory process might have suggested that all migrants operated on a large scale, which was indeed not so. While it seems that in the early years no Akawapim man was prevented by poverty from participating in the migration, for some friend or kinsman would always help him, there were many migrants who cultivated small holdings maybe on a usufructuary basis. Unfortunately, statistics of sizes of holdings are necessarily lacking, owing to the extremely wide dispersal which was often involved. Some holdings were immense; most were not very large; many were quite small (see pp.161–2 below).

The literature on Ghanaian cocoa farming is vast,[58] and it is unfortunate

migrants are proud to emphasize their continued 'strangerhood' in the cocoa-growing areas.
55. The detailed study of the history of the migration was possible because the Department of Agriculture had meticulously mapped the cocoa farms for the purposes of awarding compensation to farmers whose trees had been cut out in an endeavour to control swollen shoot disease. (Second-hand land, unlike inherited land, involved transverse division of strip farms.)
56. I am not sentimentally suggesting that all the financial activities of the creditor-farmers were beneficial to others, only that they were sometimes quite indispensable and often reasonably co-operative.   57. See Hill, 1963:186–7.
58. Thus Okali and Addy (1974), which is an incomplete bibliography, includes 325 titles.

that space permits so little reference to it here, especially as it has been estimated by the Ministry of Agriculture (how reliably?) that as much as 70% of all cultivated Ghanaian farmland south of the Northern and Upper Regions,[59] and 84% of that in Ashanti, was under cocoa in 1972.[60] But to dispel any notion that indigenous (non-migrant) cocoa farmers in all regions are relatively small (as in southern Ghana; see note on p.104 above), reference must be made to a chapter in Kotey *et al.*[61] on the development of five large cocoa holdings in Brong Ahafo (in mid-Ghana), two of which were owned by indigenes who borrowed money to start farming around 1936 and who in 1970–1 produced 875 and 542 loads (of 60 lbs) of cocoa on 7 and 4 farms respectively. If it be recklessly assumed that average yields of 6 loads per acre were obtained,[62] then these indigenes would have had c. 150 and 90 acres under cocoa respectively.

APPENDIX B
The Occupations of Migrants in Ghana

My statistical monograph *The Occupations of Migrants in Ghana* was primarily intended to show that economically motivated migration takes a much greater variety of occupational forms than is commonly supposed, and it emphasized the significance of rural/rural migration. While the analysis was expressed in terms of ethnic group, this did not reflect any belief in the immutability of ethnic occupational preferences, which undergo constant change. The monograph was entirely based on *Special Report 'E': Tribes in Ghana*, 1960 Ghana Population Census, (1964) – a uniquely excellent and informative volume which will, unfortunately, never be repeated owing to the 'politicization' of frontier-crossing migration; as I write these words, in early May 1985, it is reported that some 700,000 'aliens' are being currently expelled from Nigeria at a fortnight's notice.[63]

As many as 92 'tribes', here referred to as ethnic groups,[64] were

59. Which accounted for some two-thirds of the total area of Ghana.
60. See Rourke, 1974:21.   61. 1974:173–82.   62. *Ibid.*, 16.
63. The Ghanaian expulsion of 'aliens' in 1969 has been referred to on p.115 above; a large proportion of those expelled was Nigerian. The current (1985) Nigerian expulsion, which presumably especially involves Ghanaians, has followed hard on that of 1983. Such cruel and sudden evictions show that colonial ruthlessness in ignoring ethnicity when drawing so many of their 'straight line frontiers' has had even worse consequences than were earlier foreseen, for these frontiers 'were not seriously intended to stop the continuous flow of people and goods across them' (Hart, 1982:103). See Hart for the argument that the weaker countries will eventually be forced 'to harmonize their economic policies' with those of the stronger.
64. I have deliberately skated over the numerous difficulties associated with defining 'ethnic group', some of which are discussed in my monograph.

separately distinguished in most tables in *Special Report 'E'*. My analysis was based on 34 of these ethnic groups, whose members had a marked propensity to migrate; in 21 of these cases a substantial proportion of the members of the group had been born outside Ghana. My purpose here is to cite a few statistics from the monograph which readers may find surprising.

But first I refer to the astonishingly wide dispersal of the Yoruba (see, also, p.129 above). In 1960 representatives of this Nigerian ethnic group were found in every one of the sixty-nine Ghanaian local authority areas which then existed. So prominent were Yoruba women, in particular, in trade in market places, that a Ghanaian market place might almost have been defined as a concourse of buyers and sellers, such that at least two or three of the sellers were Yoruba women.

Twenty of the thirty-four 'migratory ethnic groups' were primarily northern or non-Ghanaian. They showed an extraordinary variation in their degree of urbanization. In four cases over 60% of the population was resident in urban areas; in three cases this proportion lay between 46% and 53%; in seven cases between 20% and 35%; leaving five cases of under 20% of which two were 1% and 2% respectively. In most cases most of these 'urbanized migrants' were in the three cities of Accra, Kumasi and Sekondi/Takoradi; but in some cases 'towns' (places with populations of 5,000 or more) were preferred.

The geographical distribution of the migrant population showed very great variation with ethnic group. Thus, in five cases the migrants were mainly concentrated in rural areas easily accessible to their homeland; in eight cases the migrants were mainly in cocoa districts; and in eleven cases (including the above-mentioned Yoruba) they were very widely dispersed throughout Ghana, with less than a quarter in the three cities.

My occupational classification, which was of course associated with the foregoing geographical classification, was into 10 groups, including 'miscellaneous', according to the predominant occupation(s) of males. *Among* these were: the migrant food farmers (3 ethnic groups); the migrant cocoa farmers (5); 'the general urban and rural proletariat', including miners (8); traders and self-employed (one – the Yoruba); and non-farming wage employees (one – the Ibo). As many as 70% of all Yoruba women migrants (15 and over) were recorded as 'occupied' of whom 91% were traders. In 9 cases the former proportion lay between 31% and 51%. Trading was usually the most important occupation of women.

CHAPTER 12

THE
NEGLECT OF
WOMEN

❧

Even before the rise of the feminist movement, anthropologists and sociologists had become ashamed of their neglect of the significance of women's work – of their inherent male bias. So a fair number of compilations resembling the pioneering *Women of Tropical Africa*[1] have appeared in the past couple of decades and more anthropologists, especially women, have concentrated their research efforts on women's roles or 'problems', producing numerous chapters and doctoral theses with such titles as 'Changing Sex Roles and Social Tensions in . . .' – though few to such good effect as Phyllis Kaberry in *Women of the Grassfields*,[2] or Mary Smith in *Baba of Karo*.[3]

Following Ardener's *Perceiving Women* (1975), two of the most modern types of approach are perhaps best exemplified by an admirable socialist debate on feminism in Africa edited by Pepe Roberts (1984) and by a much more sober compilation *Female and Male in West Africa* which tries to 'look at men's and women's behaviour symmetrically',[4] realizing that they have 'similar potential abilities and patterns of responses to incentives.'[5] As for India, general books, such as *The Position of Women in Hindu Civilization* and *Marriage and Family in India*[6] are found in every serious bookshop there; a National Committee on the Status of Women reported in 1975;[7] and Leela Gulati's *Profiles in Female Poverty* (1981) is touchingly immediate in its detail. But, apart from a general appreciation of the low pay of women farm labourers, I think that

1. Denise Paulme, ed., 1963.
2. Kaberry, 1952. A remarkable study of the economic position of women in Bamenda, in the then British Cameroons. As a member of her lineage a woman enjoyed all the advantages of a man in respect of rights of usufruct throughout her life.
3. Mary Smith, 1954; a fascinating biography of an elderly Hausa women.
4. Ed. Oppong, 1983:373.
5. The book also includes some material on the neglected subject of the economic role of children.
6. A.S. Altekar, 1938 and K.M. Kapadia, 1955 respectively.
7. The report has little to say on women in agriculture.

women is hardly more than an entry, with few page references, in the index of the ordinary Indian village survey; and that any general awareness of the neglect of the economic role of women in the countryside is lacking in that country.

I fear that the efforts that have so far been made to place women appropriately on the general map of economic underdevelopment have failed to make any impression on development economists, Boserup notwithstanding.[8] Women are neither in the indexes of textbooks like that of Ghatak and Ingersent (1984) nor in any way involved in the text, for all the terminology has a male ring. Just as I have argued (p.106) that *labour* normally implies industrial (not farm) work, so the word also indicates work performed by males. Then, the unqualified word *trader* is male in tone[9] even though, as I constantly reiterate, most of the long-distance and market traders in the forest zone of West Africa are women. As for the dread word *peasant*, its masculinity is vouched for by the Oxford English Dictionary, which defines him (as already noted) as 'a countryman a rustic' – a female countrywoman being, incidentally, a *peasantess*. Unsatisfactory though the alternative words *farmer* and *cultivator* are, perhaps they are a shade more neutral. Then, the very word *work* is seriously biased against women,[10] if only because it normally excludes domestic labour performed within the home, which is apt to include arduous food processing as well as cooking.[11] And in reference to the old-fashioned question of the backward sloping supply curve for labour, has any economist ever contemplated the preference for leisure in female terms? What would women do with their extra leisure? Would they have more children?

8. While her *Women's Role in Economic Development* (1970) contains some useful (and some bad) statistics, it is seriously flawed by such false generalizations as that plough cultivation in Asia is associated with a 'predominantly male family labour force' (p.25) and that women's farming in Africa is associated with 'shifting cultivation'.
9. If the word for an occupation has no female form, is it to be presumed that women seldom undertook that type of work? Certainly, where men's and women's work differs significantly, the words may be different – e.g. the West African *tailor* and *seamstress*.
10. Maclachlan (1983) noted that whereas in south India 'no strict distinction is drawn between work and play for girls (p.178), for boys the distinction is categorical: Work is what happens when you are separated from your friends and set to a task that is utterly unlike play with peers ...'
11. That paid prostitutes are workers whereas unpaid housewives are not is, of course, an old problem in national income studies.

The fact is that there is no agreement as to whether the economic activities of women ought to be generally included with those of men, in which case a new gender-free economic terminology is required, or treated separately on the grounds of being 'different'. This is, incidentally, a statistical problem for the first as well as for the third world where, for example, increasing participation of women in part-time paid employment sometimes leads, as in present-day Britain, to the simultaneous and confusing rise in rates of both unemployment and employment.

Nevertheless, the general neglect of the significance of women's work *is* far more serious in tropical than in industrialized countries, for which the most basic of all reasons is the high proportion of the former population that lives in the countryside where statistical material is so defective. Among the grand multitude of other reasons which account for the neglect of women, which should I select for emphasis in this very brief chapter?

In terms of the definition of *rural development*, there has been a slight move in the direction of taking some account of women's interests in the past thirty years or so, for I remember being met with incomprehension in the 1950s when I suggested that well-digging to ensure that women walked less than five miles to fetch water fell under the rubric of development. But it remains true that, except so far as the mechanical corn grinder is concerned,[12] the expressed need for improved, simple technology usually neglects domestic food processing, although the work of threshing, pounding, grinding, etc., nearly all of which is performed by women in West Africa, is just as arduous as much farm work.

In an endeavour to be more systematic in discussing this half-universe in a few pages, I now realize that I must come down firmly in favour of *differentiating* women's activities for, there being no hope of changing economists' terminology, to include them with men would be to *subsume* them *under* men. Besides, the common

12. So labour-saving is this all-purpose grinding machine that women may be prepared to walk many miles with their produce to the nearest machine to avoid hand work. (The literature on this diesel-operated machine, which used to abound in the forests of southern Ghana, and to be very rare in rural Hausaland, is astonishingly slight; I think that they were mostly bought on hire purchase by richer men or women, as an income-yielding investment.)

lack of integrated farming households, which I emphasized so strongly in Chapter 6, provides a strong reason for distinguishing male and female economic activities, as does the fact that the notion of joint conjugal property hardly exists in many tropical regions.

However, many serious difficulties impede attempts to study female economic activities separately, and I now list a few of them. First women are not only apt to be subservient in the presence of men, particularly when a third party is present, but themselves genuinely rank men above women – just as darker-skinned third world people usually assert the superiority of their lighter-skinned brothers or sisters in their own society, whatever the protestations of others. This means that three-cornered conversations, involving the conjugal pair and the statistical investigator, are no more likely to yield reliable information about the wife's economic affairs than are enquiries made of male householders who, as we have seen, are commonly biased or ignorant, partly because of female secretiveness. It may be of some assistance to employ female investigators, but not if the male householder insists on obtruding himself. In general, the occupational statistics in population censuses greatly understate the numbers of women who work on the household farmland. 'Unless enumerators are explicitly instructed to ask about the possible economic activity of the women in the household . . . they may tend automatically to enter women as home-makers . . . without asking whether they participate in any other activity.'[13]

Another difficulty, which is quite familiar, is that many female activities are less susceptible to statistical measurement, or even systematic observation, than male activities. This is not only because they are more apt to *work*[14] (whether gainfully or not) within the home, and are less frequently in wage employment, but also because they sometimes travel with their husbands,[15] becoming invisible in so doing. An interesting example is provided by the

13. *Collecting Statistics on Agricultural Population and Employment*, FAO, Rome, 1978:83.
14. The philosophical problem of the definition of work is even more intractable in the third than in the first world.
15. Although it is true that men much more often take the initiative over migrating than women, in societies like the Fante (see p.127 above), where young adults migrate, women are equally enterprising.

migrant Ewe seine fishermen of south-eastern Ghana.[16] Each member of a fishing 'company' is entitled to take a woman with him, to assist with fish preservation and marketing, which is entirely women's work; but indispensable though they are, the women are not company members and are not straightforwardly rewarded, like the men, with a share of the catch.

In the third world all 'own account work', including production of food for the household, is hard to evaluate – and economists demand such arithmetic. What is the 'value added' by head-loading a basketful of maize from the homestead to the market place? West African women, other than the secluded Muslims of the northern savannah, undertake most food-crop porterage; and in the forest zone they are largely responsible for provisioning the towns and cities with foodstuffs.[17] But how can this contribution be brought to the fore statistically?

A bizarre example of 'statistical invisibility' is provided by the 'honeycomb market' of the secluded woman of rural Hausaland, whose village trade, which may compare in importance with male trading, is conducted entirely inside their houses, which are mainly linked by children.[18]

In most though not in all communities men own or cultivate, as of right, most of the farmland; by studying the distribution of farmland between men one may assess their relative living standards, as we have seen, no such short cut being available for women. Nor is one justified in assuming that the standards of living of wives are generally closely related to those of their husbands, for anthropological enquiries have shown that, particularly in their trading activities, women are sometimes richer than their husbands, to whom they often grant loans. Another difficulty arises from uncertainty as to the extent to which husbands *in fact* provide for their wives; certainly, in many West African societies it is common for wives to receive partial maintenance only, as they

---

16. See Hill, 1970.   17. See Hill, 1985b.
18. It follows from the general neglect of women that, whereas everyone jumps at the opportunity of taking a moral view of such institutions as bonded labouring or share-cropping, no one is prepared to contemplate the cruelty of the degree of wife seclusion that is found, for instance, in rural Hausaland, where wives may not leave their houses during the day except, for special purposes, without their husband's permission.

are expected to procure some of the food required by themselves and their children, especially at certain seasons.

In monogamous south India, where households are more integrated than in polygynous West Africa, and where women are much more often wage employees than traders, it is both harder (for the first reason) and easier (for the second) to treat women's activities separately than it is in West Africa. Women's wages as farm labourers are always lower than men's for the same task; but how much significance has this got, if it is true, as always seems to be assumed on the basis of no evidence, that both sets of wages go, intact, into the husband's pocket? Certainly, Indian widows are disadvantaged compared with widowers, for they do not operate ploughs, and their lower wage rates then really matter much more; but if they happen to be the head of a joint household this distinction vanishes.

Considering, in the case of West Africa, (a) the large proportionate value added to raw food crops by elaborate processing,[19] which, as I have said, is commonly performed by women, largely by hand; (b) the large contribution made to food farming by many women who weed and generally care for much of their husband's farmland; and considering, also, (c) women's important roles in portering and trading – it is entirely conceivable that women, in that region, are responsible for a larger proportion of the gross domestic product than are men. Ought this *possibility* to be mentioned in the economic textbooks? Or should the economists wait until modern technology has sufficiently enhanced the importance of tractor-driving men?[20]

---

19. See Guyer (1984), who refers to the striking neglect in the 'aid literature' of root crops, as against grains, in the African staple food economy, one important point being that in West Africa the laborious processing of these crops, which greatly enhances their value, is largely undertaken by women. (While Guyer is dubious of the accuracy of FAO cassava statistics for Africa, it is surprising that she should feel sufficient confidence in them to emphasize the apparent stability of the rate of growth of root and tuber production – n.16 on p.34 above.)
20. In most localities this would be a long wait. But see Longhurst (1982) for the argument that modernization, in general, is apt to harm women's interests in rural Hausaland.

CHAPTER 13

THE SALE
OF
FARMLAND

༺~༻

> 'Most theories of the allocation of land take ...
> the ownership of land as given ... We shall follow
> suit.'
>
> Bliss and Stern (1982:53)

Although it is well over a century since the Krobo of the southern
Gold Coast started buying forest land on a large scale for the
purpose of establishing oil-palm plantations,[1] the widespread
belief that West Africans 'never sell land' dies so hard, despite so
much evidence to the contrary,[2] that it is necessary to include a
brief discussion of the subject. This, also, provides a welcome
opportunity of showing how farmland is now being priced out of
the market in some densely populated rural localities.

I do not propose to devote much space to citing examples of the
survival of misbeliefs about land-selling, although they are
generally reflected in modern development theory, as the above
epigraph shows. But it is necessary to point out that these
misbeliefs are often an aspect of the *sentimentalization syndrome* – the
idea that things are, touchingly, much the same as they have always
been. Thus, Harrison in his popular textbook reflects that – 'An
[African] man can own the fruit of the earth – crops and trees which
he himself planted and tended. But he cannot dispose of his plot or
sell it, there is no individual title to land, no market in real
estate.'[3]

Successful textbooks reflect prevailing orthodoxy, even if it is

---

1. Palm oil being an export crop, the purchased areas were strictly analogous to the
   European-owned plantations established in many colonies, but not (as we know) in
   Anglophone West Africa. See Hill, 1963:Appendix II (9) on the Krobo migration.
2. When I was studying the migration of cocoa farmers in Ghana in the 1950s, I suffered
   much condescension from many people who held that the farmers 'didn't *really* buy
   their land'. Yet the published evidence, particularly on litigation resulting from land-
   selling, had long been most extensive. See Chapter 11, Appendix A.
3. P. Harrison, 1984 ed.:73. See also Postscript below.

146

somewhat blurred and out-of-date, and Harrison on this subject is no exception. He comprehends the view of those of a legalistic turn of mind who, as we shall see, misunderstand the implications of land being 'vested in the state', where such is the case.[4] And he also mirrors the ideas of many successful academics and administrators of the type who are called upon to give official advice to underdeveloped countries. Thus, we read in an important report of 1969 that 'in most Nigerian villages the nature of the land tenure system is essentially communal', and that 'the theory of inalienability of land is fundamental to the indigenous land system throughout Nigeria'.[5] But as two anthropologists have put it: '"Communal tenure" is an illusion that results from viewing the systematic exploitation by kinship groups of their environment through the distorting lens of Western market-oriented and contract-dominated institutions of property and ownership.'[6]

Such is the sentimentalization syndrome that it discriminates in favour of exotic ideas which, once they have been grasped, cannot be dislodged. Thus, there *are* still many West African societies where land cannot be sold to individual cultivators, who exert individual, not communal, usufructural rights only, usually, though not necessarily, over land which is corporately owned by their patriclan or matriclan; but the point is that such land tenure conditions are no more typical of West Africa generally, as it is today or was in the past, than are circumstances where usufructural rights are unknown. And a further complication is that even in societies where land is sometimes sold outright for cash this may apply to certain categories of land only, as in Hausaland where only annually cultivated manured farmland (*karakara*) is saleable. (The sale of *karakara* was an ancient practice, certainly preceding the colonial conquest of northern Nigeria by at least a century.)[7]

Of course the ethnic heterogeneity of West Africa is so great that there are numerous other complications affecting land-

4. As in northern Nigeria, soon after its colonization was completed in 1903. Since it was wrongly supposed that all land had formerly been vested in 'chiefs', who allocated right of user to occupants, the administration felt justified in 'transferring' these rights to the Crown. See Hill, 1972:240.
5. *Strategies and Recommendations for Nigerian Rural Development 1969/1985*, United States Agency for International Development, 1969: 28 and 29.
6. Bohannan eds., 1968:88.   7. See Hill, 1972:240.

selling, especially in regions where the introduction of perennial trees, such as cocoa and coffee, necessarily led to modifications in land tenure. Such modifications may or may not have involved a greatly increased incidence in land-selling; and even if they did, as in southern Ghana, but not so much in Yorubaland,[8] then the situation may be much less straightforward than might have been expected, considering that, as we know, southern Ghanaian sales were permitted to strangers only and not to indigenes, and that 'individualized' (i.e. purchased) land was always in process of being converted into inalienable family property.

The scholarly and well-documented literature on West African land tenure is gargantuan in size and scope; in the Gold Coast, where indigenous Western-trained lawyers wrote some of the most distinguished early volumes, it was apt to be especially passionate and learned. Fortunately, it is no part of my present function to survey the literature or to attempt any generalizations regarding the conditions in which land is and is not purchasable, though readers may have picked up a few points in passing. But I must insist that 'prevailing orthodoxy' in relation to West Africa is currently coiled round on itself, simultaneously believing: (a) that the continuation of old-fashioned land tenure systems (such as prevent the sale of land, for example) *put a brake on progress*; and (b) that it was the early colonialists' concept of private property which originally destroyed the indigenous social security system.

The fact that in Hausaland all land 'ultimately belonged' to the Crown did not prevent ordinary farmers from behaving as though they were the outright owners of their farmland which, if it were *karakara* could still be freely sold or mortgaged as it had been previously; the Muslim courts recognized individual rights and compensation was paid when the government requisitioned farmland. In densely populated areas the incidence of land-selling was very high, probably accounting for much of the sub-division of farm plots that occurred. As Hart states, over the years various West African regimes 'have asserted the state's eminent domain over the land';[9] the most important recent attempt having been

8. See p.159 below.   9. Hart, 1982:91.

Nigeria's Land Use Decree of 1978 which vested all land, in the Federation, in the Governor of the state in which it was situated.

A recent article states that this Decree, which legally national-ized all Nigeria's land, was intended to remedy 'defects' in cus-tomary land tenure,[10] which were a constraining influence on agricultural development, though nobody, least of all the legis-lators, was entirely clear as to what these were. But the (then) Head of the Federal Military Government assured the farmers (p.9) that their 'right to continue to farm their lands without any encum-brances and part with their interest at will is assured', and no land registration was required; all of which meant that in a region like Hausaland the re-nationalization of nationalized land left the farmers unaffected! But in Yorubaland, where a special kind of 'permanent renting' of cocoa land had evolved,[11] the Decree actually created a good deal of insecurity among tenants – and the sale of land, which had not been very common, continued. Given the general agricultural policies of the Nigerian government, the author presented (p.24) the piquant possibility of the further development of agrarian capitalism 'being founded upon the abolition of private property in land'!

In India, where the literature on land tenure is remarkably slight compared with that of West Africa, the learned treatises have perhaps been devoted rather to the joint family and to the relations of debtors and creditors – which may, of course, involve land. Many, if not most, village surveys[12] fail to refer to land-selling at all; and when it is mentioned naif surprise at its occurrence is apt to be expressed.[13] Especially considering the significance and long history of colonial land-revenue systems,[14] the lack of general treatises dealing with land tenure is remarkable. Fortunately,

10. Francis, 1984.   11. See p.159 below.
12. Such strictures do not of course relate to anthropologists like Bailey (1957), whose central theme was land purchase – see p.76 above.
13. Thus, the experienced H.H. Mann (Mann and Kanitkar, 1921) was surprised to find how often land was sold in one village, whereas in another transfers were so rare that land values were inestimable. (I am not here discussing the transfer of land between the large hereditary *zamindars* – see Kolff, 1979.)
14. As a general rule, the colonialists taxed land in India and people (poll taxes) in West Africa.

however, our knowledge of nineteenth and twentieth-century land transactions has been improved, very recently, by the work of the historians Baker (1984), Charlesworth (1978 and 1985) and others. Considering that the individual ownership and transfer of land in south India goes back to the late Chola period,[15] that is to about six centuries ago, the time was indeed ripe for some further enlightenment on the colonial period.

In dealing with Indian farmland one ought always to distinguish irrigated from dry land, the former being far more valuable and productive, especially if it produces two or three crops annually; but, unfortunately, this is not always possible though Baker, in discussing the land market in the history of Tamilnad, does his best. Thus, he notes that in the early nineteenth century dry land was often said to have 'no pecuniary value' (p.83); in the years leading up to 1914, when the volume of transactions was said to be very small, prices of around 50 rupees were quoted. But prices were higher for land which had been 'improved' by the construction of tank or well, or by constant manuring.

In the Tamilnad valleys, where rural economies had been based on rich rice agriculture for many centuries, Baker estimates, on the basis of 'shaky' data, that, perhaps around the 1940s, about half of the population was landless,[16] a third having plots of little more than an acre. He gives the impression, which is all that he can do, that the remarkable degree of inequality was unlikely to have been due to a high incidence of land-selling by the impoverished. Which leads me to note my most important point in this chapter, which is the general evidence[17] that *the forebears of very few contemporary landless Harijans in south India had owned farmland in the colonial period*. It is often implicitly assumed that landlessness is commonly or usually due to enforced land-selling by the impoverished, but this will not wash in south India so far as the Harijans are concerned.

For Tamilnad, Baker distinguishes three different types of land transfer: first was the ordinary circulation of land within the village community, which was so commonplace that it was often forgot-

---

15. See Baker, 1984:325.
16. Baker, 1984:320. I think that in south India such high incidences of landlessness only occur with irrigated farming.   17. See Hill, 1982:271–3 and Baker, 1984:184.

ten; second was the transfer of *mirasidari* (landlord) titles; and third was the market involving enterprising agriculturists, who were interested only in improved land and special commercial crops. From the late nineteenth century onwards 'hoards of wealth' were increasingly stored as holdings of valley wet land under *mirasidari* titles; land prices far exceeded the value of the land as an agricultural investment, for people bought not only for reasons of status but also for life insurance, since it was well known that land values appreciated more rapidly than prices generally. However, the first world war boom was relatively short-lived.

Baker suggests that the main reason for the failure of the ordinary village land market to flourish, even during this century, was the absence of secure titles over land in Tamilnad.[18] The register of land deeds (*pattas*), issued by the revenue department, was so inaccurate that the courts would not accept such deeds as evidence of ownership.

It is ironic, as I have already suggested, that in a part of the world where there is an immense legal, or semi-legal, literature on land revenue and registration, land reform, the dispossession of the hereditary estate-holders (*zamindars*) and so forth, we should really know so little about land-selling.

When the Great World Inflation started to hit West Africa and (to a much lesser degree) India in the 1970s, the indications are that in well-populated areas, where all the conveniently situated land is under cultivation, the prices of farmland began to soar. As earlier in Tamilnad, farmland became *the* reliable store of wealth *par excellence*, one which was bound to rise in price and which would not rot, like so much property in the tropics where the speed of natural decay is so much more rapid than elsewhere.[19] Whether this led to much land speculation, for instance by urban residents, one cannot say; but the general indications are that it should be seen rather as having enhanced the reluctance to sell. Even the poorest landowners do their best to avoid selling: the case of the impoverished Karnataka Harijans who temporarily lend their

18. Baker, 1984:319 *et seq*. But this was not so in the princely state of Mysore – see Hill, 1982:271, n.2.
19. Hence the poignancy of the word *spoil*, which one hears all the time in West Africa.

small plots to richer people for planting casuarina trees comes to mind.[20] So the richest cultivators are usually unable to continue topping up their stock of land to provide adequately for their sons.

For West Africa I can find no reliable up-to-date statistics of land prices (which does not surprise me), but only casual statements. However, I saw the process of the stultification of the land market at work in very densely populated Dorayi as long ago as 1972, where the general level of prices may have been of the order of £60 an acre – perhaps higher near the main road.[21] While this may well seem to have been a low figure,[22] it was very high compared with (say) twenty years earlier when it might have been under £1, for the likelihood is that prices had remained very low indeed until the 1950s. As about four-fifths of all 'rich men', nearly all of whom were middle-aged or elderly, were recorded as having bought some farmland (I laboriously estimated that they had bought at least 44% of their total acreage); and as there was a remarkably close relationship between the size of holding and the proportion acquired by purchase – it can be seen that the new sluggishness of the land market, which was vouched for by a local farmer who acted as a 'land broker', had far-reaching consequences. Even in 1972 prices were absurdly high in relation to the net yield of basic crops; they are now, probably, astronomical.

For irrigated land in south India it is not surprising that we have to rely mainly on general statements on the present stultification of the land market; thus Harriss refers in passing to 'the rigidity of the land market' in Tamil Nadu.[23] But since, presumably, all irrigable land is actually under cultivation, there can be no doubt as to what is happening. As for dry land in Tamil Nadu, Harriss reports that prices had risen from 100 rupees per acre in about 1960 to 3,000 rupees around 1973 – most certainly 'real inflation'.[24]

In the Karnataka villages in 1977–8, I certainly noted the small number of land transactions that were then occurring. I was told

20. They get a loan and share the proceeds from selling the wood, at which point they regain the land.   21. Hill, 1977.
22. Even compared to the farm labourer's wage of about 5 shillings (plus food on the farm) for a 'long morning's' work.   23. J. Harriss, 1982:195.   24. J. Harriss, 1977:129.

that 3,000 rupees per acre (say £200) was a reasonable price for unimproved dry land, this being perhaps some ten times the estimated gross annual yield of the basic crop *ragi*, a very low-yielding type of millet.[25] Prices of high quality tank-irrigated paddy land might then have been of the order of 10,000 rupees per acre (say £700).

In the very densely populated coastal areas of southern Kerala, in south India, in 1982, prices of the order of 2,000 rupees per *cent* (a cent being a hundredth of an acre) – equivalent to about £13,000 per acre – were commonly quoted to me in conversation for dry farming land, such as coconut groves, situated off main roads; on main roads, and near Trivandrum city, much higher prices for agricultural land seemed to be common. Prices of irrigated paddy land in that strange looking-glass world appeared to be of the order of 10% of those for dry land, perhaps mainly because of the shortage of suitable land for house sites.[26] (In Kerala, where settlement is dispersed, a man's registered land-holding includes his house site, which is usually very much more valuable than his house; whereas in the nucleated villages of Karnataka house sites are not private property.)

There could be no better indication of the chaos caused by inflation in the rural tropical world than these Kerala land prices, which are far higher than those of high-yielding agricultural land in Britain; I gather from a recent newspaper article that the average prices of farmland in Britain were £1,327 per acre in 1978, £2,082 in 1983, falling to £1,978 in 1984 – a price which, in real terms, was some 10% lower than in 1950.

Of course in densely populated tropical localities farmland is such a reliable hedge against inflation; such a useful form of security for loans; and endows its larger owners with so much prestige – that it would be absurd to expect any close relationship between crop yield and price. So perhaps the most interesting consequence of the current inflation is that, in some localities, in a period of (say) two or three centuries, the wheel has come almost full circle; no

25. See Hill, 1982:161.   26. I even saw a house erected on stilts on a paddy field!

CHAPTER 14

RURAL CLASS
STRATIFICATION?

~∙∙∙∙∙∙∙∙∙∙~

Following the Indian anthropologist Béteille, I define the relation-ship between landlords, owner-cultivators, tenants, share-croppers and agricultural labourers as constituting the heart of what he has denoted 'the agrarian hierarchy'.[1] At the same time, I agree with Béteille that these categories derive from a conceptual framework which is no longer well suited to Indian dry grain cultivation, for in the hands of statisticians and development economists they tend to create 'a strait jacket which grossly distorts the realities of social life in rural India'.[2] Not only is there apt to be much overlap between categories, as with labourers who are also owner-cultivators; but nowadays, with the probable disap-pearance of renting on any scale, it is common for no more than two distinct categories, cultivators and *landless* labourers, to be significantly represented in any community, so that *hierarchy* is inapposite.

However, prior to recent Indian Land Reform legislation which prohibits renting,[3] and to the slightly earlier dissolution of the large hereditary estates,[4] the concept of Indian 'landlordism' certainly had much validity in some localities, so that the notion of the agrarian hierarchy, especially in districts where irrigated paddy was the main crop, was a useful differentiating mechanism. But this was not so in Anglophone West Africa in, say, 1900 where landlordism, renting, and daily-paid farm labouring were unknown. This grand inter-continental contrast means that a discussion of the appropriateness, if any, of Western notions of rural class stratification has different historical bases in the two regions.

---

1. Béteille, 1974:32.   2. *Ibid.*, p.46.
3. As Land Reform is a state not a central matter, I can only presume that this is generally so. (Actually small-scale renting presumably continues, if the example of Karnataka is a guide.) As for share-cropping, which is a type of renting, see Appendix below.
4. Generally known as *zamindars*, especially in northern India, there are many regional names for these estate owners. For the position in Tamilnad see Baker (1984).

Goody's well-known explanation for the absence of landlordism in West Africa lent heavily on the lack of a plough there.[5] But my own understanding is more generalized. It is that where differential and transmittable rights over farmland existed *or* where significant proportions of households were too poor to farm, then agrarian hierarchies were likely to occur, as formerly in south India – but that *neither of these conditions was usually satisfied in pre-colonial West Africa*. Except perhaps in certain anomalous regions where rich owners of farm-slaves had established large plantations or where high population densities had induced high incidences of land-selling, it was a general rule in pre-colonial West Africa that every free man enjoyed land rights derived either from his membership of a corporate land-holding lineage or from his residence in a rural community, whether nucleated or dispersed; furthermore, there would have been few who were so impoverished that they would have been unable to borrow a hoe and planting material in order to set themselves to work as cultivators.

A yearning to classify households qualitatively, preferably by reference to their relationship to the means of production, lies deep in the hearts of all those with any sociological pretensions, notably neo-marxists, though this is rather due to a simplistic notion of 'no classification, no articulation' than to any fear of an alternative reliance on bad statistics. But mainstream development economists, defined as those who disdain an empirical approach, regard it as beneath their dignity to make any attempt to face such an apparently awesome matter as that of West African land tenure. Yet, despite the admitted complexity of such a subject, there *are* certain general ideas or principles which might prove to be useful starting points for those of theoretical bent.

First are the implications of the fact that there is still no *landlord class*, by which I mean persons whose rights over land are *superior in kind* to those of other indigenes: in other words, no one is born into an indigenous class, resembling the erstwhile Indian Untouchables, such that as a person he is 'disqualified' from cultivating

---

5. Goody, 1971. See also Hill, 1982:276–8. Goody also emphasized the relative sparsity of West African population.

available land.[6] As there is no landlord class, and as it is only in highly anomalous circumstances, usually involving cocoa farmers, that landowners in fact have rights over land which is surplus to their requirements, so it is generally still the case that there are no West African tenants proper, share-cropping proper being equally rare. Why is 'surplus land', except in some circumstances with cocoa farmers, a misleading concept? Because, in general, cultivators have no means of asserting their continued rights over land which they are not themselves cultivating. And because also, as we have seen, the contemporary farm-labouring system, which requires supervision, has long set a limit to the size of farm-holding.

Second, it has to be accepted as a fact that farmland is saleable in some localities and not in others and that this is mainly a function of ethnicity. Formerly, there were some chiefs who sold land – maybe to the horror of their superiors.[7] Nowadays the sellers are all individuals, the evidence being that land is not sold because it is 'surplus' but because the vendor is in need of money. In regions like the more densely populated sections of Hausaland, where farm-selling was very common until recently, much farmland was transferred by sale from poorer to richer cultivators and the incidence of landlessness consequently increased. But the concept of landlessness does not exist in localities where every indigene is a member of a corporate land-holding lineage from which he is entitled to claim individual rights.

Third, the pledging (mortgaging) of farmland should be seen, especially in the forest zone, as serving one of the main functions of renting, but in reverse: it is a system which enables the pledgor, who is in need of money but does not own surplus land, to retain the ownership of his pledged land while it is temporarily cultivated by someone else.

Fourth, the reluctance of members of many ethnic groups to work as farm labourers, so that there may be, as we have seen, a consequential dependence on stranger-labourers, sometimes has

6. This was a *de facto* rather than a legal disqualification, as shown by the fact that Untouchable village officials were apt to be partly rewarded with land.
7. In Akim Abuakwa, in southern Ghana, the helpless paramount chief was outraged by the profligacy of his inferiors in 'selling away' their forest land for ever.

implications for land tenure if such strangers evolve into farmers on their own account.

Finally, the very great variations in population density which characterized pre-colonial West Africa, and which remain significant today, led to much planned migration of farmers; it is even arguable that radical economic change in the countryside had usually involved the migration of actual or aspirant farmers.

I now expand on some of the above points, starting with the general lack of tenancy and share-cropping. If there were any localities where tenancy might have been expected to have developed in colonial times, as did daily-paid farm labouring, these were in densely populated central Hausaland[8] at the time of the collapse of farm-slavery, c. 1920–30, when many ex-slave-owners found themselves possessing much more land than they could cultivate with the aid of daily-paid farm labourers; but the evidence[9] is that these slave-owners all sold or gave away their surplus land sometimes to their ex-slaves who had evolved into free men and had not migrated, retaining no more than a maximum of about 40 to 50 acres, the only exceptions having been city-based members of the aristocracy who were probably rare in most Provinces other than Sokoto. It is true that there is a land-*borrowing* system (*aro*) in Hausaland; but this is most certainly not tenancy proper, small plots being lent, mainly to needy relatives for a single season, for a notional payment which may not be made until after harvest.[10]

I have laid so much emphasis on the migration of cocoa farmers that it is easy to overlook the significance of indigenous (non-migrant) cocoa farmers, who certainly produce a considerable, though indeterminate, proportion of the Ghanaian crop; especially as their trees happened to have been less affected by swollen shoot disease than those of the migrants, probably for geographical reasons. Despite the modifications in land tenure

8. As distinct from the peripheral area of southern Hausaland studied by M.G. Smith, where land-tenure conditions were peculiar – see Smith, 1960 and Hill, 1977.
9. See Hill, 1977:Chapter 13.
10. The etymology of *aro* also makes it abundantly clear that borrowing not tenancy is involved; but such is the economists' yearning for qualitative differentiation, and the strength of the belief that private ownership inevitably leads to tenancy, that one's evidence is seldom taken seriously.

resulting from migration, the practices of indigenous cocoa farmers remained unchanged when, after an interval, they imitated the migrants by starting to grow much cocoa; so far as I know, they never to this day either sell or rent their cocoa or food farms. Nor did the migrant cocoa farmers of southern Ghana ever rent out portions of the land they had bought, although they often sold them.[11] But in Yorubaland, where the incidence of land-selling to migrant cocoa farmers was low, a species of rent[12] (*isakole*) evolved from the 1920s; such annual payments for the use of land by strangers were enforceable in the native courts.

To my mind the exception that proves the rule that land is ordinarily not rented relates to the renting of shallot beds[13] in the Anloga area of Eweland in south-eastern Ghana, where ordinary farmland is neither sold nor rented; these beds are not farmland in the customary sense, but are composed of sand, transported by head-load at great expense, into low-lying, otherwise unculti-vable, coastal or lagoon areas. Significantly, systems of share-cropping (proper) also exist there.

On the matter of the general lack of share-cropping in West Africa, this is clearly an aspect of the lack of tenancy. I deplore the fact that the *abusa*-man (see p.116 above), who is conventionally rewarded with a one-third share of the cocoa he plucks, is so commonly regarded as a share-cropper. A share-cropper proper (see Appendix below) necessarily receives some inputs, besides land, from his landlord, which is why the south Indian tenant whose rent happens to be a portion of the crop is not to be classified as such.[14] The *abusa*-man is a law unto himself, a special kind of stranger; thus, as already mentioned, he receives land for growing food crops from his landlord, for which he pays no rent.

Such is the importance of the concept of strangerhood in West Africa, and such the lack of general as distinct from ethnographic

11. It was largely because the rich migrant farmers of Akwapim helped their poorer fellow townsmen by selling them 'second-hand land', on easy terms, that virtually everyone participated in the migration.   12. See Francis, 1984:17.
13. See Grove, 1966. This is one of the most intensive examples of bulb cultivation in the entire world, cultivation methods, which involve many kinds of manure, having been developed by the farmers themselves.
14. In the Karnataka villages, such renting systems were quite common.

discussion of the subject, that it is unfortunate that Fortes's chapter 'Strangers'[15] never became a book. In reference to Ahafo in mid-Ghana, Fortes distinguished *permanent guests* (otherwise *internal strangers*, who came from the same cultural and political community, in the widest sense, as their hosts) from *foreign* or *alien* strangers, who belonged to some ten different northern ethnic groups and who were commonly Muslims: the former were the stranger cocoa farmers, the latter (who lived in strangers' quarters) were the cocoa farm labourers, who were definitely not aspirant farmers. Here was an example of ethnic differentiation of an apparently permanent kind.

But in other circumstances and places, large numbers of *foreign strangers* who began work as labourers did evolve into cocoa or coffee farmers. Thus, in Bongouanou in the southern Ivory Coast, where the indigenes were matrilineal people, as in Ahafo, Boutillier reported that many strangers from north of the Ivory Coast rapidly achieved this change of status.[16] (As many as a third of the total population consisted of strangers, who belonged to at least twenty-six ethnic groups.) The northern strangers lived in separate sections of the towns or hamlets; they sought a symbiotic relationship with the indigenes, not assimilation into their lineages, their natural pride in their origins enabling them to accept their somewhat inferior social status as strangers.

The case of Bongouanou is an especially good illustration of the idea that rapid economic development necessitates the influx of strangers who, it must be emphasized, are invariably made welcome in West Africa, at least on their first arrival, if only because they are seen as enhancing the status of the local chief. The strangers fell into four overlapping categories: they were farmers who assisted in extending the area under export crops; they were traders, both large and small, who filled the niche created by the reluctance of male indigenes to work in this way; they were artisans and butchers; and, of course, they were agricultural labourers who worked on the farms of strangers as well as indigenes. Here, as elsewhere, rapid economic development was triggered by the arrival of the actual or aspirant farmers, who were soon joined by people with no such ambition, such as the Nigerian cocoa buyers who flooded into the southern Ghanaian forests after the stranger farmers had established their farms. *Strangerhood, not class, was the basis of differentiation.*

While it would be possible to give many other positive illustrations of this phenomenon, I have to conclude my discussion of the function of strangers by making the negative point that socio-economic conditions may remain remarkably stable over the decades, if not the centuries, if no strangers arrive to leaven relationships between people and their local natural resources. Thus, the land-tenure system of the rural Edo-speaking peoples in south-western Nigeria[17] remained remarkably static, despite their full integration in the cash economy and their production for export of rubber, cocoa, coffee and so on.

I now turn to the far more general and indeed almost hopelessly difficult question of the kinds of consideration which should be taken into account in deciding whether the 'type of inequality' which is found in any community implies Western-style class stratification, when we know that neither landlordism, nor strangerhood, is involved. Because it *is* often contended that very pronounced inequality (one man owning half a square mile, another one acre) among Ghanaian cocoa farmers is evidence of such stratification, I query this supposition by reference to a group of matrilineal kin.[18]

In 1912 a famous cocoa farmer, known as Kofi Pare,[19] in association with six kinsmen, bought an area of over 2 sq. miles for planting cocoa – in 1959 the surveyed portion of this land measured 1,152 acres. Kofi Pare, who gave his name to the land, originally owned some 372 acres, the shares of the other six, who would have put up less money, varying between about 201 and 42 acres. By 1959 I found that as many as 137 farmers, virtually all of whom were probably related, by birth or marriage, to one of the seven original purchasers, were registered as owning land; two of these original seven men were still alive, and they, together with the successors of the other five, owned about 40% of the surveyed area

17. See Bradbury, 1959.
18. Partly because patrilineal farmers bought their land through 'companies', and brothers were wont to join different groups, I cannot present any statistics for them.   19. See Hill, 1963:92 *et seq.*

(466 acres); some fifty-five other maternally related people owned about 30% (362 acres); and nineteen sons or daughters owned 8% (97 acres). Many farmers had tiny plots of one or two acres.

Although it is true that some of these 137 farmers in 1959 had cocoa farms in other localities, it is unlikely that any of the many small plot owners who were resident at Kofi Pare had significant acreages elsewhere. My question is, therefore, whether such a degree of inequality among kinsfolk is compatible with any conventional notion of class stratification? I think not.

Lloyd's important book on perceptions of social inequality among the urban Yoruba is very relevant, although it is much taken up with the superior position of the *educated* urban elite, with whom I am not here concerned.[20] I would say that Yorubaland is representative of West Africa generally in that 'the wealth of a prosperous trader was not usually replicated in any one of his sons' (p.190). More relevantly to present purposes, Lloyd concludes that 'the practice of polygyny effectively prevented a closed society, for the higher the status of the individual, in terms of power or wealth, the greater was the number of his children and the greater the likelihood that collectively they would in the next generation constitute a cross-section of the population, ranging from rich to poor, powerful to weak' (p.190). (See also p.96, n.6.) If there is a high degree of inequality among brothers in any community, does this in itself connote a lack of stratification?

This question was always in my mind in Dorayi, where, owing to the refusal of fathers to agree that any son should migrate, there were many resident sets of brothers whose situations were readily comparable.[21] The wealth classification (see pp.74–5 above) did show that few poorer sons, with fathers who had retired from farming, had rich brothers – and *vice versa*. This looked like stratification. But yet when I noted that: (a) only the sons of elderly rich men stood any significant chance of prospering during their father's lifetime; and (b) that most of the sons of rich men were not themselves rich – was 'incipient stratification' perhaps the correct

---

20. Lloyd, 1974. Of course a villager with educated sons in the city enjoys considerable prestige as a result, but in the smaller villages where there are no secondary schools, *where most of the rural population lives*, I think that the proportion of such men is seldom high enough to constitute a local *class*.   21. Hill, 1977.

term? But then again, if looked at from the point of view of the rapidly growing proportion of landless households and the virtual impossibility of upward mobility for such households, this was stratification with a vengeance.

Dorayi was a most anomalously overcrowded place – to the degree that it lacks all relevance for forecasting purposes.[22] In Batagarawa, which was a more ordinary village, I found that as rich men had many more wives during the course of their lives and accordingly more sons than other men, that these sons were not particularly favoured at the time of inheritance.[23] But this was partly compensated for by the superior ability of the sons of certain rich fathers to establish themselves as successful farmers on their own account during their father's lifetime, and by the superiority of their non-farming occupations. Whether this, too, has proved to be incipient stratification, perhaps mainly depends on the degree of stultification of the land market which has occurred meanwhile.

Most discussions of class stratification forget women. Lloyd does not, claiming that the status in the community of an adult woman depends 'as much on the prestige of her own descent group and of her wealth as a trader as on her husband' (p.180). Of course, *status* and *prestige* do not alone connote *class*. But is class usually bound up with male landownership? I fear that it is.

Turning, extremely briefly, to the Indian sub-continent, we find ourselves (as it were) on a different planet, where: first, the rigidities of caste (including strict rural caste endogamy); second, the maldistribution of farmland in favour of the upper castes; and third, the poor prospects of advancement for rural Harijans – are certainly sufficient reasons for regarding caste as a kind of cruel caricature of class, although one with its own peculiar characteristics. I here concentrate on the second and third of these considerations.

Many writers have provided evidence, which is mainly qualitative, for the maldistribution of landownership between castes as

22. See Hill, 1977 for justification for this.   23. Hill, 1972.

groups,[24] which is sometimes so striking that one is justified in thinking in terms of there being only one or two significant land-holding castes in a community. In south India, where there is everywhere a considerable sprinkling of Harijans, it is doubtful whether there are any communities such that there is not at least one *dominant* land-holding caste.[25] And wealth is to such a degree a function of land-holding, especially if the land be irrigated, that the case for expressing inequality in terms of *caste stratification* is not in doubt.

But, as already noted, statistical material relating to intra-caste landownership is remarkably scanty, which is why it is all too easy to assume, quite wrongly, that the pattern of land distribution by household for any dominant caste is unlikely to be widely dispersed. Yet the scanty evidence is that membership of a 'rich caste' is not, in itself, sufficient to assure a comfortable standard of living; and that it is not only in densely populated localities that much may depend on how many inheriting brothers a householder had when his father died. Small though the sample is, I cite estimated statistics relating to fifty-seven high caste (Reddy) households in two of the villages I studied in Karnataka, which show a high degree of intra-caste inequality;[26] the proportions of households which were landless or owned under 2 acres, between 2 and 5 acres, between 5 and 10 acres and 10 acres or more were, respectively 11%, 26%, 31% and 31%. (Of course the statistics for other castes, particularly for the Harijans, showed very much higher proportions of households who were landless or had hold-ings under 2 acres.)

Attracted by the large size of the sample (1,743 Tamil Nadu farm-holdings), I cite some statistics presented by Mencher, even

24. I am astonished that I could find so few reliable statistical sources. These include Epstein (1962:24), who found that in Wangala, in Karnataka state, 128 households of the Vokkaliga caste owned 89% of the farmland (average 4.4 acres), compared to the 28 Harijan (Adikarnataka) households who owned 7% (average 1.5 acres); and (for Karnataka) two official *Village Survey Monographs* (Nos. 16 and 29) which followed the 1960 population census. I also mention the case of one of the six Karnataka villages (Nanjapura) that I studied (Hill, 1982:56), where the 30 Harijan households together owned slightly less land (estimated at 37 acres) than the single richest individual (estimated at 44 acres).
25. In each of the six Karnataka villages one or two castes were unquestionably dominant in terms of wealth, size and other factors. See Hill, 1982:126 *et seq.*   26. *Ibid.*: 127.

though she herself has reservations as to their accuracy.[27] These
show a very considerable degree of intra-caste variation in landownership for the two highest castes (other than the Brahmins, for
whom the sample was too small): thus, if we take the size-ranges of
(a) 1 acre and under; (b) 1.1 to 2.5 acres; (c) 2.51 to 5.5 acres; (d)
5.51 to 10 acres; and (e) over 10 acres – the proportion of Reddiar
and Vellalar households respectively which fell into these groups
were: (a) 4%, 37%; (b) 10%, 23%; (c) 24%, 18%; (d) 36%, 13%; and
(e) 27%, 11%. In contrast, the intra-caste variation for the
Paraiyans, the mainstream Scheduled Caste, was very small: (a)
94%; (b) 4%; (c)2%; (d) nil – only 2 out of 574 Paraiyans owned
more than 2.5 acres.

'Caste in action' is indeed seen with a vengeance in relation to
the Harijans. Before discussing this, I need to mention that strict
caste ladders, of the textbook type, seem to have little relevance in
the middle reaches to the matter of economic inequality, whatever
members of the local community may feel about inter-dining,[28] for
example; so in multi-caste villages there is apt to be a fairly large,
undifferentiated grey area between the dominant and Scheduled
Castes, where caste may have little significance in terms of class
stratification.

I also need to emphasize that caste stratification does not
nowadays imply that the richest castes, at least in well-populated
areas, continuously get richer, in absolute terms, at the expense of
the poorer. The main reason for this is the growing unwillingness
of most landowners, however poor, to sell land so that, as already
noted, many high-caste men with several sons cannot top up their
holdings as much as they would wish by land purchase. Although
land, even dry land, is far from being a homogeneous factor,
particularly as a rich man may derive a considerable income from a
small acreage if he invests in an electrically operated pump set,[29] it
yet remains true that no man is considered wealthy by his peers

27. These consisted of unchecked figures obtained from village accountants, most of
which related to irrigated land (Mencher, 1978:138).
28. People being unwilling to accept food from those of lower caste than themselves.
29. There is a very great variation in the extent of the ownership of pump sets in south
India. Whereas in parts of Tamil Nadu they are so common that they are in danger of
upsetting the hydro-ecological balance, in the six Karnataka villages (population
c. 2,700) there were only 5 such sets.

(this attitude being an important element in anyone's standard of living) unless he owns a decent acreage. Indian rural society differs from the industrialized West in that in the latter there is (money apart) no scarce factor, corresponding to farmland, which rich men must acquire or lose all face.

Turning to the Harijans in ordinary villages in south India, they are locked in their poverty to an even greater degree than were factory workers in Britain two centuries ago, despite the efforts of successive Indian governments to relieve their plight. One trouble is that the decision made some twenty years ago, at least in some localities, to grant these generally landless men small plots of farmland came far too late, land prices having already risen so high that they had no hope of building up their holdings from a tiny base: the grant of one acre to a householder with three sons *is* a mere sop. As the evidence is that Harijans mainly depend on farm-labouring and other odd jobs[30] – that few of them have superior non-farming occupations – it follows that they can seldom better themselves except by migrating to town or city as educated or skilled men. But, despite the educational priorities they are accorded, relatively few Harijan parents can afford to send their sons to secondary schools and the number of Harijans who are in elite urban jobs is a tiny proportion of the vast Harijan population, which amounts to perhaps a fifth of the entire Indian population of over 700 million. Because most Harijans are too poor to migrate constructively, the likelihood is that they will become increasingly concentrated in the countryside. The statistics relating to the distributions of Harijans[31] in Bangalore District cited on p.132 above may well resemble those for other huge cities and neighbouring countryside.

To my mind, the matter of the appallingly low and worsening living standards of most rural Harijans is one of the world's most horrible problems, in both size and intractibility. Is it even conceivable that a massive programme of rural development, includ-

---

30. I refer to the 'mainstream Harijans' (who in Karnataka were the Adikarnatakas and Adidravidas), and not to certain much smaller castes who, despite having certain skills, for instance in stone quarrying or stone dressing, had been 'Scheduled'.
31. And, for all we know (since caste names are only very rarely mentioned in the census), many of these people may not be mainstream Harijans.

ing suitable industries[32], would be more than a palliative? Nor does
it seem likely that 'Harijan revolt' might spark off favourable and
sustainable developments, considering the huge dimensions of
this widespread problem and the jealousy of many other groups of
underprivileged people. Perhaps it is partly because some members of the urban elite, notably university students, make a
deliberate effort to expunge caste from their consciousness, that
rural rigidities are insufficiently appreciated? Certainly within the
villages any notion of an upwardly mobile Harijan is usually a con-
tradiction in terms.

Realizing that the query in this chapter's title still remains, I conclude by citing R.H.T. Smith, who believes that while 'Class is an
appropriate concept for anthropological analysis and, in some
circumstances an indispensable one', 'fine-grained analyses of
class formation in the modern world have not [yet] reached the
necessary degree of ethnographic specificity'.[33]

APPENDIX

Indian Share-Cropping

To condemn share-cropping outright, in the manner of many popular
writers,[34] would be as thoughtless as any blanket condemnation of tenancy
or agricultural labouring. In any particular instance moral judgements
have to be suspended, pending examination of the terms and conditions
as well as of the alternative strategies open to landless tenants and
landlords.

Ironically, many instinctive critics of share-cropping are unaware of the
correct definition of this form of tenancy. Systems such that the tenant
pays out a share of the crop as rent are not share-cropping proper *unless the
landlord provides some inputs*, such as plough animals or fertilizers, *additional
to land*. This was made quite clear by both Adam Smith[35] and Alfred

32. It is conventional in India to refer to the need for 'cottage industries', whereas modern
    factories are required.
33. R.H.T. Smith, 1984:490 – 491.
34. Including Myrdal (1968) on, for example, pp.1065 *et seq.*
35. 'The proprietor furnished them with seed, cattle and instruments of husbandry, the
    whole stock, in short, necessary for cultivating the farm' (Adam Smith, 1776
    (1970 ed.:490)).

Marshall,[36] each of whom pointed out that *métayage* (share-cropping) was unknown in England – hence the ignorance of so many British economists. Definitional confusion is compounded in India, where there are not *necessarily* any words in regional languages which distinguish share-croppers proper from annual labourers (in some instances) or from tenants (in others).

The recent ethnographic literature on share-cropping being less abundant than one might expect, I start by citing Buchanan who, when travelling in present-day Tamil Nadu, distinguished annual labourers (*pudial*) from share-croppers (*pungal*).

The *Pungals* go to a rich farmer and for a share of the crop undertake to cultivate his lands. He advances the cattle, implements, seed, and money or grain, that is necessary for the subsistance of the *Pungals*. He also gives each family a house. He takes no share in the labour, which is all performed by the *Pungals* and their wives and children . . .'[37]

If a farmer employed six *pungals* they were rewarded with six-fifteenths of the produce, from which share they had to repay any sums advanced for their subsistence. Buchanan added that farmers preferred to employ *pudials* when they were available, but that 'among the labourers the condition of the *Pungals* is considered as preferable to that of the *Pudials*'.

Kumar referred to a type of share-cropper (*parakudi*) in the Madras Presidency (now Tamil Nadu) in the nineteenth century, who was a tenant from outside the village, his lease being usually for a single year. All the capital was provided by the landlord, who might even have granted a loan for the tenant's living expenses. 'The incomes of the poorest crop-sharer and the agricultural labourer were frequently the same . . . Indeed the same person might play both parts.'[38] Also, the *parakudi* might have received daily wages during the harvest.

Baker, referring to the Tamilnad valleys, emphasized that there was 'a range of labour relationships'[39] from indentured labour (at the one extreme) to various stages of *waram*[40] (share-cropping) at the other. The share-croppers' percentage varied inversely with the quality of the land and the quantity of fixed and working capital provided by the landlord: thus the tenant might get only 20% if the land were rich and all capital were provided. While *waram* was to be distinguished from *kuthagai* tenancy,

---

36. Métayage 'enables a man who has next to no capital of his own to obtain the use of it at a lower charge than he could in any other way, and to have more freedom and responsibility than he would as a hired labourer. . .' (Marshall, 1890:731).
37. Buchanan, 1807, vol. II:320.
38. Kumar, 1965:29.   39. Baker, 1984:172.   40. More usually rendered *varam*.

which involved fixed grain rents payable to landlords who were usually absentees, the latter type of landlord might have provided manure and seed. In 1946 the *waramdars* in one district revolted (p.195) and seized the whole crop, as a result of which their share rose from one-third to 45% – they were also allotted the straw since their landlords no longer provided the cattle.

Mencher, writing about a later period, distinguished between *al-varam*, such that the landlord provided all inputs save labour, the tenant possibly getting a quarter share of the crop, and the much commoner *per-padi varam*, with lower landlords' inputs and equal division of the crop.[41] She noted that the demand for *al-varam* land sometimes exceeded the supply. If the land were irrigated from a tube-well, then one-third shares might go respectively to the tenant, the landlord and (to finance) the tube-well.

Since the advent of Land Reform, which commonly made tenancy illegal[42], share-cropping (where it existed[43]) had, presumably, declined in importance and been driven underground where it still persists – which is not to imply that it has everywhere sunk into insignificance.[44]

For the landlord the advantages of share-cropping *as a system* are evident enough, for he receives a share of the crop without having either to work on the land himself (though he ought to be around at harvest time) or to supervise daily-paid labourers – but he is apt to incur some risks, such as the mishandling of his plough animals. The landless tenant of small means who owns no plough animals may well prefer the security of share-cropping to the insecurity of day-labouring; and his rewards may be somewhat higher, especially as he and members of his family may also work as day-labourers on other farms. As the evidence seems to be that share-cropping tenancies are very short-term, the supply of potential tenants is, presumably, commonly adequate.

One of the few writers to attempt an objective assessment of Indian share-cropping generally is Hanumantha Rao. He points out that 'Economists have, by and large, viewed sharecropping arrangements as inefficient and owner farming and leasing on a fixed-rent basis as conducive to the efficient use of land.'[45] While his own conclusions are, unfortunately, very generalized, involving such a notion as 'the scope for decision making' in any *locality*, it seems to be the responsibility of his

41. Mencher, 1978:84 *et seq.*
42. Even if it is not illegal (which is by no means clear), the farmers commonly believe that it is – see Bliss and Stern, 1982:132, n.6.
43. As noted in Hill (1982:58), share-cropping has apparently been rare in Karnataka for at least the last century.
44. Hanumantha Rao (1971:579, n.) claimed that 'despite public legislation to discourage share tenancy, many resident landlords in rice-growing as well as wheat-growing regions continue to lease out land...'   45. *Ibid.*: 578.

opponents to dispute the truth of his final sentence: '*When the relevant alternatives are specified* [my italics], the evidence examined does not indicate significant inefficiencies in the use of land under share-cropping.' After a theoretical discussion, running to no less than nineteen pages, Bliss and Stern (1982) come to much the same conclusion about Palanpur village.

As for the moral issues involved, these are surely matters of fact not principle?[46] Just as the wages of farm labourers are *commonly* far too low, in terms both of the standard of living they provide and the ability of the employer to afford them, so the same may be *commonly* true of the croppers' share – but we need more information.

46. Schendel (1981:112) has pointed out that the system of borrowing a cow and paying a calf in return (see Hill, 1982:163) is analogous to share-cropping: but it excites no moral revulsion.

POSTSCRIPT
DOOMSDAY ECONOMICS

One reason for the sharply declining interest of the Western world in general problems of underdevelopment is the false belief, which I have discussed above, that conditions in the third world are already so catastrophic as to have passed the point of no return: the terrible famines in Ethiopia and Sudan are widely regarded as indicative of things shortly to come in many other African regions. Such attitudes are fostered by numerous academic and popular doom-mongers, marxists and non-marxists alike, whose amorphous despair, apparently compassionate but actually very denigratory of the third world, appeals to a wide public which has hardly any knowledge of Africa's geography. Before starting to write this book I asked a well-known Cambridge bookseller to identify the best-selling author on developing countries for first-year students and was unhesitatingly referred to Paul Harrison's *Inside the Third World*.[1] On glancing at this work, by an author who is not an economist[2] but who had undertaken five years' research and travel in Asia, Latin America and Africa, I at once realized that it is an example of doomsday economics *par excellence*, its approach being indicated by the citation from Tagore at the head of Chapter I: 'We live under the tyranny of the tropics, paying heavy toll every moment for the barest right of existence.'

What is doomsday economics? It is the simple conviction that, mainly owing to very rapid population growth, crop yields per acre have been declining so fast for the past few decades that living standards in the rural tropical world generally are already so catastrophically low that only a wholly unrealistic 'package of reforms'

---

1. *Inside the Third World: The Anatomy of Poverty* (1984). This book of 512 pages was first published by Penguin in 1979; the second edition of 1981 had been reprinted five times by 1984. See, also, Harrison's *The Third World Tomorrow* (1980).
2. The author is described as 'a freelance writer and journalist'; at one time he lectured in French at the University of Ife, Nigeria.

could conceivably prevent uncontrollable chaos. Essential elements in Harrison's 'package' are that co-operative farming
should be introduced;[3] that birth-rates should be immensely
reduced; that conservation should take priority everywhere; and
that Western aid should be increased – far beyond any scale which
would be acceptable to the complacent peoples of the West and
their mainly reactionary governments. Most of Harrison's book is
concerned with the hopelessness of any less fundamental 'sol-
utions', which would usually only succeed in making things
worse;[4] speaking on behalf of the third world, the author behaves
like a sick man who rejects all the foods and medicines offered by
his well-wishers.

It is mainly by means of citation and reference that I must briefly
justify my knowledge that doom-mongering of this kind (which
leans so heavily on the 'prevailing orthodoxy' exposed on pp.68–9
above) is as intellectually unsound as it is demoralizing to world
sentiment. I start with population factors.

Harrison does not sufficiently emphasize that the population of
sub-Saharan Africa is sparse on world standards (pp.63–4 above),
as well as being unevenly distributed. There is no evidence for the
'population explosion' which he regards as a fact in Nigeria; certainly, population is likely to have been increasing fast there in the
past few decades but (pp.60–5 above) *explosion* is not the word, and
there have never been any reliable censuses.[5] In discussing the
various incentives to have larger families, Harrison states that 'In
most of traditional Africa[6] the man with three or four sons is

3. The author refers (p.420) to the need for 'co-operatively worked estates' without
   regard to the facts that, contrary to common prevailing belief, there is no evidence
   that communal arable farming (as distinct from communal grazing) has ever found
   favour in Africa or south India, and that 'socialist communal farming' has always failed
   wherever it has been imposed on African people – even, on Nyerere's own admission,
   in Tanzania.
4. It is most unfortunate that *Indigenous Agricultural Revolution: Ecology and Food Production in
   West Africa* by P. Richards (1985) did not appear until this book had gone to press, for it
   provides fascinating evidence of the ability of ordinary farmers to intensify their
   agriculture by means of experimentation, investment and hard work – evidence which
   should greatly encourage governments, for their part, to do much more in the way of
   providing improved seeds, chemical fertilizers, etc. In other words, as this knowledge
   about the farmers spreads, 'decreasing returns' should become increasingly
   avoidable.
5. The earliest censuses were to such a degree under-counts (and not only because farm-
   slaves went unenumerated) that it is by no means certain that the widespread belief
   that the Nigerian population has quadrupled during this century is justified.
6. The expression 'traditional Africa' sometimes relates to the past, sometimes to
   the present.

allocated [my italics] more land to work' (p.222); but such an allocation system, far from being usual, is unknown in West Africa (for
example), where, in any case, land is not generally allocated by any
authority. Then, how can he possibly know that 'In most places it
still costs less to raise an extra child than the potential gain from
his labour, his marriage alliance, or his support in old age'? Or that
a contributory factor to high child-mortality rate is that 'children
get lowest priority in the share-out of family food supplies'
(p.263)?

While it is true that Harrison does very occasionally express
doubts about the quality of official statistics relating to the rural
tropical world, his book is crowded with unqualified statements
such as the following: that between 1969–71 and 1981 the demand
for food in third-world countries grew 0.2% faster than production; that 1,210 million people were 'seriously poor' in 1976;
that the number of people 'short of fuelwood' in 95 countries was
1,395 million in 1980; that developing countries got 22% of the
world's income in 1976; and that 'estimates of the extent of
poverty in the Third World show considerable agreement,
whatever the particular measure that is used' (p.405).

When dealing with land tenure and allied matters in Chapter 4
('Eco-Catastrophe in Africa') and elsewhere, Harrison confuses
shifting cultivation with bush fallow; asserts that 'everywhere in
Africa, as population has grown, fallow-periods . . . have shrunk'
(p.65);[7] holds that dry (unirrigated) land is 'unproductive' (p.404);
asserts that the general spur to African migration to the cities is the
exhaustion of the soil; believes that 'traditional forms of land
tenure [generally] brake technological progress' (p.73); supposes
that in Africa it is only *now* that 'private property in land is emerg-
ing' (p.74) and that land still cannot be sold;[8] and is seen to hold the
conventional idea that there was a former Golden Age of
'egalitarianism' (p.419), which indeed still often prevails (p.73).[9]
All these are misbeliefs which I have dealt with above.

Such a conventionally emotional approach means that no
attempt can be made, by the author or anyone else, to fit the

---

7. Only in a *very* small number of localities, at least in West Africa, is there *any* firm
   evidence on fallow periods.   8. See citation on p.146 above.
9. Elsewhere in the book he deplores inegalitarianism which is never innate, so that it is
   always necessary to look for individual scapegoats in a community.

BRIEF GLOSSARY WITH
A LIST OF PLACE NAMES, ETC.

❧

* *Asterisks refer the reader to other entries*

abusa	Meaning 'one-third' in Akan* languages, the word is applied to workers on cocoa farms who receive a one-third share of the crop.
Accra	The capital of Ghana*.
Accra plains	An anomalous coastal plain, centred on Accra*, where cattle-rearing is possible.
affines	Persons related by marriage not blood.
Akan	A cluster of ethnic groups (and languages) in southern Ghana* and the Ivory Coast, including the Akim, the Fante and the Ashanti*.
Akwapim	The polyglot state in southern Ghana*, mainly situated on a high scarp near Accra*, which was the home of most of the earliest migrant cocoa farmers.
Ashanti	An ancient kingdom, situated in the north of the Ghanaian forest zone.
Bangalore	The huge city which is the capital of Karnataka* state in south India.
Batagarawa	A Hausa* village, some 6 miles south of Katsina* city. See Hill, 1972.
bonded labourer	An 'attached' Indian farm labourer* who contracts to work for his employer for a year or more; he may or may not be indebted to his employer.
Brahmin	The highest caste* throughout India.
bush fallow	A farming system such that the farmland has to revert to 'bush' (to be fallowed) after one or two crop-plantings for a period of some years.
caravan	The long-distance trading caravans of savannah West Africa* were often composed of many traders, and other people, with their transport animals.
cash crop	A useless and also a misleading term, since all crops are apt to be sold for cash and since, nowadays, it is so often wrongly equated with 'export crop'.
cassava (manioc)	A root crop grown very widely in the West African forest zone, which is something of a 'luxury crop' in the savannah.

caste	A system of social ranking such that a population is divided into hierarchically ranked corporate groups, according to criteria of ritual purity and pollution; in rural India most caste members are endogamous*.
casuarina	In south India the casuarina tree, which grows very rapidly, provides much-valued fuel; especially near cities, there is an increasing tendency for casuarina plantations to replace arable plots. See Hill, 1982.
clan	A corporate group claiming descent from an unknown or mythical ancestor, through either the male or the female line.
cocoa	*Theobroma cacao*. The cocoa bean grows in pods hanging from the trunks of long-lived orchard trees which first come into bearing, according to variety, some five years or more after planting.
crop mixtures	Two or more crops grown simultaneously on the same farm-plot*.
descent group	A corporate clan* or lineage*.
donkey	The ubiquitous beast of burden in much of the West African savannah*.
Dorayi	The name given to a very densely populated farming locality of dispersed settlement just south of Kano* city. See Hill, 1977.
dry season	The period(s) when no rain falls: it extends to considerably more than half the year in Hausaland.
endogamy	Marriage systems such that spouses belong to the same caste* or descent group*.
ethnic group	The modern synonym for 'tribe' in West Africa*.
Ewe	The homeland of the Ewe people is in south-eastern Ghana* and nearby Togo.
exogamy	Marriage systems such that spouses belong to different descent* or caste* groups.
family property	Property, such as farmland, over which individual lineage* members exert usufructural* rights only.
FAO	Food and Agriculture Organization; one of the UN's specialized agencies.
farm	An ambiguous word meaning either farm-holding* or farm-plot*.
farmer	Strictly a man or woman who cultivates land for the direct benefit of his/her household, but often identified with householder*.
farm-holding	The set of farm-plots* cultivated by any farming household.
farm labourer	A hired agricultural worker; usually a day-labourer unless otherwise stated.

farm-plot	A set of non-contiguous farm-plots, or fields, comprises a farm-holding*.
farming household	A kin group which usually lives in the same house and cultivates the same land.
fertilizers	Chemicals, not organic manure such as dung.
forest	Owing to clearing for cultivation, little high or even thick forest remains in the West African forest zone.
fragmentation	The division, on inheritance, of tiny farm-plots* into even smaller portions.
gandu	A Hausa* farming organization such that married sons continue to work on their fathers' farms.
Ghana	The name assumed by the Gold Coast* when it achieved its Independence in 1957.
Gold Coast	See **Ghana**.
grain	Unless otherwise stated, 'grain' refers to sorghum (guinea corn) and millet only.
green revolution	A somewhat outmoded term which particularly relates to the introduction of new high-yielding varieties of irrigated paddy* and to associated new technologies in South Asia.
Harijan	Mahatma Gandhi's euphemistic term for the former Untouchable castes* in India; synonymous with Scheduled Caste*.
Hausa	Strictly a northern Nigerian language rather than an ethnic group; much the largest linguistic group in sub-Saharan Africa*.
Hausaland	For a tentative map of Hausaland see Hill, 1972.
household	(i) Nuclear; this basically consists of a conjugal pair, or widowed person, together with unmarried children. (ii) Joint; this Indian term is here applied, in vague general principle, to households which include either dependent married sons of the householder or one or more of his married brothers.
householder	The household head.
Ibo (Igbo)	An important eastern Nigerian* ethnic group*.
inter-cropping	See **crop-mixtures**.
Kano	An enormous Hausa* city in northern Nigeria*.
Kano Close Settled Zone	A huge farming area of dispersed settlement around Kano* city. See Hill, 1977.
Karnataka	A large and populous modern state in south India, mainly on the Deccan plateau; much larger than the former princely state of Mysore which formed its basis.
Karnataka villages	Six villages in Anekal Taluk in south-eastern Karnataka*, which lie some 15 to 20 miles south of

Bangalore city; see Hill, 1982. Hullahalli and Nanjapura are two of these villages.

Katsina   A large Hausa* city in northern Nigeria*.

Kerala   A narrow, populous, coastal state in the extreme south-west of India, with many special characteristics.

kola-nuts   An important item of long-distance trade in West Africa, since the nuts grow in the south and are largely consumed in the north; a stimulant with many ceremonial uses.

Krobo   A southern Ghanaian ethnic group* which led the way in the large-scale purchase of farmland.

landless   An ambiguous word, best related to whole households which cultivate no land on their own account.

landless labourer   A term best avoided since in both south India and West Africa many day-labourers are not members of landless households.

landlord   A person whose rights over farmland are superior in kind to those of other indigenes.

Land Reform   The legislation which was introduced by individual Indian states from the 1960s; intended to effect a more equable distribution of farmland, its results have been generally disappointing.

land revenue   The Indian system of taxing registered farmland which was introduced by the British Raj during the last century, and is still intact.

lineage   A group of kin tracing its descent, through either the male or the female line, from a named forebear; hence matrilineal*, patrilineal*.

market place   An authorized concourse of buyers and sellers, meeting at a certain place at an appointed time; rural periodic market places, unlike city markets, are open only on certain days of the local 'market week'.

Marketing Board   Statutory West African authorities with a sole right to purchase (through their licensed buying agents) certain produce including cocoa, which is usually for export, at fixed minimum prices.

matrilineal   Systems of succession and inheritance such that offices and property pass only to those claiming descent in the female line.

moneylender   Best used to denote only non-cultivators whose main business is lending money at interest, maybe in connection with trade; a far less general word than 'creditor'.

monogamous	Marriage systems such that men only have one wife at any time. (Although in this book south Indian societies are generally regarded as 'monogamous' in contrast to West African societies which are 'polygynous', there is actually a small incidence of polygyny* in rural south India.)
mortgage	In many West African and south Indian regions farmland is commonly mortgaged (pledged) in return for a loan, the mortgagee usually having the right of cultivation until the farm is redeemed.
Nigeria	An immense West African country, which includes hundreds of ethnic groups, most notably the Hausa*, the Yoruba* and the Ibo*; even though official population estimates are far from reliable, it is safe to affirm that Nigeria is far and away the most populous country in sub-Saharan Africa*. Her economy is most precarious since over four-fifths of the total value of her rapidly declining exports currently consists of oil.
oil palm	The wild palm is ubiquitous in the West African forest zone, usually scattered, but also in pure stands; the source of palm oil, palm kernel oil and palm wine.
paddy	Rice in its raw, unhusked, state.
padial	A Tamil (south Indian) word for a bonded or 'attached' farm labourer*; also known as *panniyal*.
panchayat	Nowadays usually a group of Indian revenue villages*.
patrilineal	As matrilineal*, but in the male line.
peasant	Generally indefinable in the rural tropical world.
polygynous	A man is polygynous if he has more than one wife; a society is regarded as such if most married men, other than the young, *aspire* to have two or more wives.
revenue village	For the purposes of taxing Indian farmland (see **land revenue**), revenue villages, with fixed boundaries, were identified.
Sahel	The relatively sparsely populated West African Sahel is the zone intermediate between the savannah and the Sahara, where pastoralism has long been far more important than arable farming.
savannah (savanna)	The West African* savannah zone is a vast elevated grassland, which is commonly dotted with useful trees; unlike the forest zone, which lies to the south, it has one rainy season; in some regions there is a

	considerable intermediate zone, between forest and savannah, sometimes known as 'orchard bush'. Grains* and groundnuts are the staple crops. See Morgan and Pugh, 1969.
Scheduled Castes	The lowest castes*, former Untouchables, which for their advancement are Scheduled in the Indian Constitution.
self-acquired property	Property, such as land for cocoa farming, which the owner had bought for himself, so that he may dispose of it as he wishes.
share-cropping	A form of renting (*métayage*) such that the tenant retains only a portion of the crop and the landlord provides some inputs additional to land.
subsistence farmer	A derogatory, confusing and old-fashioned term which is best avoided since it is often held to imply both household self-sufficiency and no crop-selling – in short 'aboriginal equilibrium'.
sub-Saharan Africa	Colloquially known as 'Black Africa', this 'part continent' consists of West Africa* (except insofar as it extends into the Sahara) and of all countries farther south other than South Africa; Ethiopia, Sudan and Somalia are excluded.
surplus	This word is best avoided in the sense of 'sale of surplus crops', since its use often wrongly implies that all sales are of produce in excess of household requirements.
Tallensi	A small ethnic group in north-eastern Ghana made famous through the work of M. Fortes (1945, 1949).
Tamilnad	Literally the land of the Tamil-speaking peoples of south India; as defined by Baker (1984) it excludes part of the modern state of Tamil Nadu.
tank	The English word for an Indian or Sri Lankan communal irrigation reservoir, usually created by damming streams.
trypanosomiasis	A disease transmitted by the tsetse fly which still makes cattle-rearing impossible in the West African forest zone.
usufructural right	The right as cultivator to the use of the land's produce.
West Africa	There are sixteen West African states extending from Mauritania in the north-west to Nigeria* in the south-east; the four (Anglophone) ex-British colonies are the Gambia, Ghana*, Nigeria* and Sierra Leone. Despite the general unreliability of population

estimates, it is certain that Nigeria alone accounts for at least a half of West Africa's population, Ghana (the next most populous country) for less than 10%.

yam A much-coveted West African root crop, the distribution of which is far less widespread than that of cassava*; the individual tubers are grown in mounds, the vine being staked.

yield When unqualified this word usually relates the volume of crop production to the area under cultivation.

Yoruba An important ethnic group* in south-western Nigeria*.

zamindar A former hereditary estate-holder in north India and also in certain other regions, including Madras Province.

REFERENCES

～✺～

(Official publications are not listed.)

Aboyade, O. *Integrated Economics: A Study of Developing Economies*. Addison-Wesley, London, 1983

Abu, Katherine. 'The Separateness of Spouses: Conjugal Resources in an Ashanti town', *in* Oppong (ed.), 1983

Addo, N.O. 'Employment and Labour Conditions on Ghana's Cocoa Farms', *in* Kotey *et al.* (eds.), 1974

Altekar, A.S. *The Position of Women in Hindu Civilization*. Motilal Banarsidass, Delhi, 1973

Amin, S. (ed.) *Modern Migrations in Western Africa*. Oxford University Press, London, 1974

Ardener, Shirley (ed.) *Perceiving Women*. Dent, London, 1975

Bailey, F.G. *Caste and the Economic Frontier*. Manchester University Press, 1957

'Capital, Saving and Credit in Highland Orissa (India)', *in* Firth and Yamey (eds.), 1964

Baker, C.J. 'Debt and the Depression in Madras, 1929–36', *in* Dewey and Hopkins (eds.), 1978

The Tamilnad Countryside. Clarendon Press, Oxford, 1984

Bayly, C.A. *Rulers, Townsmen and Bazaars: North Indian Society in the Age of British Expansion 1770–1870*. Cambridge University Press, 1983

Beckett, W.H. *Akokoaso: A Survey of a Gold Coast Village*. London School of Economics, Monographs on Social Anthropology, 1944

Beckman, B. *Organizing the Farmers: Cocoa Politics and National Development in Ghana*. The Scandinavian Institute of African Studies, Uppsala, 1976

Beneria, L. (ed.) *Women and Development: The Sexual Division of Labor in Rural Societies*. ILO. Praeger Publishers, New York, 1982

Bernard, H.R., Kilworth, P., Kronenfeld, D. and Sailer, L. 'The Problem of Informant Accuracy: The Validity of Retrospective Data', *Annual Review of Anthropology*, 13, 1984

Berry, Sara S. *Cocoa, Custom and Socio-Economic Change in Rural Western Nigeria*. Clarendon Press, Oxford, 1975

Béteille, A. *Studies in Agrarian Social Structure*. Oxford University Press, London, 1974

Bliss, C.J. and Stern, N.H. *Palanpur: The Economy of an Indian Village*. Clarendon Press, Oxford, 1982

Bohannan, P. and Dalton, G. (eds.) *Markets in Africa*. Northwestern University Press, 1962

Bohannan, P. and Laura. *Tiv Economy*. Longman, London, 1968

Bose, A. (eds.) 'Migration Streams in India'. *International Population Conference*. Sydney, 1967

Boserup, Ester. *The Conditions of Agricultural Growth*. Allen & Unwin, London, 1965

    Women's Role in Economic Development. Allen & Unwin, London, 1970

Boutillier, J.-L. *Bongouanou Côte d'Ivoire*. Berger-Levrault, Paris, 1960

Bradbury, R.E. *The Benin Kingdom and the Edo-Speaking Peoples of South-Western Nigeria*. Ethnographic Survey of Africa, International African Institute, London, 1957

Breman, J. *Patronage and Exploitation: Changing Agrarian Relationships in South Gujarat*. University of California Press, 1974

Bromley, R.J. *Periodic Markets, Daily Markets and Fairs: A Bibliography*. Centre for Development Studies, University College of Swansea, 1977

    Supplement to Bromley (1977), University College of Swansea, 1979

Bruce-Chwatt, L.J. *Essential Malariology*. Heinemann Medical Books, London, 1980

Buchanan, F. *A Journey from Madras through the Countries of Mysore, Canara and Malabar*. β vols. London, 1807

Cassen, R.H. *India: Population, Economy, Society*. Macmillan, London, 1978

Chambers, R. *Rural Development: Putting the Last First*. Longman, London, 1983

Chandra, R.D. (ed.) *Critical Reviews in Tropical Medicine*, Vol.2. Plenum Press, New York, 1982

Charlesworth, N. 'Rich Peasants and Poor Peasants in late Nineteenth-century Maharashtra', *in* Dewey and Hopkins (eds.), 1978

    Peasant and Imperial Rule: Agriculture and Agrarian Society in the Bombay Presidency, 1850–1935. Cambridge University Press, 1985

Charsley, S.R. *Culture and Sericulture: Social Anthropology and Development in a South Indian Livestock Industry*. Academic Press, London, 1982

Chaudhuri, K.N. and Dewey, C.J. (eds.) *Economy and Society: Essays in Indian Economic and Social History*. Oxford University Press, Delhi, 1979

Chayanov, A.V. *The Theory of Peasant Economy*. 1925 translated for American Economic Association, 1966

Connell, J., Dasgupta, B., Laishley, R. and Lipton, M. *Migration from Rural Areas: The Evidence from Village Studies*. Institute of Development Studies, Oxford University Press, Delhi, 1976

Dalton, G. *Economic Anthropology and Development: Essays on Tribal and Peasant Economies*. Basic Books, New York, 1971

    (ed.) *see* Bohannan and Dalton (eds.), 1962

(ed.) *Primitive, Archaic and Modern Economies: Essays of Karl Polanyi*. Anchor Books, New York, 1968

Derrett, J.D.M. (ed.) *Studies in the Laws of Succession in Nigeria*. Oxford University Press, London, 1965

Dewey, C. '*Patwari* and *Chaukidar*: Subordinate Officials and the Reliability of India's Agricultural Statistics', *in* Dewey *et al.* (eds.), 1978
see Chaudhuri and Dewey (eds.), 1979

Dewey, C. and Hopkins, A.G. (eds.) *The Imperial Impact: Studies in the Economic History of Africa and India*. The Athlone Press, University of London, 1978

Djurfeldt, G. and Lindberg, S. *Behind Poverty: The Social Formation in a Tamil Village*. Curzon Press, London, 1975

Dumont, L. *Homo Hierarchicus: The Caste System and its Implications*. Weidenfeld, London, 1970

Dunn, J. and Robertson, A.F. *Dependence and Opportunity: Political Change in Ahafo*. Cambridge University Press, 1973

Dupire, Marguerite. 'Planteurs autochtones et étrangers en Basse-Côte d'Ivoire orientale'. *Etudes Eburnéennes*, Abidjan, 1960

Dyson, T. 'Infant and Child Mortality in Developing Countries', *in* Chandra (ed.), 1982

Enke, S. *Economics for Development*. Dennis Hobson, London, 1964

Epstein, T. Scarlett. *Economic Development and Social Change in South Asia*. Manchester University Press, 1962
South India: Yesterday, Today and Tomorrow. Macmillan, London, 1973

Etienne, G. *India's Changing Rural Scene 1963–1979*. Oxford University Press, Delhi, 1982

Fallers, L.A. 'Are African Cultivators to be called "Peasants"?' *Current Anthropology*, April, 1961

Farmer, B.H. (ed.) *Green Revolution? Technology and Change in Rice-Growing Areas of Tamil Nadu and Sri Lanka*. Macmillan, London, 1977

Firth, R. (ed.) *Man and Culture: An Evaluation of the Work of Bronislaw Malinowski*. Routledge & Kegan Paul, London, 1957

Firth, R. and Yamey, B.S. (eds.) *Capital, Saving and Credit in Peasant Societies*. Allen & Unwin, London, 1964

Forde, D. 'The Rural Economies', *in* Perham (ed.), 1946
Yakö Studies. Oxford University Press, London, 1964

Fortes, M. *The Dynamics of Clanship among the Tallensi*. Oxford University Press, London, 1945
The Web of Kinship among the Tallensi. Oxford University Press, London, 1949
'Kinship and Marriage among the Ashanti', *in* Radcliffe-Brown and Forde (eds.), 1950
Time and Social Structure and other Essays. The Athlone Press, University of London, 1970

'Strangers', *in* Fortes and Patterson (eds.), 1975

'An Anthropologist's Apprenticeship'. *Annual Review of Anthropology*, 7, 1978

Fortes, M. and Patterson, Sheila (eds.) *Studies in African Social Anthropology*. Academic Press, London, 1975

Francis, P. 'For the Use and Common Benefit of all Nigerians: Consequences of the 1978 Land Nationalization.' *Africa*, 54(3), 1984

Fröhlich, W. 'Das afrikanische Marktwesen'. *Zeitschrift für Ethnologie*, 1940

Galletti, R., Baldwin, K.D.S. and Dina, I.O. *Nigerian Cocoa Farmers: An Economic Survey of Yoruba Cocoa Farming Families*. Oxford University Press, London, 1956

Geertz, C. *Agricultural Involution*. University of California Press, Berkeley, 1963

'Culture and Social Change: The Indonesian Case'. *Man*, Dec. 1984

Ghatak, S. and Ingersent, K. *Agriculture and Economic Development*. Harvester Press, Brighton, 1984

Goody, J.R. *Technology, Tradition and the State in Africa*. Cambridge University Press, 1971

(ed.) *The Developmental Cycle in Domestic Groups*. Cambridge University Press, 1958

(ed.) *Changing Social Structure in Ghana*. International African Institute, London, 1975

Gosal, G.S. 'Redistribution of Population in Punjab 1951–61', *in* Bose (ed.), 1967

Gough, Kathleen. 'Agricultural Labour in Thanjavur', *in* Mencher (ed.), 1983

Grillo, R. and Rew, A. (eds.) *Social Anthropology and Development Policy*. Tavistock Publications, London, 1985

Grove, Jean M. 'Some Aspects of the Economy of the Volta Delta (Ghana)'. *Bulletin de l'IFAN*, Jan. to April 1966

Gulati, Leela. *Profiles in Female Poverty: A Study of Five Poor Working Women in Kerala*. Hindustan Publishing Corporation, Delhi, 1981

Gutkind, P.C.W. (ed.) *see* Jongmans and Gutkind (eds.), 1967

Guyer, Jane I. 'Women's Work and Production Systems'. *Review of African Political Economy*, 27/28, 1984

Hancock, W.K. *Survey of British Commonwealth Affairs*, Vol. II, Part II. Oxford University Press, London, 1940

Hanumantha Rao, C.H. 'Uncertainty, Entrepreneurship and Share-cropping in India.' *Journal of Political Economy*, 79, 1971

Harris, M. 'The Cultural Ecology of India's Sacred Cattle'. *Current Anthropology*, Feb. 1966

Harrison, P. *Inside the Third World*. Penguin, Harmondsworth, 1984 edition

Harriss, Barbara. *Agricultural Marketing in the Semi-Arid Tropics of West Africa.* University of East Anglia, 1982
Exchange Relations and Poverty in Dryland Agriculture: Studies of South India. Concept Publishing, New Delhi, 1984

Harriss, J. 'The Limitations of HYV technology in North Arcot District' *in* Farmer (ed.), 1977
Capitalism and Peasant Farming: Agrarian Structure and Ideology in Northern Tamil Nadu. Oxford University Press, Bombay, 1982

Hart, J.K. 'Migration and the Opportunity Structure: A Ghanaian Case Study', *in* Amin (ed.), 1974
The Political Economy of West African Agriculture. Cambridge University Press, 1982

Higgins, B. *Economic Development.* Constable, London, 1959

Hill, Polly. 'The Creditors Come Too'. *West Africa*, 21 Nov. 1953
The Gold Coast Cocoa Farmer. Oxford University Press, London, 1956
The Migrant Cocoa-Farmers of Southern Ghana: A Study in Rural Capitalism. Cambridge University Press, 1963
'Notes on Traditional Market Authority and Market Periodicity in West Africa'. *Journal of African History*, VII, 2, 1966a
'Landlords and brokers: A West African trading system'. *Cahiers d'Études Africaines*. 1966b
'Hidden Trade in Hausaland'. *Man*, Sept. 1969
Studies in Rural Capitalism in West Africa. Cambridge University Press, 1970a
The Occupations of Migrants in Ghana. Museum of Anthropology, University of Michigan, Ann Arbor, 1970b
Rural Hausa: A Village and a Setting. Cambridge University Press, 1972
'The West African Farming Household', *in* Goody (ed.), 1975
Population, Prosperity and Poverty: Rural Kano 1900 and 1970. Cambridge University Press, 1977
'Food-farming and Migration from Fante Villages'. *Africa*, 48(3), 1978
Dry Grain Farming Families: Hausaland (Nigeria) and Karnataka (India) Compared. Cambridge University Press, 1982
'The Poor Quality of Official Socio-economic Statistics Relating to the Rural Tropical World: With Special Reference to south India'. *Modern Asian Studies*, July, 1984
'The Practical Need for a Socio-economic Classification of Tropical Agrarian Systems', *in* Grillo *et al.* (eds.), 1985a
Indigenous Trade and Market Places in Ghana 1962–64. (Edited oral material.) Jos Oral History and Literature Texts, University of Jos, Nigeria, 1985b

Hirschman, A. *The Strategy of Economic Development.* Yale University Press, New Haven, 1958

Hogendorn, J.S. *Nigerian Groundnut Exports: Origins and Early Development.*

Ahmadu Bello University Press, Zaria, 1978

Hopkins, A.G. *An Economic History of West Africa*. Longman, London, 1973

(ed.) *see* Dewey and Hopkins (eds.), 1979

Hopper, W.D. *The Economic Organization of a Village in North Central India*. PhD Thesis, Cornell University, 1957

Humphrey, Caroline. 'Barter and Economic Disintegration'. *Man*, 20, 1, March 1985

Husain, S.A. *Agricultural Marketing in Northern India*. Allen & Unwin, London, 1937

Iliffe, J. *A Modern History of Tanganyika*. Cambridge University Press, 1979

Ingersent, K. *see* Ghatak and Ingersent (eds.), 1984

Isichei, Elizabeth. *A History of Nigeria*. Longman, London, 1983

Jongmans, D.G. and Gutkind, P.C.W. (eds.) *Anthropologists in the Field*. Van Gorcum, Assen, 1967

Kaberry, Phyllis M. *Women of the Grassfields: A Study of the Economic Position of Women in Bamenda, British Cameroons*. Colonial Office Research Publication No. 14, 1952

Kapadia, K.M. *Marriage and Family in India*. Oxford University Press, Calcutta, 1955

Keatinge. G. *Rural Economy in the Bombay Deccan*. Longmans, Green, London, 1912

Kerblay, B. 'Chayanov and the Theory of Peasantry as a Specific Type of Economy', *in* Shanin (ed.), 1971

Klein, M.A. (ed.) *Peasants in Africa: Historical and Contemporary Perspectives*. Sage Publications, London, 1980

Köbben, A.J.F. 'Le planteur noir.' *Etudes Eburnéenes*, Abidjan, 1956

Kolff, D.H.A. 'A Study of Land Transfers in Mau Tahsil, District Jhansi', *in* Chaudhuri and Dewey (eds.), 1979

Kotey, R.A., Okali, Christine and Rourke, B.E. (eds.) *The Economics of Cocoa Production and Marketing*. Proceedings of Cocoa Economics Research Conference, 1973. University of Ghana, Legon, 1974

Kumar, Dharma. *Land and Caste in South India: Agricultural Labour in the Madras Presidency during the Nineteenth Century*. Cambridge University Press, 1965

Leach, E.R. 'The Epistemological Background to Malinowski's Empiricism', *in* Firth (ed.), 1957

Pul Eliya: A Village in Ceylon. Cambridge University Press, 1961

'An Anthropologist's Reflections on a Social Survey', *in* Jongmans and Gutkind (eds.), 1967

Lenin, V.I. *Collected Works*. Vol. 3: *The Development of Capitalism in Russia*. Lawrence & Wishart, London, translation of 2nd edition of 1918

Lewis, W.A. 'Economic Development with Unlimited Supplies of Labour.' *Manchester School*, 1954

The Theory of Economic Growth. Allen & Unwin, London, 1955

Lipton, M. *Why Poor People Stay Poor: A Study of Urban Bias in World Development.* Temple Smith, London, 1977

'Migration from Rural Areas of Poor Countries: The Impact on Rural Productivity and Income Distribution.' *World Development,* 8, 1980

'Urban Bias Revisited'. *The Journal of Development Studies,* 20, 3, 1984

Lloyd, P.C. *Yoruba Land Law.* Oxford University Press, London, 1962

Power and Independence: Urban Africans' Perception of Social Inequality. Routledge & Kegan Paul, London, 1974

Long, N. *Creating Space for Change: A Perspective on the Sociology of Development.* Inaugural lecture, the Agricultural University, Wageningen, Netherlands, 1984

Longhurst, R. 'Resource Allocation and the Sexual Division of Labor: A Case Study of a Moslem Hausa Village in northern Nigeria', *in* Beneria (ed.), 1982

The Energy Trap: Work, Nutrition and Child Malnutrition in Northern Nigeria. Cornell University, Program in International Nutrition, 14, 1984

MacCormack, Carol. 'Primary Health Care in Sierra Leone'. *Society of Scientific Medicine,* 3, 1984

Maclachlan, M.D. *Why They Did Not Starve: Biocultural Adaptation in a South Indian Village.* Institute for the Study of Human Issues, Philadelphia, 1983

Mann, H.H. *Land and Labour in a Deccan Village.* Series No. 1. Oxford University Press, 1917

Mann, H.H. and Kanitkar, N.V. *Land and Labour in a Deccan Village.* Series No. 2. Oxford University Press, London, 1921

Marshall, A. *Principles of Economics.* Macmillan, London, 1890

Meek, C.K. *Land Law and Custom in the Colonies.* Oxford University Press, London, 1946

Mencher, Joan. *Agriculture and Social Structure in Tamil Nadu.* Allied Publishers, Delhi, 1978

'Agricultural Labourers in Peasant Societies', *in* Mencher (ed.), 1983

(ed.), *Social Anthropology of Peasantry.* Somaiya Publications, Bombay, 1983

Morgan, W.B. and Pugh, J.C. *West Africa.* Methuen, London, 1969

Morris, J. 'Agrarian Structure Implications for Development: A Kano (Nigeria) Case Study.' *Oxford Agrarian Studies,* X, 1981

Mote, F.W. 'The Transformation of Nanking', *in* Skinner (ed.), 1977

Mukhtyar, G.C. *Life and Labour in a South Gujarat Village.* (ed. C.N. Vakil.) Longman, London, 1930

Musgrave, P.J. 'Rural Credit and Rural Society in the United Provinces, 1860–1920', *in* Dewey and Hopkins (eds.), 1978

Myrdal, G. *Asian Drama: An Inquiry into the Poverty of Nations,* 3 vols. Penguin, Harmondsworth, 1968

Nadel, S.F. *A Black Byzantium: The Kingdom of Nupe*. Oxford University Press, 1942

Nakane, Chie. *Kinship and Economic Organization in Rural Japan*. The Athlone Press, London, 1967

Norman, D.W. 'Crop Mixtures under Indigenous Conditions in the northern part of Nigeria', *in* Ofori (ed.), 1973

Oculi, O. 'Multinationals in Nigerian Agriculture in the 1980s.' *Review of African Political Economy*, 31, December 1984

Ofori, E.D. (ed.) *Factors of Agricultural Growth in West Africa*. University of Ghana, Legon, 1973

Okali, Christine. 'Costs and Returns for the Cocoa Farmer', *in* Kotey *et al.* (eds.), 1974

 'Kinship and Cocoa Farming in Ghana', *in* Oppong (ed.), 1983

Okali, Christine and Addy, P.L.N.A. *Economics of Cocoa Production and Marketing with Special Reference to Ghana: An Annotated Bibliography*. University of Ghana, Legon, 1974

Okali, Christine, Owusuansah, M. and Rourke, B.E. 'The Development Pattern of some Large Cocoa Holdings in Ghana', *in* Kotey *et al.* (eds.), 1974

Okoye, S. 'Mortality Levels and Differentials in Sierra Leone.' *Census Analysis Project*, Central Statistics Office, Freetown, 1980

Oppong, Christine (ed.) *Female and Male in West Africa*. Allen & Unwin, London, 1983

Ottenberg, S. 'Inheritance and Succession in Afikpo', *in* Derrett (ed.), 1965

Owusuansah, M. *see* Okali and Owusuansah (eds.), 1974

Paulme, Denise (ed.) *Women of Tropical Africa*. Routledge & Kegan Paul, London, 1963

Peil, Margaret with Mitchell, P.K. and Rimmer, D. *Social Science Methods: An African Handbook*. Hodder & Stoughton, London, 1982

Pelissier, P. *Les paysans du Senegal: Les civilisations agraires du Cayor à la Casamance*. Imprimerie Fabregue, Saint-Yrieix (Haute-Vienne), 1966

Perham, M. (ed.) *The Native Economies of Nigeria*. Faber, London, 1946

Polanyi, K. *The Great Transformation*. Beacon Press, Boston, 1957

Pugh, J.C. *see* Morgan and Pugh, 1969

Radcliffe-Brown, A.R. and Forde, D. *African Systems of Kinship and Marriage*. Oxford University Press, 1950

Raj, K.N. *in* Robinson and Kidron (eds.), 1970

Rew, A. *see* Grillo and Rew (eds.), 1985

Rimmer, D. 'Official Statistics', *in* Peil *et al.*, 1982

 The Economics of West Africa. Weidenfeld & Nicolson, London, 1984

Roberts, Pepe. 'Feminism *in* Africa: Feminism *and* Africa'. *Review of African Political Economy*. Nos. 27/28, 1984

Robertson, A.F. *see* Dunn and Robertson, 1973

Robinson, E.A.G. and Kidron, M. (eds.) *Economic Development in South Asia*. Macmillan, London, 1970

Rourke, B.E. 'Profitability of Cocoa and Alternative Crops in Eastern Region, Ghana', *in* Kotey *et al*. (eds.), 1974

Roxborough, I. *Theories of Underdevelopment*. Humanities Press, New Jersey, 1979

Rudra, A. and Sen, A. 'Farm Size and Labour Use: Analysis and Policy'. *Economic & Political Weekly*, Annual Number, 1980

Schendel, W. van. *Peasant Mobility: The Odds of Life in Rural Bangladesh*. Van Gorcum, Assen, 1981

Schildkrout, Enid. 'Women's Work and Children's Work: variations among Moslems in Kano', *in* Wallman (eds.), 1979
 'Dependence and Autonomy: The Economic Activities of Secluded Hausa Women in Kano, *in* Oppong (ed.), 1983

Schultz, T.W. *Transforming Traditional Agriculture*. Yale University Press, New Haven, 1964

Sen, A. *see* Rudra and Sen, 1980
 Poverty and Famines: An Essay on Entitlement and Deprivation. Clarendon Press, Oxford, 1981.

Shanin, T. (ed.) *Peasants and Peasant Societies*. Penguin, Harmondsworth, 1971

Skinner, G.W. 'Marketing and Social Structure in Rural China.' 3 parts. *The Journal of Asian Studies*, Nov. 1964, Feb. 1965, May 1965
 (ed.) *The City in Late Imperial China*. Stanford University Press, Stanford, 1977

Smith, A. *The Wealth of Nations*, Books I to III, 1776. Penguin, Harmondsworth, 1970

Smith, Mary. *Baba of Karo: A Woman of the Muslim Hausa*. Faber, London, 1954

Smith, R.H.T. (ed.) *Periodic Markets, Hawkers and Traders in Africa, Asia and Latin America*. Centre for Transportation Studies, University of British Columbia, Vancouver, 1978

Smith, R.T. 'Anthropology and the Concept of Social Class.' *Annual Review of Anthropology*, Vol. 13, 1984

Stansfield, R.G. 'Operational Research and Sociology: a Case-Study of Cross-Fertilizations in the Growth of Useful Science.' *Science and Public Policy*, 4, 1981

Stern, N.H. *see* Bliss and Stern (eds.), 1982

Tax, S. *Penny Capitalism*, 1953, reprinted Chicago University Press, 1963

Todaro, M.P. 'A Model of Labour Migration and Urban Unemployment in LDCs.' *American Economic Review*, 59, 1969
 Economics for a Developing World: An Introduction to Principles, Problems and Policies for Development. Longman, London, 1977

Todaro, M.P. and Harris, J. 'Migration Unemployment and Development: A Two-Sector Analysis.' *American Economic Review*, 60, 1970

Udo, R.K. 'The Migrant Tenant Farmer of Eastern Nigeria.' *Africa*, Oct. 1964

Vakil, C.N. (ed.) *see Mukhtyar, 1930*

Van Hear, N. ' "By-Day" Boys and Dariga Men: Casual Labour versus Agrarian Capital in Northern Ghana.' *Review of African Political Economy*, 31, 1984

Vitebsky, P. *Policy Dilemmas for Unirrigated Agriculture in Southeastern Sri Lanka: A Social Anthropologist's Report on Shifting and Semi-Permanent Cultivation in an Area of Moneragala District.* Centre of South Asian Studies, University of Cambridge, 1984 (photocopy)

Wallace, Tina. 'Agricultural Projects and Land in Northern Nigeria.' *Review of African Political Economy*, 17, 1980

Wallman, Sandra (ed.) *Social Anthropology of Work.* Academic Press, London, 1979

Wanmali, S. 'The Regulated and Periodic Markets and Rural Development in India.' *Transactions of the Institute of British Geographers*, 5, 1980

 Periodic Markets and Rural Development in India. B.R. Publishing Corporation, Delhi, 1981

Wills, J.B. (ed.) *Agriculture and Land Use in Ghana.* Oxford University Press, London, 1962

Wolf, E.R. *Peasants.* Prentice-Hall, Englewood Cliffs, 1966

Wolfson, Freda. *Pageant of Ghana.* Oxford University Press, London, 1958

World Bank. *Accelerated Development in Sub-Saharan Africa: An Agenda for Action* (Berg Report). The World Bank, Washington DC, 1981

Yamey, B.S. *see* Firth and Yamey (eds), 1964

Zachariah, K.C. and Conde, J. *Migration in West Africa: Demographic Aspects.* A Joint World Bank—OECD Study. Oxford University Press, Oxford, 1981

INDEX

Aboyade, O., 52n
Abu, Katherine, 78, 79n
abusa, 174; men, in cocoa-farming, 116–17, 159
Addo, N. O., 116, 118n
agrarian hierarchy, 155 ff
agrarian systems: plea for typology of, 67–9; and population growth, 61–2
agricultural labourer: *see* farm labourers
agriculture: division of labour in , 79; growth rates and population growth, 49–50; Indian Royal Commission on, 44, 58; indigenous, intensification of, 172n; multinationals in W. African, 10n; productivity in, 50; 'traditional': defined, 17; Schultz's concept of, 25
Ahafo, strangerhood in, 160
Akan, 174; societies and inheritance, 98–9
Akim Abuakwa, 157n
Akwapim, 174; migration of cocoa farmers from, 94, 134, 135n, 137
aliens, expulsion of: Ghanaian, 115–16, 138n; Nigerian, 138
All-India National Sample Survey, 33, 34, 38, 39n, 40n
Altekar, A. S., 140
Amin, S., 129–30
Anloga, shallot farmers, 27, 159
anthropology, economic, and development economics, xi
Ardener, Shirley, 140
area, indigenous units of, 37
aro, Hausa land-borrowing, 158
artisans: farmers as, 10; *see also* occupations
arziki, Hausa concept of, 75n
Ashanti, households, 79

Bailey, F. G., 76n, 92, 97n, 131, 149n
Baker, C. J., 38n, 58, 62n, 62, 83, 85, 86, 87n, 91n, 112, 113n, 115, 150–1, 155n, 168
Bangalore: Harijans in, 166; population and migration, 133n
Bangladesh: credit-granting in, 86; village inequality in, 75–6
bania, Indian trader, 85
barter: and long-distance trade, 55; and market places, 59
Batagarawa, 174; daily wage rates in,

110–11n; economic inequality in, 74–5, 83, 163
Bayly, C. A., 131
Beckett, W. H., 104, 117n, 119n
Beckman, B., 1, 3n
Berg Report, 49–50, 60n, 63n, 64n
Bernard, H. R., 31
Berry, Sara, 120
Béteille, A., 19n, 155
blacksmiths, 10, 27
Bliss, C. J., 21–4, 93n, 146, 169n, 170
Bohannan, P., 55n, 147
borrowing, rural, 83 ff; and default, 88; and interest rates, 88; and usury 87; and written records, 88; *see also* indebtedness
Boserup, Ester, 27, 30, 66, 141
Boutillier, J.-L., 120, 160
Bradbury, R. E., 161
Breman, J., 114n
bridges, cocoa farmers', 94
Bromley, R. J., 57
Bruce-Chwatt, L. J., 65n
Buchanan, F., 59, 108, 168
bullocks: *see* cattle
bush fallow, 37, 174

cadastral surveys, 37
capital: household, 38, 41; migrant farmers' concept of, 135–6
capitalism: and farm-slavery, Nigerian, 52; and the migration of cocoa farmers, 135–7; penetration of 'subsistence sector' by, 51–2
caravans, long-distance trading, 56, 174
carts, Indian bullock, 59n
cash: circulation in villages, 12, 71, 76; economies, and 'peasant', 12; and the market principle, 58; transactions and market places, 57; types of, 57; *see also* barter
cassava, 174; processing by women, 145n; statistics on, 34, 145n
Cassen, R. H., 19n, 34, 60, 60n, 61, 62–3, 65n, 123n, 131, 132, 133
castes, Indian, 175; and class stratification, 163–7; dominant, 164; economic inequality within, 164–5; and farm-labouring, 111; and land-ownership, 77, 163–6; and occupation, 10n; and